1001
ways
to meet *mr. right*

...d date flea market reunion restaurant tattoo parlor wedding auction ho...
...ub baby shower casino hibachi ladies night café bake sale brunch riverb...
...ambake double date culinary festival smorgasbord tavern church service...
...mal hospital roommates yacht club school courthouse nudist colony bee...
...val baseball game car show firefighting fishing tailgating poker campgro...
...ating contest bowling weight room military cigar shop airport london brid...
...s eiffel tower vacation hotel cruise mardi gras times square central park...
...f america mount rushmore hollywood safari smithsonian online animal r...
...ue blood drive volunteering special olympics toy drive red cross soup kitc...
...rt gallery book club cooking class library museum college campus orches...
...nature walk planetarium political rally shakespeare festival disney world...
...uarium water park caroling parents playground mini-golf county fair cou...
...use laundromat grocery store beach gym subway deli yard sale liquor s...
...post office personal ads company picnic conference water cooler bartend...
...oncert scavenger hunt karaoke comedy club biking karate softball paint...
...iling ymca square dancing boardwalk cookout whale watching farmer's...
...et party friends cafeteria open house singing group bars beach house w...
...sting blind date flea market reunion restaurant tattoo parlor wedding au...
...ospital club baby shower casino hibachi ladies night café bake sale bru...
...iverboat clambake double date culinary festival smorgasbord tavern chu...
...service spa animal hospital roommates yacht club school courthouse nud...
...ony beer festival baseball game car show firefighting fishing tailgating...
...campground eating contest bowling weight room military cigar shop airp...
...ndon bridges bus eiffel tower vacation hotel cruise mardi gras times sq...
...ntral park mall of america mount rushmore hollywood safari smithsonian...
...e animal rescue blood drive volunteering special olympics toy drive red c...
...up kitchen art gallery book club cooking class library museum college ca...
...orchestra nature walk planetarium political rally shakespeare festival dis...
...orld zoo aquarium water park caroling parents playground mini-golf co...
...air coffeehouse laundromat grocery store beach gym subway deli yard s...
...iquor store post office personal ads company picnic conference water coo...
...rtending concert scavenger hunt karaoke comedy club biking karate sof...
...intball sailing ymca square dancing cookout whale watching farmer's ma...
...rty friends cafeteria open house singing group bars beach house wine ta...
...nd date flea market reunion restaurant tattoo parlor wedding auction ho...
...ub baby shower casino hibachi ladies night café bake sale brunch riverb...
...ambake double date culinary festival smorgasbord tavern church service...
...imal hospital roommates yacht club school courthouse nudist colony bee...
...val baseball game car show firefighting fishing tailgating poker campgr...
...ating contest bowling weight room military cigar shop airport london bri...
...s eiffel tower vacation hotel cruise mardi gras times square central park...
...f america mount rushmore hollywood safari smithsonian online animal...
...ue blood drive volunteering special olympics toy drive red cross soup kit...
...rt gallery book club cooking class library museum college campus orche...

1001
ways
to meet *mr. right*

elizabeth shimer bowers

avon, massachusetts

Copyright © 2008 by F+W Publications, Inc.

All rights reserved.
This book, or parts thereof, may not be reproduced in any
form without permission from the publisher; exceptions
are made for brief excerpts used in published reviews.

Published by Adams Media, an F+W Publications Company
57 Littlefield Street
Avon, MA 02322
www.adamsmedia.com

ISBN-10: 1-59869-422-7
ISBN-13: 978-1-59869-422-2

Printed in Canada.

J I H G F E D C B A

Library of Congress Cataloging-in-Publication Data
is available from the publisher.

This book is available at quantity discounts for bulk purchases.
For information, please call 1-800-289-0963.

contents

1   social**ways**

83   travel**ways**

119   online**ways**

139   life-enriching**ways**

149   intellectual**ways**

169   kid-friendly**ways**

187   everyday**ways**

235   work-related**ways**

249   entertaining**ways**

265   active**ways**

295   outdoor**ways**

For your Mr. Right Seeking Convenience, each Way is rated using the following criteria:

How much **TIME** you will need to invest in a particular Way: If there is one ⏱, this Way can be completed in less than one day (some can be done in less time than it takes you to get a cup of coffee!). If there are two ⏱⏱, you'll need a week to a month. And if there are three ⏱⏱⏱, you'd best clear your calendar—this Way is going to take you a while.

How many **FRIENDS**—if any—you'll need to bring along for a particular Way: If there is one 👤, this one can be done solo. If there are two 👤👤, you'll need to bring along one or two trustworthy friends. And if there are three 👤👤👤 icons, plan for a group outing.

How much **MONEY** you will need to invest in a particular Way: If there is one $, this Way will cost you less than one drink (and some are absolutely free!)! If there are two $$, plan on spending what you would on one night out on the town. And if there are three $$$, you need to save a bit— this Way will set you back a few.

Have a blast!

d date flea market reunion restaurant tattoo parlor wedding auction ho
ub baby shower casino hibachi ladies night café bake sale brunch riverl
mbake double date culinary festival smorgasbord tavern church service
mal hospital roommates yacht club school courthouse nudist colony beer
val baseball game car show firefighting fishing tailgating poker campgro
ting contest bowling weight room military cigar shop airport london bri
s eiffel tower vacation hotel cruise mardi gras times square central park
f america mount rushmore hollywood safari smithsonian online animal r
e blood drive volunteering special olympics toy drive red cross soup kitc
rt gallery book club cooking class library museum college campus orches
ature walk planetarium political rally shakespeare festival disney world z
uarium water park caroling parents playground mini-golf county fair co
use laundromat grocery store beach gym subway deli yard sale liquor s
post office personal ads company picnic conference water cooler bartend
oncert scavenger hunt karaoke comedy club biking karate softball paint
iling ymca square dancing boardwalk cookout whale watching farmer's
et party friends cafeteria open house singing group bars beach house w
sting blind date flea market reunion restaurant tattoo parlor wedding au
ospital club baby shower casino hibachi ladies night café bake sale bru
iverboat clambake double date culinary festival smorgasbord tavern chu
service spa animal hospital roommates yacht club school courthouse nu
ony beer festival baseball game car show firefighting fishing tailgating
campground eating contest bowling weight room military cigar shop airp
ndon bridges bus eiffel tower vacation hotel cruise mardi gras times sq
ntral park mall of america mount rushmore hollywood safari smithsonian
e animal rescue blood drive volunteering special olympics toy drive red
up kitchen art gallery book club cooking class library museum college ca
orchestra nature walk planetarium political rally shakespeare festival dis
orld zoo aquarium water park caroling parents playground mini-golf co
air coffeehouse laundromat grocery store beach gym subway deli yard
iquor store post office personal ads company picnic conference water coo
rtending concert scavenger hunt karaoke comedy club biking karate so
intball sailing ymca square dancing cookout whale watching farmer's m
rty friends cafeteria open house singing group bars beach house wine ta
nd date flea market reunion restaurant tattoo parlor wedding auction ho
lub baby shower casino hibachi ladies night café bake sale brunch river
ambake double date culinary festival smorgasbord tavern church service
imal hospital roommates yacht club school courthouse nudist colony bee
val baseball game car show firefighting fishing tailgating poker campgr
ating contest bowling weight room military cigar shop airport london bri
s eiffel tower vacation hotel cruise mardi gras times square central park
of america mount rushmore hollywood safari smithsonian online animal
ue blood drive volunteering special olympics toy drive red cross soup kit
rt gallery book club cooking class library museum college campus orche

socialways

1. FRIEND'S PARTY

$

It can be tough with a busy schedule, but if you are in the market for a guy, you should do your best to go to every social event you are invited to. A party atmosphere is more desirable than the fix-up one-on-one date. For maximum guy exposure, open things up: "Women tend to group together, talk in a circle, go to the bathroom together—this is intimidating to men," says Lori Gorshow, president of Dating Made Simple (*www.makedatingsimple.com*). So if you go to a restaurant, bar, or other social place with your girlfriends, "look around the room, make eye contact, and smile," she says.

O PRO *If things aren't going well, you can always escape with the "I need to get a drink" excuse. Also, if you don't get a phone number or vice versa, you have at least one friend in common.*

O CON *The friend in common can work against you, too. If things aren't going well, things could become awkward.*

2. FUNERAL

$

It may sound morbid, but an after-funeral gathering may present some eligible strangers, and as long as you stay within the lines of decency and respect, you may be able to meet them. After a funeral, people want to—and are supposed to—talk about the deceased. So it's perfectly acceptable for you to ask someone how he knew the person whose life you are celebrating . . . and then go from there.

O PRO *You have at least one person in common.*

O CON *Some guys may not be in the mood for chitchat at a funeral, especially if they knew the deceased well. Tread lightly.*

3. HOME SHOW

$

A lot of successful singles are buying homes these days. And even if they aren't springing for a home yet, they may be in the market for things they can use to improve their apartments or condos. From kitchen counters to window boxes, a home show is one of the best places to find items you can use to improve your own living space . . . or to find single guys with the same idea.

O PRO *A home show is the type of outing a couple usually attends together, so if you see a guy looking at curtain rods by himself, the odds are good that he is single. And then there are the guys working at the home show. . . .*

O CON *If you are not the home improvement or decorator type, you could be pretty bored at a home show.*

=Time ♦=Friends $=Expense

4. HOSPITAL CAFETERIA

There is a reason that hospitals are the center of most daytime soap operas—they are a hot spot for social interaction. You may not be in the mood to socialize if you are the patient yourself, but if you are visiting a friend or are in the hospital for a routine procedure and stop in the cafeteria, you're in a good place to meet men. Doctors, nurses, physicians' assistants, visitors, patients—they are all people you can get to know better. So look around you in the cafeteria for people you may want to share your meal with.

O PRO *All the well-educated eligible guys (doctors).*

O CON *Unless you work in a hospital or are visiting a chronically ill friend or relative, you probably don't frequent them too often. Also, germs.*

5. REAL ESTATE OPEN HOUSE

Most single, successful professionals are in the market for real estate these days. And where can you find these catches is at real estate open houses. So peruse your local newspaper for Saturday and Sunday afternoon open houses in your area. As you check out the furnace and the back yard, check out your bidding competition. It helps if you are actually in the market for a house or condo, however, because real estate agents are usually pretty good at picking out "lookers only" and will quickly become annoyed.

6. SINGING GROUP

Community choirs and choruses join people together who love to sing. Sometimes, singing groups travel together to perform—a great way to bond with fellow group members. If you are blessed with a good voice, a singing group is a fabulous forum for meeting new people—including new men—with whom you share a passion.

O PRO *Music is one of the strongest bonds between people.*

O CON *Singing groups tend to attract a lot of men who are gay.*

=Time =Friends $=Expense

7. SINGLES DINNERS

Clubs around the country will set up dinner parties for four single men and four single women who share interests and a common desire to meet new members of the opposite sex. These clubs include Eight at Eight (*www.8at8.com*), Table for Eight (*www.table foreight.com*), and Dinner at Eight (*www.dinnerat8.com*). Worst case scenario: You don't make a connection, but you enjoy a great meal.

8. MARTINI BAR

There is just something about a night out at a martini bar. It gives you an excuse to get dressed up, try tasty martini creations such as chocolate mint and extra dirty, and maybe even smoke a cigar. . . . The unique martini recipes are a great conversation starter, and the alcohol buzz will help take away some of your shyness. Dr. Hu Fleming, a national relationship coach who has worked with hundreds of singles, gives women who are having trouble finding men the following piece of advice: "Don't try too hard," he says. "Men can see through overly aggressive behavior. Relax, take a deep breath, and put yourself in positions to meet guys. The rest will follow."

○ PRO *A trip to a martini bar will be a fun night out, even if it is just with your girlfriends.*

○ CON *Drunk guys and a potential hangover.*

9. SUMMER BEACH HOUSE

Summer shares between groups of singles are becoming increasingly more popular, and Margee M.'s experience is evidence that these shares are the perfect place to meet guys. "During my summer share, I met a ton of new friends . . . and I found a romantic relationship that will probably turn into a marriage," says Margee, who lives in the notoriously difficult dating city of New York, New York.

○ PRO *Even if you don't meet the man of your dreams, a summer share will bring many memories and friendships.*

○ CON *With numerous people with different personality types coming together, summer shares can lead to some conflict.*

10. WINE TASTING

$ $

Wine tastings are fun, festive bonding experiences you can share with fellow wine lovers. Great minds think and taste alike, so if you and the guy next to you both find the robust 2000 berry-infused merlot the most pleasing to your palate, you may agree on a lot more than wine. And men are impressed and intrigued by women who are up for trying new things, wines included.

○ PRO *Wine tastings are a great way to educate yourself on wines, and they offer a fabulous opportunity for meeting new people.*

○ CON *If you are not a wine drinker, steer clear. The whole point of a wine tasting is to try and comment on wines, and true wine lovers will pick up on the look of disgust on your face in a hurry.*

11. THIRTIETH BIRTHDAY PARTY

$

There is something about a guy's thirtieth birthday that makes him, well, a grownup all of a sudden. It's as if he wakes up one day and says, "Unless I want to be single for the rest of my life, I better start taking women more seriously." Where better to find a guy who has recently snapped out of the wildness of his 20s than at a thirtieth birthday party? In addition to the birthday boy himself, there will be numerous friends of his who are teetering around the thirty mark themselves. So if you get an invitation to a thirtieth birthday party, by all means, do not turn it down. Also, keep in mind that friendliness goes a long way. "Saying 'hi' and smiling are the easiest and most nonthreatening ways to draw in a man," says Lori Gorshow, president of Dating Made Simple (*www.makedatingsimple.com*). "And realize that if a man doesn't respond to you right away, it's probably just taking him a little longer to notice your signals," she says. So go a little further. "Ask him a question or make a comment that invites conversation. For instance, if you are at a chair lift, say, 'It's pretty crowded here—do you know of any slopes in the area that usually aren't so full?' or make a comment about your passion for skiing," she says.

12. BLIND DATE

Sure, you might be going up against some odds—be it foul breath, rudeness, or simply a bad match. Most people have a nightmare blind date story. But if you're being fixed up by someone whose judgment you trust, a blind date is worth a shot. So as your trust-worthy friends and relatives set you up, keep your mind open, and try to have a great time. Who knows—you two may just hit it off.

❂ PRO *All you have to lose is a few hours . . . and if the guy is a gentleman, you will get a free dinner. Even if the two of you don't get along on a romantic level, you may have a great time as friends.*

❂ CON *You might have the sudden urge to run out the door when you see him, and if it's that bad, you may just want to. . . .*

13. HOLIDAY PARTY

The holidays can be a busy time, and it's tempting to say "no" to some holiday party invitations in order to have more time to shop. But the invitation you turn down could be for the one the man of your dreams decides to attend . . . and you'll miss him. So throw on a festive holiday dress and enjoy the eggnog and cookies. Who knows . . . you might find yourself standing under the mistletoe.

❂ PRO *You could leave the party with a date for New Year's Eve.*

❂ CON *You may spend a lot of money on gifts for multiple hostesses.*

14. FLEA MARKET

Love to spend hours perusing a mix of antiques, knockoff sweatshirts, and other random but potentially valuable items? You are likely to bump into a guy who shares your passion. With all those items to look at, you have lots of conversation starters to choose from: "Do you think this is a good price for this set of German beer steins?" or "Do you think these Polo shirts are real?"

Five great flea markets:
1. Crown Market Center and Flea Market, Archbald, PA
2. Tri Town Flea Market, Agawam, MA
3. Atwater Flea Market, Atwater, CA
4. Hillbilly Flea Market, Ashland, KY
5. Jamie's Flea Market, Amherst, OH

❂ PRO *Flea markets offer a fun after-noon of bargain hunting.*

❂ CON *You will have to sift through some junk to get to the good stuff . . . which may be true of the men at the flea market as well.*

 =Time ♟=Friends $=Expense

15. HALLOWEEN PARTY

At a Halloween party, there is the allure of the mystique—he could be fabulous to talk to, but what does he look like behind the costume? A Halloween party also gives you a glimpse into a guy's personality. Is he a funny, quirky costume guy? A scary costume guy? An excuse to dress in women's clothing costume guy? And there is no requirement to commit. If you are bored by the conversation, you can leave without revealing yourself from behind the mask.

O PRO *Good Halloween parties—parties where people actually put some thought and time into their costumes—are a really fun time.*

O CON *Cheesy costume guys or worse—guys without costumes.*

16. HIGH SCHOOL REUNION

Whether it's yours or you tag along with a friend to hers, a high school reunion is a juicy place to meet men, to say the least. The surprising thing is that the guy you wouldn't give the time of day to ten or twenty years ago (or vice versa) may be the one you totally click with now. And even if you don't make a love connection, it will be fun to see who's lost his hair, who's gained a lot of weight, and who's made his or her first million already . . .

O PRO *You may hook up with your long-lost love.*

O CON *If you hated high school, a high school reunion may be a can of worms you don't want to open.*

17. IRISH PUB

There are thousands of Irish pubs across the country, and they all have a few things in common: They are full of guys (Irish guys who like to drink beer and non-Irish guys who like to drink beer), and they always have Guinness on tap. So if you like Guinness and friendly, beer-drinking guys who may or may not have Irish roots, head out to the Irish bar on a Friday night and enjoy a pint or two. The luck of the Irish may strike and make you lucky in love.

O PRO *Authentic Irish pubs usually have a menu full of tasty authentic Irish fare, such as pasties and shepherd's pie.*

O CON *Because of the alcohol and the number of men these places draw, this is not a great place to go to alone—to be safe, bring a friend or two and watch out for each other.*

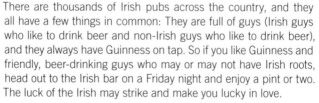

18.   JUICE BAR

Juice bars offer the bar-style counter and enticing beverage con-coctions of a regular bar . . . but without the alcohol. Who knew that carrot juice mixed well with papaya, or that orange juice actu-ally can taste better with a splash of spinach? There are hundreds of tasty juice concoctions . . . and as you sit at the juice bar sipping your creation, you are bound to be in the company of a fellow juice lover; hopefully, a single male one. Where can you find a juice bar? A lot of malls have juice bar kiosks, and some juice bars can be found on city streets and in some health spas.

○ PRO *A guy who is open to try new juices is most likely adventur-ous and into his health—a good combination.*

○ CON *Juice bars can be on the pricey side. Even without the alco-hol, you may shell out the same money as you would for a cosmo.*

19.   NEARBY TOWN

Let's face it—if you continue to hang out in the same area and frequent the same places, you will hurt your chances of meet-ing someone new. So instead of going to the coffee shop, grocery store, or post office right around the corner from your house, head to the next town over now and then for a change of scenery and a fresh crop of single guys. And even better, go to towns that tend to attract singles rather than towns heavily populated with families and/or senior citizens. If you drive down the main street and spot numerous retirement homes and Buicks, move on to a town with nightclubs and outdoor cafés. If you are in the market for Mr. Right, be ready to meet him at any time. It may sound shallow, but if you are single and looking for a man, you want to look somewhat pre-sentable wherever you go, be it the grocery store, the post office, or the dry cleaners. Because the way things go, the day you decide to run out in sweats without showering will be the day you spot the man of your dreams. Try not to let your guard down.

○ PRO *You may discover some fun new restaurants and shops where you can meet new men or that you can simply enjoy by yourself of with girlfriends.*

○ CON *If you live in the middle of nowhere, you may have to drive for awhile.*

20. SINGLES PARTY

$

An increasingly popular way to get single people together is for single people to throw a "singles party" for each other. Only people who are available and open to mingling and dating are invited to these parties. That way, the guesswork is gone—any guy you meet and like at the party is guaranteed to be unattached. So if you get an invitation to a singles party, by all means, get yourself all dolled up and go. And consider throwing one of these shindigs yourself. Your single friends will be so glad you did . . . and so will you. To set up the party, invite all the single people you know and ask them to bring at least one single guest of honor. You might be surprised at the number of people who show up.

○ PRO *You know all guys at the party are fair game.*

○ CON *Because all the girls at the party will also be fair game, the competition level will be raised. Also, if you're not interested in any of the guys, you might be bored.*

21. SUSHI RESTAURANT

$ $

Sushi restaurants are popping up on every corner like Starbucks. There are two factors that make sushi restaurants great places to meet guys. One, most sushi restaurants have a sushi bar that you can sit down at solo without feeling like you're wearing an "I'm dining alone" stamp on your forehead. And two, they say that guys who are daring with what they eat are daring in other ways as well (wink-wink).

○ PRO *If the thought of raw fish turns your stomach, there are vegetable or cooked sushi options. Try a vegetable roll or a California roll.*

○ CON *If you are not great with chopsticks, sushi can be a challenge to eat with grace.*

22. TATTOO PARLOR

$ $ $

If you are a girl who loves ink (on yourself and on your men), this may be a good forum. If you are getting a tattoo, you will be dying for something to get your mind off the pain—whether it is a conversation with the tattoo artist himself or a fellow patron. And if things work out, you will have a permanent memento to remind you of when and where you met your love.

○ PRO *You'll leave with a new design.*

○ CON *Hepatitis, although most parlors are clean these days.*

⏱=Time ♟=Friends $=Expense

23.   WEDGING

When you get that wedding invitation in the mail that says you and "guest," you have a choice—you can find a guy friend or someone you may or may not have fun with and drag him along . . . or you can go alone, be seated at the singles table, and hang out with whomever you want. At the wedding you will be dancing, possibly downing some champagne, and celebrating the union of two friends: a perfect backdrop for romance with a fellow guest who decided to go stag. And you already have a suitable icebreaker: "Friend of the bride's or the groom's?" Things not working out with the wedding guests? You can always strike up a conversation with the bartender or band leader.

◑ PRO *If you hit it off with a guest, with the drinks, dinner, and dancing, you will have your first date out of the way.*

◐ CON *Some weddings don't attract too many single guests. Consider the group of friends you're dealing with. If everyone is bringing a date, you may be bored alone.*

24.   ANTIQUE AUCTION

Not only is it possible to meet a man or two at an antique auction, it's possible to meet a man who is interested in antiques—potentially, a rich man. Believe it or not, there are books geared toward helping women talk to rich men. Even if he isn't rich, you are likely to meet someone who shares a similar interest in antiques.

◑ PRO *If you are an antique lover, you will be excited by the potential buys alone.*

◐ CON *If you don't have much money to spend, this isn't a great place. Auctions can get boring fast when you can't make bids.*

25.   BACHELORETTE PARTY

Nothing draws attention faster at a bar or a club than a group of women surrounding a bachelorette in a white veil. Suzanne P. from Philadelphia knows—she met her boyfriend Scott when she asked him for his boxer shorts to give to the bachelorette. "When I asked him for his underwear, Scott obliged, took his boxers off in the bathroom, and went commando for the night . . . he was a good sport. We've been together ever since!" she says. This isn't to say you have to ask for a guy's underwear to strike up a conversation, but it's worth your while to take advantage of the attention you and your group will get.

26. BAR NEAR A HOSPITAL

After a hard day at the hospital, male doctors, nurses, and physicians' assistants often like to unwind over a drink or two. The ones who are out after work are most likely the ones who don't have a wife and/or kids to head home to. If you would like to meet one of these available medical professionals, the best place for you to be between about four and six in the afternoon is at one of these bars, enjoying an after-work drink yourself. So even if your office is a bit of a drive from the closest hospital, it may be worth your investment in gas and time.

27. CHINESE BUFFET

When you are really hungry for Chinese food and you just can't decide between the lo mein and the chicken and broccoli, your best bet is to head to your local Chinese buffet and get both . . . plus six or seven other selections. And because they provide unlimited amounts of food, Chinese buffets tend to attract a lot of men, particularly single men because Chinese buffets aren't on the top of most people's favorite places to go on a date. If you spot someone nice next to you in the buffet line, you can always break the ice by asking him his favorite dish.

◐ PRO *If you hit it off with someone, you can always skip the buffet dessert and grab some ice cream or a coffee and get to know each other better.*

◑ CON *Some Chinese buffets are more quantity than quality; you may need to try a few before you find the winner in your area—both food-wise and men-wise.*

28. COUNTRY CLUB

Between the golf course, tennis courts, pool, and clubhouse, a country club offers a multitude of opportunities to meet established single men. People hear the term *country club* and automatically think big bucks, but country club membership fees range anywhere from a few thousand dollars a year to tens of thousands, so you can choose one in your area that you can afford.

29. OYSTER BAR

$ $

Chic seafood restaurants are great places to meet successful guys who appreciate good seafood. You can enjoy classy cocktails, engage in some people watching, and maybe meet someone interesting with whom you can share a good conversation and an order of raw oysters.

O PRO *You know what they say about oysters—after you eat a few, you will be feeling particularly amorous.*

O CON *Bring your wallet.*

30. TALL CLUB

$ $

If you're over 5'10" and have trouble finding men whom you don't tower over when you're wearing heels, consider the Tall Club, a social organization for tall adults. Guys in the Tall Club must measure at least 6'2", and the 3,000 members are scattered throughout the United States and Canada. The Tall Club sponsors events and Tall Club Weekends at hotels, campgrounds, and other locations for tall people to meet and socialize. For more information, check out *www.tall.org*.

31. TOASTMASTERS

$

Because public speaking still ranks above death as most people's biggest fear, a lot of people who have to engage in public speaking decide to join Toastmasters, a club aimed at improving members' overall confidence level and public speaking skills. Toastmasters attracts a lot of professionals, and the supportive group atmosphere is wonderful for making new friends . . . and maybe more. For more information on Toastmasters or to find a chapter in your area, check out *www.toastmasters.org*.

O PRO *Even if you don't meet someone, you will learn how to deliver great presentations, to lead teams, and to be a better listener.*

O CON *If you have a severe phobia of public speaking, you may not want to practice in front of guys you'd like to date, no matter how supportive they may be.*

=Time =Friends $=Expense

32. BABY SHOWER

Times have changed, and baby showers aren't just a group of new mothers anymore, oooing and aahing over footed pajamas and the latest bottle nipple designs. Today, women have a range of male and female friends and as a result, some are throwing coed baby showers. Instead of dainty tea shops, these women are holding their showers in chic restaurants or microbreweries. The point is that a baby shower may be a good venue for meeting a nice guy. If a man comes to a baby shower with only a gift in tow (not a girl-friend, fiancée, or wife), he's single. Men generally do not attend events involving babies solo unless they are unattached.

33. BYOB MUSIC VENUE

There are some venues out there where you can see excellent live music . . . and bring your own booze. These places tend to draw bands with a cult following and free-thinking, laid-back patrons—usually guys—who prefer to spend money on good music than on five dollar beers. Wait until a band is playing the style of music you enjoy—that way, you will be likely to meet a guy who has a similar taste in music.

34. CASINO BUFFET

If you are on a winning streak and just want to grab a quick bite, you'll head to the casino buffet; on the other hand, if you are on a losing streak and want a distraction in the form of a free meal, you will go to the casino buffet. Either way, these buffets are full of fellow gamblers for you to meet. And the larger tables in these establishments will force you and your friends to sit with people you don't know . . . so scan the room for a group of men you'd like to meet.

O PRO *These buffets are often complimentary, and casinos draw men of all ages and economic backgrounds.*

O CON *Casinos tend to attract a mixed (or sometimes weird) crowd; you may have to search for a while to find a table of guys you'd like to sit with.*

35. CATHOLIC CLUB

If it is important to you to find someone of the Catholic faith, the Catholic Alumni Clubs International, an organization of single Catholic professionals, is worth checking out. Each of the thirty Catholic Alumni Clubs across the country provides opportunities for Catholic singles to meet and develop friendships (and maybe more). There is also an annual national convention where more than 200 Catholic singles join together for tours, sporting events, dinner-dances, liturgies, seminars, and parties. For more information, check out *www.caci.org*.

○ PRO *You won't have to wonder (or ask) whether or not he is Catholic.*

○ CON *If you are not a strict Catholic, this organization is not for you.*

36. THE CHEESECAKE FACTORY

The Cheesecake Factory is an extremely popular upscale chain restaurant that specializes in uniquely flavored and delicious cheesecakes. In addition, they also serve 200 tasty menu items and specialty drinks. Why should you go to the Cheesecake Factory to meet men? Because the average wait (even on a weeknight) is a few hours, which will leave you with plenty of time to talk with fellow waiting diners—including potentially single guys—at the bar. To find a Cheesecake Factory in your area, go to *www.cheesecake factory.com*.

37. COUNTRY-WESTERN BAR

Want to show men your most adventurous, fun-loving self without having to say a word? Ride the bull at a country-western bar . . . then do some country line dancing. Even if country-western music is not really your thing, you will still have fun with your girlfriends at a rodeo bar . . . and you may meet some handsome cowboys to boot! Bull riding and country line dancing are interactive, lively activities that pave the way for socializing.

○ PRO *Bull riding and line dancing are both great workouts.*

○ CON *If cowboys aren't your type, you'll be wasting your time at a country-western bar.*

=Time =Friends $=Expense

38. | CRAB HOUSE

$ $

To get the best crabs and freshest seafood you've ever tasted, you're sometimes better off going to a restaurant that is a little rough around the edges—the paper towel roll on the table, beer in plastic cups type of place. These places tend to attract people who are willing to sit on a picnic table bench to get some really good crabs, including seafood-loving guys. Plus, the picnic table seating arrangement often forces these venues to seat strangers together at the same table, which could definitely work in your favor if those strangers are attractive. Go at the busiest night and time to increase your chances of sitting with someone you don't know (but who you'd like to know).

39. | HIBACHI RESTAURANT

$ $

At a hibachi Japanese restaurant, your meal will be prepared by a chef right in front of you as you and seven or so other diners sit around a U-shaped grill. Not only do hibachi restaurants serve delicious food, they present an opportunity for you to get to know your table mates. Unless you show up with eight people, you will be seated with people you don't know. And the cooking show you watch together is a fun bonding experience—by the end of the meal, you may be exchanging phone numbers . . . which will be exciting if one of your fellow diners is a handsome single guy! So head out to a hibachi restaurant with a friend or two and see what happens.

O PRO *Not a fan of ethnic foods? Japanese food offers some of the most basic choices, such as stir-fried beef and fried rice—even the pickiest of eaters are bound to find something on the menu.*

O CON *These restaurants tend to attract a lot of families. To catch the more "adult" hour, go after 9:00 P.M.*

40. | LADIES' NIGHT

$ $

Even though it sounds counterintuitive, ladies' night at your local bar or club can actually be a pretty good place to meet gentlemen. First, your drinks will be cheap. Second, the men who hang out at bars on ladies' night are in the market for ladies, so you and your girlfriends are bound to meet a friendly crew of guys.

O PRO *Drinks at the average ladies' night are $2 or less; some are even free.*

O CON *Unlike a normal night at a bar, you may have a lot of competition in the form of other women.*

=Time =Friends $=Expense

41. MEXICAN RESTAURANT

There's the festive atmosphere, the refreshing margaritas, and delicious authentic food . . . and then there are the single men who love Mexican food as much as you do. Grab a girlfriend or two and head to the best Mexican restaurant in your area at the peak hour. That way, you will be forced to enjoy a margarita or soda and hopefully, a conversation with a handsome stranger, before your table is ready.

❍ PRO *Guys love Mexican food so they will be present at a fabulous Mexican restaurant on a Friday or Saturday night.*

❍ CON *Mexican food could make you gassy. Eat it with some Beano in case you hit it off with someone cute.*

42. WATER TAXI

Whether you climb on a water taxi to commute or to sightsee, you are guaranteed to be on board with some single guys in the same boat (no pun intended). Water taxis are a fun alternate form of public transportation, and most taxis in major cities hold hundreds of people. So hop on and enjoy the ride, and to get the most out of it, make sure to look around at your fellow passengers as well as out at the water.

43. WINE BAR

For a warm, relaxing, classy place to meet new people, you simply cannot beat a wine bar. Wine bars pride themselves on their extensive lists of eclectic wines, so they're havens for wine lovers. If you glance over at a handsome stranger as you sip your 1999 California Cabernet, you can rest assured that you have at least one thing in common—a love of fine wine. And wine is a great conversation starter. Ask your handsome stranger about his favorite region and grape . . . and see where it goes from there. Who knows, in a year the two of you might be sipping wine in Napa Valley . . . on your honeymoon.

❍ PRO *Wine bars tend to draw a professional, classy crowd.*

❍ CON *Due to the extensive selection, you will pay a little more per glass of wine than you would at your standard bar.*

44. COUNTRY CLUB DANCE

If you belong to a country club yourself or know someone who does, don't turn down the opportunity to attend a country club dance. These affairs are full of single men who love to golf, play tennis, swim, and socialize . . . and they are there to meet women who like to do the same. Even if you don't make a love match, you may find a partner for your next match of tennis.

45. DIVE BAR (WITH YOUR FRIENDS)

Now and then, you want a low maintenance night where you and your friends can go out in jeans (maybe even sneakers, too) and T-shirts, have a cheap domestic beer and a burger, and play the jukebox all night. And where better to do this than at your local dive bar? By nature of being cheap and dirty, dive bars tend to draw a lot of guys . . . guys who will be instantly attracted by you and your friends' choice to hang at a low key place.

O PRO *You can get a whole night out for under twenty bucks.*

OCON *Some dive bars can get pretty seedy—travel in a group.*

46. INDOOR BEACH PARTY

Nothing will brighten your spirits in the dead of winter faster than an indoor beach party. If you can't convince a friend to throw one of these shindigs, consider doing it yourself and ask your friends to bring as many single guys as they can. Decorate your place with blow-up palm trees and hand out grass skirts to your swimming-suit clad guests. The off-season theme will put everyone in high spirits, and you may meet the wintertime beach cutie of your dreams.

O PRO *Fun, fun, fun.*

O CON *Bathing suit in the winter—you may have to do prep work.*

47. KENTUCKY DERBY PARTY

The race itself only lasts a minute, but the buildup to the Kentucky Derby—both on the field and in private homes—is quite an event. People who love horse racing and betting on horse racing often throw Kentucky Derby parties. These gatherings, usually complete with good food and good mint juleps, often bring together people of all ages and walks of life . . . including single guys who want to throw down a few bucks on a horse and enjoy the party. Don't know of any Kentucky Derby parties? Consider hosting one yourself.

=Time =Friends $=Expense

48. MARINA RESTAURANT

If you are lucky enough to live near the ocean, you should regularly dine at a marina restaurant. Not only will you be able to watch the water glistening as you eat fresh seafood, you will get a nice view of guys pulling in on their boats. And where are those guys going to head after they step back on land? The marina restaurant, of course, for a drink and a snack. So scope out who you want to talk to from the window, and then approach him and tell him how much you were admiring his boat once he walks in.

49. OUT-OF-THE-WAY CAFÉ

Take a drive to a nearby town and sit down at an outdoor café you've never been to before. Consider ordering something you would never ordinarily order on the menu. Sometimes we need to get out of our routines to spark some newness in our lives, both in terms of our habits and the people we meet.

50. VINTAGE CLOTHING STORE

Vintage clothing stores are great for Halloween shopping or when you're searching for an outfit that is a little more eccentric. They say fashion is cyclical, so if you devote enough time to sifting through vintage duds, you are bound to find something cool. And while you are looking, you may find your male counterpart . . . in other words, someone who appreciates vintage fashion as much as you do. If you're looking for an icebreaker, ask your fellow shopper what his favorite clothing era is . . . it could be the beginning of a beautiful vintage clothing relationship.

○ PRO *Vintage clothing is not only cool, it's relatively inexpensive.*

○ CON *Some guys who are interested in vintage clothing may be a little too eccentric for your liking.*

51. ANNIVERSARY PARTY

It could be for your parents, your friends, or whoever, but an anniversary party is always a festive and romantic event for all involved . . . not to mention a great place to meet someone. If you meet a guy at an anniversary party, first you will know he knows someone you know, so you can rest assured he's not a serial killer, and second, you will both be in the mood to celebrate love—a great start if things progress beyond the party.

=Time   =Friends $=Expense

52. AROUND-THE-WORLD PARTY

$

Around-the-world parties are fun, interactive parties where each guest brings an item from a particular region of the world. If you don't know anyone who will host one of these parties, host one yourself. Ask each guest to bring something—for example, a type of food—from a certain country . . . and one single friend. Between the travel stories and getting to know each other, people will have plenty to talk about.

53. BAKE SALE

$

At a bake sale, you can donate money to a good cause and get some tasty treats. You can also potentially meet some good-hearted, giving guys who love sweets—guys who would like to get a cupcake or two in return for their charitable donations. If you spot an attractive guy at a bake sale, ask him if he'd like to grab a cup of coffee to go with his cookie . . . with you.

54. CONDO AUCTION

$ $ $

If you are in the market for a condo, either to live in yourself or for an investment, it's worth your while to check out a condo auction. Not only for the condo, but for the attractive single men who are also making a bid. Who knows—you might even meet your future neighbor!

○ **PRO** *You may get a great deal on a nice new place to live.*

○ **CON** *Make sure you're serious about buying. These auctions are not for people who are "just looking" . . . for men or for condos.*

55. COUNTRY CLUB BRUNCH

$ $

If you belong to a country club or have a friend or family member who does, don't pass up the chance to attend a country club brunch. Not only will you get a bountiful display of wonderful breakfast foods, you will most likely get a bountiful display of male country club members fueling up before golf . . . some of whom are likely to be unattached.

○ **PRO** *Depending on the country club, some members may be quite affluent (which is great, if that's your thing).*

○ **CON** *The price will be higher than your average Denny's breakfast, but it will be well worth it.*

⏱=Time 👤=Friends $=Expense

56. GERMAN RESTAURANT

Unless you're a vegetarian, surely you enjoy a good German bratwurst now and then . . . and where better to get one than at a German restaurant? In addition to your bratwurst, you are likely to stumble upon some single men. The combination of giant mugs of beer and endless sausages and potatoes tends to attract members of the opposite sex. For maximum man exposure, enjoy your sausage and beer at the bar, where you will be more approachable.

57. HIPPIE STORE/HEAD SHOP

Aside from the incense and tie-dye, some hippie stores actually have a lot in terms of art and cool jewelry. So if colorful and laid-back is your thing, browse through one of these stores once in a while . . . you may find someone who catches your eye and shares your uninhibited sense of style.

58. THE MELTING POT

By nature of its name and its setup, the Melting Pot is a guaranteed fun evening. A fondue restaurant, the Melting Pot serves a range of dips, from cheese to chocolate, along with endless dipping foods, from vegetables to bread to pieces of cheesecake. The restaurant seats groups, so consider going with a girlfriend or two, scoping out a group of guys at the bar, and then asking them if they'd like to share your table. With all the sharing and dipping, you'll be off to an intimate start! To find a Melting Pot in your area, go to *www.meltingpot.com*.

59. RIVERBOAT

Take a small journey on a riverboat with a few friends, and you are guaranteed to have a fun evening. If you meet a nice guy on the trip, well, you will just have to be stuck with him for the duration of the sail. Oh well. Most major rivers offer riverboats, many of which have bars on board, so if you live near one don't miss this opportunity for romance.

◯ PRO *Because there is booze and water involved, guys seem to flock to riverboat bars.*

◯ CON *Seasickness.*

=Time �=Friends $=Expense

60. SQUARE-DANCING CLUB

Remember those fun days in elementary school music class when you got to put down your recorders, put on the country-style music, and do some good, old-fashioned square dancing? Well, you can bring those days back to life by joining a square-dancing club. Not only is square dancing great exercise, it's a great, wholesome way to meet your partners. To find a square-dancing club, check out *www.dosado.com*.

○ PRO *The "Swing your partner" move is a good preview of whether the two of you have chemistry.*

○ CON *Square dancing is a dying art in some parts of the country, so you may have some trouble finding a club, especially one that involves people under the age of 60.*

61. UNDER THE MISTLETOE AT A CHRISTMAS PARTY

Mistletoe gives you the perfect excuse to kiss a stranger . . . if you want to. If you spot someone interesting at a Christmas party and you get the sense that he might be interested too, see if you can work it so the two of you are conveniently under the mistletoe at the same time. Then glance up and say, "well, we're here . . . " You don't have to make out with him—just a quick peck to let him know he's piqued your interest.

62. EIGHT-MINUTE DATING

With eight-minute dating, you will have eight one-on-one dates that last eight minutes each . . . then you decide which of your eight dates you would like to get to know better and, if the guy feels the same way about you, the 8minuteDating.com organization provides you with contact information so you can set up another date. If you don't meet someone you click with, 8minute-Dating will pay for your next event. For more information, check out *www.8minutedating.com*.

○ PRO *A room full of eligible singles and eight chances to meet someone you click with in one night.*

○ CON *If you're not terribly outgoing, 8minuteDating could be intimidating.*

63. ANTIQUE TOY SHOW

If seeing toys that you loved to play with as a kid sparks some excitement in you, don't miss the chance to check out an antique toy show. Guys love their toys, and some of them might want to check out the toys they played with as a kid as well. So after you check out the Barbies and Breyer horses, make sure you spend some time in the G.I. Joe section—you might get excitement from more than just the toys.

64. BLACK FRIDAY

They call it Black Friday because it's the first day of the year that stores actually start to make a profit—going from red to black in their books. And they call it Black Friday for another reason—the stores are packed. The more packed the stores, the better your chances of scoring a date in addition to a stack of bargains. To maximize your guy exposure on the busiest shopping day of the year, go where the guys are—the benches in the mall, the bars, or coffee shops in or near the mall, in line at CD or DVD stores, or, for the guy who can shop 'til he drops, the men's stores.

◑ PRO *The sales are great, especially if you go early.*

◐ CON *The crowds can be downright overwhelming, putting you in no mood to be friendly.*

65. BRING-YOUR-OLD-BOYFRIEND PARTY

It's not unusual for a man and woman to remain friends after they've broken up. If you have a significant number of friends who have kept in touch with their exes, it may be worthwhile for you to host a bring-your-old-boyfriend party, where you ask your guests to bring one or more old flames that they wouldn't mind seeing hook up with another party guest.

◑ PRO *If you're interested in a guy your friend has dated, you can get some background info on him before you decide whether or not you want to go out.*

◐ CON *If anyone still has feelings for an ex, jealously is bound to rear its ugly head.*

66. CHRISTMAS TREE SHOW

If you're planning to decorate your place with a tree this year, you might want to gather some creative ideas at a Christmas tree show. Not only will you think about how to expand beyond the traditional ornaments and lights, you might bump into some fellow single people who, like you, don't need a partner to put up a tree. A solo guy you see at a Christmas tree show is nearly guaranteed to be single. So don't be afraid to approach him and ask him which tree style he finds the most appealing. You might find yourself sharing some eggnog soon after.

67. CLAMBAKE

There is just something about a giant steamer full of shelled sea-food that really makes a party. And better yet, men love clams. Whether it's the potential for an eating contest—who can put down the most dozen clams???—or the fact that littlenecks go well with beer, you need not worry about why guys flock to clam bakes. You just need to get yourself to one or more of them so you can meet and mingle with these guys . . . and enjoy a few dozen clams yourself, of course.

○ PRO *Lots of men coupled with good eating and outdoor fun.*

○ CON *The potential for a "bad clam," which could put an end to your clambake fun real quick. If you spot a black clam or a shell that hasn't fully opened, throw it away ASAP.*

68. DOUBLE DATE

Blind dates have definitely gotten a bad rap—and for good reason, in some cases. But if a friend offers to fix you up with someone and will come along to watch the success or crash and burn of the union of you and a complete stranger, it takes some of the pressure off. So if a friend whose judgment you trust (this part is key) offers to fix you up with one of her single male friends and wants to double date, take her up on it.

○ PRO *All you have to lose is one night, but you'll still be out with your pal.*

○ CON *If things don't go as your fixer-up friend planned (especially if her guy is good friends with your reject), things could get awkward between the two of you.*

69. HOLIDAY DANCE

If you receive an invitation to a holiday dance, don't turn it down. These formal events are full of much more than holiday cheer—they are filled with single men, particularly when they are held by charitable organizations. So don't miss it.

○ PRO *A great excuse to spring for a festive holiday ball gown.*

○ CON *These events usually require a donation, which can be a stretch for some people at the holidays.*

70. FRENCH RESTAURANT

For delightful ambiance and scrumptious food—the perfect romantic atmosphere to meet the man of your dreams—go to a French restaurant. Dress up, take a single girlfriend or two with you, and have a wonderful meal. For prime guy exposure, go at the most popular dinner hour and have a few drinks or sodas at the bar before you sit down. That way, you'll increase your chances of meeting some guys before dinner and get a good preview of the menu, so to speak.

71. NEW YEAR'S DAY PARTY

For a nice alternative to the New Year's Eve party, consider attending or hosting a New Year's Day party. If you eat your pork and sauerkraut, your luck may kick in immediately . . . in the form of a handsome, single guy at the same party.

○ PRO *If you've made a resolution to improve your love life, you may be able to cross it off your list on the first day of the year!*

○ CON *If you over-imbibed the night before, you might not be at your freshest.*

72. PONTOON BOAT PARTY

Set sail on a pontoon boat party with a few friends, and you are guaranteed to have a fun day. If you meet a nice guy on the trip, what a great bonus! And if you don't, there will always be the men on the other boats you pass along the way. Don't miss this opportunity for romance.

○ PRO *Because there is booze and water involved, guys seem to love pontoon boat parties.*

○ CON *If you're not having fun, you'll be stuck on the water for the duration of the trip.*

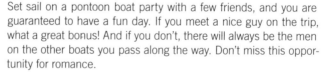
=Time ♥=Friends $=Expense

73. ST. PATRICK'S DAY PARTY

Whether you're actually Irish or you just enjoy pretending you're Irish or you're celebrating the fraction of your heritage that bleeds green on St. Patrick's Day, you'll be at a St. Patrick's Day party with bells on . . . drinking green beer, of course. And St. Patrick's Day is one of those holidays that seem to appeal to guys. Maybe it's the bagpipes, maybe it's the excuse to wear a skirt, or maybe (again) it's the green beer. No matter what gets them there, you are guaranteed to be surrounded by guys at a St. Patrick's Day party.

○ PRO *Irish people know how to throw a fantastic party.*

○ CON *Some really drunk guys . . . possibly in kilts.*

74. TOGA PARTY

It is virtually impossible to have a bad time at a toga party. First of all, anyone who would throw one is obviously a fun-loving person with lots of fun-loving guy friends for you to meet. And second, you're completely free of any uncomfortable shoes or other accessories . . . you're wearing a toga, for God's sake. So throw on your favorite old sheet and sandals and have a ball.

○ PRO *No stressing about what to wear.*

○ CON *Because the guys will all be wearing togas, you won't get a great sense of their physique or fashion sense (if that matters to you). Potential for wardrobe malfunction if you're not properly pinned.*

75. PRETZEL FACTORY

For a combination of a wonderful smell, delicious samples, and an interesting tour, consider a visit to a pretzel factory. This is a fun place to take the kids or to go with a few friends. And because pretzel factory tours involve food and food samples (most men love pretzels), you will find some men in your tour group or buying fresh pretzels in the gift shop.

Five great soft pretzel factories:
1. Philly Soft Pretzel Factory, Philadelphia, PA
2. Intercourse Soft Pretzel Factory, Lancaster County, PA
3. Sturgis Pretzel House, Lititz, PA
4. It's a Wrap Pretzel Factory, Hamilton, NJ
5. Benzel's Pretzel Factory, Altoona, PA

○=Time ✚=Friends $=Expense

76. BLUES BAR

Whether you love blues or you just feel the need for a little mellow-ing out, a blues bar will do the trick. So grab a bar stool or a couch, relax over a smooth cocktail or beer, and let the blues soothe your soul. After all, your soothed soul just might find its mate a few stools over.

77. CHAMPAGNE BREAKFAST

On a Sunday when you're just not ready to let the weekend end, head out for a festive champagne breakfast. A lot of restaurants are getting into hosting champagne breakfasts. Enjoy a combina-tion spread of breakfast and lunch foods, a glass or two of cham-pagne (or perhaps a mimosa!) and take a look around you at the many guys feasting on eggs and ham. Men love eating breakfast out, and the champagne is an added bonus.

78. CHRISTMAS EVE SERVICE

There are some Americans who only attend church once or twice a year. These people are sometimes called "Chreasters" because they reserve their church-going for Christmas and Easter. Whether or not you yourself are a Chreaster, you could benefit from attend-ing a Christmas Eve service because of all the male Chreasters who have come out of the woodwork to worship on the night before Jesus' birthday.

79. COUPLES' WEDDING SHOWER

Instead of the traditional party where a room full of women watch the bride open gifts, some couples are opting for a joint shower these days. And these couples' showers, sometimes called Jack and Jills, are wonderful places to meet single guys. The groom invites his closest friends and groomsmen—plenty of guys for you to meet. So if you get an invitation to one of these modern-day wedding showers, go.

○ PRO *The guys at the wedding shower will be a preview of who will be at the wedding a few weeks later.*

○ CON *If you go on a few dates with someone from the shower and it doesn't work out, you will be forced to see him again at the wedding.*

 =Time =Friends $=Expense

80. CULINARY FESTIVAL

You may just find your match—in and out of the kitchen—at a culinary festival. Whether you love to cook or you just love to eat good food, you'll enjoy the cooking demonstrations, samples, and food/wine pairings at a culinary festival. And these outdoor events tend to attract single men . . . better yet, single men who cook.

○ PRO *If you meet someone special, you can use your new skills to make him dinner.*

○ CON *There may also be quite a few married or attached guys at a culinary festival—keep your eyes out for rings and girlfriends.*

81. DOG BIRTHDAY PARTY

If you have a dog, you've probably celebrated a few of his or her birthdays. So you will understand when a friend loves his or her pooch enough to celebrate its birthday in a big way. A dog birthday party is not only a great opportunity to allow your dog some play-time with fellow four-legged friends; it also allows you the opportunity to mingle with fellow dog owners. So bring a basket of bones and a bottle of wine and have a ball.

○ PRO *If you and he both love dogs, you are off to a great start.*

○ CON *Not all dogs are good in a party environment—if your dog is particularly hyper or a serious crotch sniffer or leg humper, consider attending the birthday party without him.*

82. GRILL-YOUR-OWN RESTAURANT

Most guys love meat. Most guys love meat on the grill. And most guys love cooking meat on the grill. So a grill-your-own restaurant will attract plenty of meat-eating guys who would rather cook their own steak to perfection than leave it in the hands of a chef. So pick out a good-looking cut of meat (or chicken or veggie kabobs) and sidle up next to a good-looking guy at the grill.

83. SMORGASBORD

On a night when you are feeling particularly hungry, consider heading out to your local smorgasbord. Not only will you pay one price to sample limitless portions of any type of food, you will pile food on your plate alongside a lot of men. Guys love to eat, especially when there is no limit to the amount. And many men are impressed by women who eat more than a side salad for dinner.

=Time =Friends $ =Expense

84.   TAVERN ON A RAINY SATURDAY

On a rainy Saturday when you have nothing to do, grab a fun-loving girlfriend and head to a cozy tavern for lunch. If there's a good football or baseball game on, the place will probably be full of guys. Even if you don't meet the man of your dreams, you can enjoy a good burger.

85.   WINE AND CHEESE PARTY

For a more sophisticated night out, head to a wine and cheese party. As you feast on a selection of perfectly aged wines and cheeses, you will mingle with the more refined side of the male species. If guys who shotgun beers and chomp on wings aren't your type, you may just find your ideal match at a wine and cheese event.

86.   COMMUNITY PLAY GROUP

For those of you who have always dreamed of acting on stage but never got the chance, you'll be happy to know that it is never too late. Most cities and towns host community playhouses that take auditions from both experienced and novice actors and actresses. Plus, these groups are a fabulous way to meet new people—both your fellow actors, the people designing the stage, the lighting guys . . . the list goes on and on. So watch your local paper for auditions . . . you just may be the next Juliet.

○ PRO *You will get to enjoy the experience of performing on stage, which is life changing in and of itself.*

○ CON *Because they are usually fairly professionally done, these plays will require a lot of your time.*

87.   COSTUME PARTY

It doesn't have to be Halloween for you to throw or attend a fabulous costume party. Costume parties are some of the most fun parties, because the dress-up theme puts everyone in a good mood. A costume party also gives you a quick glimpse into a guy's personality based on the type of costume he chooses. Does he use the costume as a means to express himself in a big way, or does he use it in a more subtle way? And at a costume party, there is no requirement to commit to a conversation—if you're bored, you can slip away without revealing your true face. If you are bored by the conversation, you can leave without revealing yourself from behind the mask.

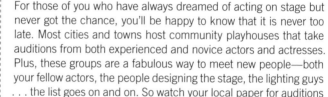

=Time =Friends $=Expense

88. ENGAGEMENT PARTY

Instead of the traditional split between men and women for a shower or bachelor/bachelorette party, many engaged couples are choosing to throw an engagement party to celebrate their impending union. These parties are wonderful places to meet men in the form of the groom's closest friends. Who knows—you might get an early date for the wedding!

89. DAY AFTER CHRISTMAS SHOPPING

Next to Black Friday, the day after Christmas is one of the busiest shopping days of the year. If you hit the mall on December 26, you are guaranteed to bump into single men returning gifts. So to cope with the crowds and increase your chances of meeting a fellow shopper, take frequent breaks in the mall coffee shops or restaurants, where a lot of guys will be hanging out.

○ PRO *You'll get your returns finished, so you won't be faced with bags of unwanted gifts.*

○ CON *If a guy is at the mall returning most of his gifts, he could be the fussy type. Plus, you're sure to battle some major crowds.*

90. EASTER MORNING CHURCH SERVICE

There are some men who only attend church for major holidays, one of them being Easter morning. And hey, that's better than never going to church at all, right?

91. ESPRESSO BAR

It's a rare breed who prefers to throw down a super-strong shot of coffee to sipping a cup. If you fit into this unique breed, you obviously don't like to mess around when it comes to getting your caffeine . . . and you just might have things other than a love of strong coffee in common with the people sitting next to you at an espresso bar. So even if your coffee is down the hatch, spend some time in the espresso bar. Jump on the Wi-Fi Internet, enjoy a muffin or scone, read a magazine—whatever you have to do to increase your chances of meeting a single, attractive espresso drinker.

○ PRO *Some espresso bars have happy hours; a nice alternative if you don't drink alcohol or are sick of the bar scene.*

○ CON *Espressos and gourmet coffees are significantly more expensive than a 16-ounce coffee at a convenience store.*

=Time =Friends $=Expense

92. FONDUE PARTY

To get your friends to mingle, eat, and dip, host a fondue party. Chop foods into bite-sized pieces, pull out the old fondue pot and skewers, and invite your single friends. To better your chances, ask each of your friends to bring a single guy friend.

O PRO *The interactive nature of the fondue party will make it easy for all your guests to get to know each other.*

O CON *Because some people tend to double dip or lick their skewers, fondue parties are not for germiphobes.*

93. HOUSE SITTING

If a friend asks you to watch his or her house while he or she is away, don't look at it as a burden—look at it as an opportunity. In a new neighborhood or town, your possibilities for meeting men will be completely refreshed. So don't spend your entire week sitting inside watching your friend's HBO—get out there and explore the restaurants, shops, and parks . . . just to see who you bump into.

O PRO *You will be doing your friend a favor and opening up your dating possibilities at the same time.*

O CON *If your friend lives on a farm in the middle of nowhere, your chances of meeting people will be a lot slimmer.*

94. NEWLY OPENED RESTAURANT

When a restaurant first opens its doors, it usually attracts a flurry of curious diners in the area. To meet some of the inquisitive single male diners, don't miss these crucial first few weeks. For best results, go at prime time on a Saturday and have a drink at the bar before you sit down—that way, you'll meet the drinkers and the diners. And remember, try to keep a positive attitude. "You can be dropped naked into the middle of a group of single men and if you have a terrible attitude about yourself and men, you're going to end up turning them off," says Karen Jones, president of the Heart Matters and author of *Men Are Great*. "Energetically, we understand things about each other instantly. So the minute you catch yourself thinking or saying things like, 'I'm never going to find Mr. Right' or 'all men are looking for 22-year-old women,' stop yourself," she says. Instead, remind yourself that you are worthy of a happy, healthy relationship and the right guy is out there and just as eager to meet you as you are to meet him.

95. VINEYARD TOUR

$ $

On a sunny spring or summer afternoon, consider a trip to your local (or not-so-local) vineyard. These tours tend to draw single people who like to try wine, and they usually include a pleasant ride around the vines followed by a "tour" of the wines they create there. So get to know an attractive tour-mate on the ride . . . then get to know him better over a glass of wine.

◑ PRO *Vineyard tours are usually fairly inexpensive for the combination of education and tastings they include.*

◑ CON *These tours also tend to attract some wine snobs.*

96. WRITING YOUR WILL

$ $ $

No matter what your age, if you have assets, you should have a will. On the plus side, drawing a will gives you the opportunity to have a face-to-face meeting with a handsome, eligible lawyer. So do a little research and find a single, male lawyer (who also has the reputation of being good at what he does, of course) and set up a meeting. There's no telling what could happen.

◑ PRO *You will accomplish an unpleasant but necessary task and meet someone you could potentially date at the same time. Talk about killing two birds . . .*

◑ CON *Lawyers may not be your type.*

97. CITY HALL

$

Important men wearing suits. Need we say more? People think of City Hall as a place for a couple to get hitched fast or where criminals are immediately sentenced, but City Hall is crawling with young lawyers and district attorneys. You can always go into City Hall and simply pretend you're sightseeing. Then ask some unsuspecting young prosecutor for directions.

98. JEWELRY STORE

$ $

You may think that couples go to jewelry stores to pick out wedding rings and necklaces that glisten and all that bling. But guess who also goes there? Men! It's true—men have plenty of women in their lives who make it known that jewelry is the ONLY gift for them. Often, men are shopping for aunts, mothers, sisters, and grandmothers, so don't be shy—see if he has a ring and see if he's ring shopping. If not, dazzle him with your brilliant personality.

=Time =Friends $=Expense

99.   RESTAURANT DISTRICT

If you have a restaurant district in your town, you simply have to hit it regularly with your girlfriends on peak nights and times. For one, there's the large range of menus to choose from. And more importantly, there is a large range of men looking for a tasty bite. Bring your appetite, but also bring your glasses so you don't miss any of the men!

100.   RETIREMENT HOME

More and more single people are volunteering these days. This is an outstanding way to do something positive in your community first and possibly meet the man of your dreams second. Call around to some of the retirement communities in your area and learn how you can lend a hand. Then ask how many volunteers are normally there and what you would be doing. Even if you don't meet Mr. Right, you'll instantly meet a lot of new friends and do a wonderful service for your community.

101.   SADIE HAWKINS DANCE

A Sadie Hawkins dance is based on Sadie Hawkins, a woman who lived in the 1930s who got tired of waiting for a man to ask her out, so she took matters into her own hands. At a Sadie Hawkins dance, all the women follow in Sadie's brave footsteps and do all the approaching. So if you prefer to ask a man to dance to vice versa, this will be your kind of event.

O PRO *The ball will be in your court, so you can dance with whomever you choose.*

O CON *This format opens you up to the possibility of rejection. If you're feeling less than self-confident, skip it.*

102.   WEGMANS

Wegmans is an excellent place to meet men. Everyone loves food and many people don't know how to cook. If you do, you could offer some pointers as you spot a guy gazing confusedly at the shallots. If you don't cook and you find yourself gazing confusedly at the shallots, you could always ask the advice of a handsome stranger. And the beauty of Wegmans is that the vast variety of foods they offer can lead to food confusion, which, when it comes to meeting men, is a good thing. To find a Wegmans store near you, go to *www.wegmans.com*.

=Time =Friends $=Expense

103. CRIME SCENE

$

Not exactly the storybook meeting one would hope for, but when a crime is committed, people do tend to gather and chat. Walk right up and take a peek around to see if there are any men hanging around. Just stay behind the crime scene tape. Don't forget, cops need love too.

104. FRIENDS

$

One of the most foolproof ways to meet a man is through your friends. While this may seem obvious, many women do not let enough friends know that they're single and looking. Of course, your close friends know. But what about your friends at work? You don't need to wear a scarlet "S," indicating you're terribly lonely. Just give subtle hints that you're available. Make it known you're open to being set-up, but do not make it sound like every potential meeting is one step closer to a lifetime of bliss. Just enjoy a cocktail with your friend's friend. A good conversation goes a long way in the beginning.

○ PRO *If things work out, you'll have a nice little posse to hang out with.*

○ CON *If things don't work out, it could be a little awkward between you and the friend(s) who set you up.*

105. GLASS-BLOWING COMPANY

$ $

If you're into arts and crafts, design, or simply appreciate how glassware is made, you're off to a good start. There are a number of places where you can learn how to blow glass. One of the more popular places is called Simon Pearce (*www.simonpearce .com*). Obviously, if it's Sunday at 1 P.M., you're not likely to find the majority of men at a glass-blowing establishment. However, if you prefer men with an artsy flair, you just might find what you're seeking here. Plus, some of the men working in these businesses are both artsy and masculine. They are the type to appreciate a painting and they can fix a flat. This type isn't easy to find. Worst case, you'll find the perfect vase for 50 percent off because of a miniscule scratch on the bottom.

106. POTTERY-PAINTING STORE

Haven't you heard? Pottery painting is the "in" thing. Well, somewhat. Pottery painting has become more popular thanks to some of the dating shows on TV. But could you actually meet someone there? There is only one way to find out. Drop in with a friend and grab something off the shelf to paint and see who comes and goes. Also speak with the manager there and see if he or she ever notices any single guys in there.

O PRO *If anything, you've found yourself the perfect spot to bring your next date.*

O CON *It could be brimming with couples, but you don't know until you try.*

107. SANTA'S LAP

You've seen the throngs of people lined up to meet Old St. Nick. But did you ever notice that there are a number of men there? It's true. Many of these men are divorced or even the uncles of the children they're bringing to the jolly wonder. The question is, how do you meet these men? One way to meet them is to volunteer your time as one of Santa's elves. But if that seems a bit too time-consuming, then grab a box of candy canes and hand them out to those in line. Just tell them you bought too many and you're giving them away. In the meantime, start chatting away with the people in line. Not only will they think you've truly mastered the whole "Christmas spirit" thing, but you'll begin to learn who's naughty, who's nice, and who's single.

108. SPA

Spas come in many forms these days. There are more natural, holistic spas specializing in massage, facials, manicures and pedicures, waxing, and more. And there are also "med spas," which offer non-invasive laser surgery, Botox, microdermabrasion, and even teeth whitening. Now more than ever, men are paying close attention to the appearance of their bodies. And you can find men in spas, but they're still not highly common. However, if a man who goes to a spa interests you, then don't hesitate. Get to know some of the female employees at your local spa and spread the word that you're on the prowl. Women in spas are more than happy to play matchmaker!

 =Time =Friends $=Expense

109. ANIMAL HOSPITAL

Timing is definitely a factor here, as an animal hospital isn't crawling with single men at all times. But, many single men have dogs, cats, and even birds, so if you can just determine the best possible time to go, you might meet up with a fellow animal lover. Think about your own schedule. Now, factor in where your local animal hospital is located. If you're greatly attached to your hospital, then there is no point in finding a new one. However, if you're up for a new one, find an animal hospital in a busy part of town where you know many single professionals live. You're guaranteed to find something waiting for you in the waiting room. Go ahead, touch his monkey.

O PRO *If you both love animals, you have a very important thing in common.*

O CON *Some animal hospital trips may be emergencies, in which case it may not be the right time, or you may not be in the right mood, to meet a handsome stranger.*

110. CATERING A PARTY

Feeling a little adventurous and a little short on spare cash? Call a few of the premier catering companies in your area and see if they need some servers. You'll refresh the water glasses, bring out extra silverware, pour wine, and serve food to interesting people of all kinds, including single men! It's a fun way to meet new people and you might even make some contacts for your full-time career too.

O PRO *You'll put a nice little chunk of cash in your pocket.*

O CON *You will give up some valuable weekend nights.*

111. HIGH SCHOOL OR COLLEGE YEARBOOK

Although it may be ten, twenty, or even thirty years since high school, take a half hour and flip through your yearbook. Not only will it rekindle some memories of yesteryears, but chances are there are a few guys in there with whom you'd absolutely love to reunite. The hard part is tracking them down, but through sites like classmates.com and reunion.com, you just might be able to do it.

O PRO *You might be able to close the loop with your first love.*

O CON *It may rekindle the low self-esteem you had as a brace-faced teenager.*

=Time =Friends $=Expense

112. ON-SITE RADIO PROMOTION

They're always up to something outrageous and they're often right around the corner. Your local rock, hip-hop, or sports talk station is throwing a promotion near you. You just need to find it. Find some of your favorite station's Web sites and look to see where they're having special promotional events. Men and women come out in droves to see their favorite DJ, enjoy food and drink specials, improve the community, lend a hand with a food or toy drive, and more. Why not check it out?

O PRO *These events can give out some really cool prizes.*

O CON *If you live in the middle of nowhere, your local radio station's events may not be so happening.*

113. PAINT STORE

Remember when you swore you were going to paint the bathroom? How about that old dresser that you wanted to give a faux finish? Head over to your local paint store and get the 411 on these projects and more. And not just for home beautification purposes. More than likely, a handsome and knowledgeable customer-service man will be there to lend a hand. But if he's not your shade of gold, peek around the store. Surely you'll bump into someone who can not only help you with your questions, but he just might give you a hand with the labor.

114. RESTAURANT SUPPLY STORE

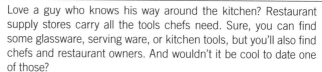

Love a guy who knows his way around the kitchen? Restaurant supply stores carry all the tools chefs need. Sure, you can find some glassware, serving ware, or kitchen tools, but you'll also find chefs and restaurant owners. And wouldn't it be cool to date one of those?

115. SORORITY CONNECTIONS

Remember your closest friends from your college sorority? Some of them are married and their husbands have single friends. Some of them work in busy offices filled with single men. And some of them have simply made new friends over the years who happen to be male and single. Catch up with an old friend, have a few laughs, and see if your college confidante knows any cute guys—all in one shot.

116.   SPECIALTY FOOD STORE

Want a guy who can whip up something delectable for you? Pop in a specialty food store. Whether it's a cheese shop, spice shop, bread shop, or a store that caters to Asian, Middle Eastern, or another international cuisine, you can find professional and amateur chefs in these stores. Catching the male crowd requires that you pop in between 5 and 7 P.M. on weeknights, just when most people are getting out of work. Just browse the aisles and find what you like. Then find something for dinner.

117.   VIP PARTIES

Everyone loves a party. But if you're looking to meet men with a little influence and perhaps a healthy bank account all while having the time of your life, start attending VIP parties. Not sure how? Do an online search for "VIP" parties and see where you can find some.

118.   YOUR ROOMMATE

Did you ever actually discuss your singlehood with your roommate? Maybe you should find out more about where they work, who they know, if they've ever wondered about setting you up, and, most importantly, if they have any friends or coworkers who happen to be male, attractive, and even mildly interesting. It's an easy one everyone forgets. The worst that happens? He ends up sleeping over on a regular basis. Then your roommate has to see him 24/7.

119.   MATERNITY WARD

This is certainly not to suggest that you should pick up a new papa in a maternity ward. But in addition to proud dads, there are proud uncles, brothers, and friends in a maternity ward. A guy who shows up to see a friend's newborn baby probably has a sensitive side, so you'll be off to a good start. For best results, head to the maternity ward toward the end of visiting hours—when you are given the boot, everyone will have to walk out at once, which will give you a good chance to exchange some words with fellow visitors in the elevator.

=Time =Friends $=Expense

120.   PLACE OF WORSHIP

"For nearly twenty years, I have taught undergraduate and gradu-ate students and these days, most of the students are female," says Michael Ray Smith, Ph.D., professor in the Department of Mass Communication at Campbell University in North Carolina. "And I have found that my single female students say they have the best opportunities to meet men at a place of worship," he says. "The venue may sound hopelessly dated, but it is still the absolute best place to meet people who prove to be good people. The wor-ship venue has a built-in support network and the activities tend to be low stress and interactive," he says.

121.   WINE-TASTING GROUP

If you love tasting new wines, you will enjoy a wine-tasting group. Wine-tasting groups usually meet biweekly, monthly, or quarterly to taste and discuss various wines from around the world. With more than 100,000 types of wines worldwide you will have plenty of tasting to do. Members all love wine, so they have at least one thing in common . . . and the conversation usually flows as smoothly as the wine from there. And because more and more men are getting into wine these days, you are likely to meet some interesting ones in a wine-tasting group. If you can't find a wine-tasting group in your area, consider forming one yourself.

122.   COMMUNITY ORCHESTRA

If you can play a string instrument well but you'd rather not play professionally, consider trying out for your community orchestra. Community orchestras are comprised of people who love to play classical music . . . but have not quit their day jobs. And they usu-ally include some single musical men. So to expand your musical talents and your social circle, don't let this opportunity pass you by. If nothing more, you will meet a wonderful group of friends who share your passion.

=Time =Friends $=Expense

123.   FRIENDS OF THE OPPOSITE SEX

$

If you are lucky enough to have a few guy pals to bounce things off of and share a few laughs and/or beers with, don't overlook them as sources for men you might actually be interested in dating. Drop a couple of hints about being in the market for a man, and make sure you join in for guys' night out once in a while. Who knows . . . one of the men you once considered just a friend may become a potential date himself.

124.   GREEK FOOD FESTIVAL

$ $

Greek food is one of the tastiest ethnic fares in the world. So if you are lucky enough to live in an area that sponsors an annual Greek food festival, by all means, go. Choose from Caesar salad, baklava, stuffed grape leaves, or feta . . . your taste buds will be pleased. And because Greek men are some of the most charming and good looking around, your eyes will be pleased as well. So use the food as an opportunity to ask questions of the male Greek festivalgoers . . . or even the non-Greek guys who are there for the tasty gyros.

○ **PRO** *A Greek food festival promises to be a rewarding activity—you'll get some culture and a stomach full of delicious food.*

○ **CON** *Garlic breath.*

125.   GYRO STAND

$ $

Scattered throughout cities, authentic Greek gyro stands are gold mines. If you are a gyro lover, you will no doubt know where these places are, and you should frequent them more often because . . . men love gyros. Gyro stands are great for meeting someone: Just shoot a few glances as you are ordering, and then walk in the same direction—gyros in hand—if you find the fellow customer interesting. If not, you can make a quick getaway.

126.   IN A WEDDING PARTY

If a friend asks you to be in her wedding party, you may get more out of the experience than a thank-you gift and a dress you'll never wear again—you may get a man. If you're lucky, the gentleman you're paired with will be single, and you two will hit it off. If you're not so lucky, there will be three to ten others to choose from. So go into the wedding party experience with an open mind and an open heart.

127. NEW YEAR'S EVE PARTY

There are a few things about a New Year's Eve party that make it a great situation for meeting a man. First, you've got goals for the new year, one of which is probably to meet a nice guy—so why not start as soon as the clock strikes midnight? Second, you are probably a little buzzed, which will make you less shy and more daring. And third, when the ball drops and the countdown gets to "1," you have the perfect excuse to kiss someone!

◯ PRO *If you hit it off with a man at a New Year's Eve party, you will always have an excuse to celebrate on your anniversary.*

◯ CON *Beer goggles (females can wear them, too).*

128. SINGLES CONDO

As the show *Melrose Place* pointed out, living in a happening condo complex can do wonders for your social life. When it comes time for you to look for a new place, ask your realtor which condo complexes house the most singles in your age group. If you move into a complex with lots of single men, the trip to the mailbox, lounging by the pool, and walking to your car will seem much more exciting.

129. SLOT MACHINES

Next time you visit a casino, don't overlook the slot machines as an opportunity for love. As you walk into a row of slots, scan the machines to see if any of them house a handsome gambler. If so, slide up to the machine next to him and throw a low bill in the slot. You can always throw in more money if things pan out . . . or quickly slip away if the guy turns out to be a creep. Good luck!

130. YACHT CLUB

Enjoy nice boats, boat races, and socializing with rich men? Consider joining a yacht club. The club-sponsored social events and water sports will provide the perfect opportunity to mix and mingle with boat-owning members of the opposite sex. If you don't have the funds or the boating interest to join a club yourself, tag along with a friend or relative who is a member.

Five great yacht clubs:
1. The New York Yacht Club: *www.nyyc.org*
2. The California Yacht Club: *www.calyachtclub.com*
3. The Chicago Yacht Club: *www.chicagoyachtclub.org*
4. The Seattle Yacht Club: *www.seattleyachtclub.org*
5. The Annapolis Yacht Club: *www.annapolisyc.org*

⏱=Time ♦=Friends $=Expense

131. CRAB FESTIVAL

For fun in the sun including delicious fresh crabs and other seafood, beer, crafts, boat rides, single men, and more, head to a crab festival. Men tend to love events that combine water activities, food, and beer, so a crab festival is a sure bet for attracting them. So grab a fun girlfriend and have a wonderful day out in the fresh air.

Five great crab festivals:

1. Dungeness Crab and Seafood Festival, Port Angeles, WA: *www.crabfestival.org*
2. Little River Blue Crab Festival, Little River, SC: *www.crabfestival.com*
3. Kodiak Crab Festival, AK: *www.kodiak.org*
4. Baltimore Crab & Beer Fest, MD: *www.mdcrabfest.org*
5. Delmarva Blue Crab Festival, Milton, DE: *www.delmarva bluecrabfestival.com*

132. PRESS CONFERENCE

If a politician, sports figure, or other person of interest is coming to your area and holding a public press conference, consider attending. Not only to get a look at the person up close, but to get a load of the men who are also interested enough in the person to check them out. Studies show that couples who have a lot in common fare better than those who don't; by meeting a man at a press conference, you will know you have at least one topic in common.

133. CANDLE SHOP

Studies have shown that men get turned on by certain scents, including vanilla and cinnamon. So if you catch a man sniffing scented candles in a candle shop like Yankee Candle, you may be off to a good start. Smile and ask him if he'd like to grab a vanilla or cinnamon latte at a nearby coffee shop to keep his juices flowing.

134. DOG SUPPORT GROUP

If you are a dog owner, you know how much responsibility Fido or Spot requires. From waking up at 6:00 A.M. to the walks to making sure you haven't been gone for more than eight hours at a time, being a single dog owner can be tough. To share some of your woes and to meet fellow dog owners, consider joining a dog support group such as the San Diego Beagle Meetup Group. You will learn tips on training and feeding, and could possibly meet the male dog owner of your dreams.

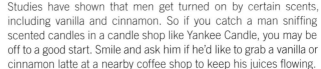

=Time ♦=Friends $=Expense

135. HOMEMADE DOG-BISCUIT BAKERY

$ $

Although these places aren't on every street corner, they do exist, and if you have a dog with allergies or you're just extra conscious of what you feed him or her, you may want to swing into a homemade dog-biscuit bakery where you will find peanut butter, whole wheat, molasses, and other delicious dog biscuits. Plus, you may bump into a health-conscious, kind dog owner in the form of a single man. With all the biscuits, you have an instant icebreaker—ask him which flavors his dog prefers.

◐ **PRO** *These places are usually dog friendly, so you can let your pooch break the ice between you and a handsome dog-owning stranger.*

◑ **CON** *If you ask him which flavor his dog prefers and he says, "Actually, I come here for myself," run.*

136. HEMP JEWELRY STORE

Whether you are in the market for a cute pair of dangly earrings, a hemp necklace, or a patch for your bag, a hemp jewelry store is a good bet. In addition to the hemp merchandise, these stores attract laid-back, long-haired dudes looking for incense, candles, or unique items with which to decorate their pads. So if the hippie type turns you on, do some shopping at a hemp jewelry store.

137. NEW YEAR'S DAY BRUNCH

$ $

To ease the pain of a hangover and the sting of not having had a date the night before, invite a few girlfriends to join you at a popular New Year's Day brunch. These brunches usually offer a gigantic spread of all-you-can-eat food for one entry price, along with beers and mimosas; in other words, guy magnets. So despite your headache, be friendly as you wait in line for your omelet, and offer to share your table with a few eligible bachelors. Your year will be off to a great start.

138. OFF-LIMITS RESTAURANT

Everyone has that restaurant in their area that they steer clear of when they're single. Either they avoid it because they think everyone who goes there is on a date, or they went there with a past love and don't want to be reminded of a love gone bad or, even worse, a combination of both reasons. But by restricting yourself from this restaurant and its fine food and atmosphere, you could be limiting some opportunities to meet men. Businessmen—both local and out of town—often choose this kind of restaurant to hold dinner meetings because they know their clients will be impressed. So dress up and head to the off-limits restaurant with a girlfriend or two and get an interesting man's attention by sending a nice bottle of wine to his table (provided he isn't actually on a date, that is). It very well could be money—and an evening—well spent.

139. PRADA

For an upscale man, take a walk through Prada now and then. There's a reason *Vogue* editor Anna Wintour is such a fan of the brand—they make fabulous high-end sunglasses, handbags . . . and yes, men's clothing. But it is pricey. So if he's shopping at Prada, he's probably got a pretty nice car parked out front; if you're into men with money, you may want to approach him.

140. TREE-TRIMMING PARTY

To gather some singles together to celebrate the holidays with eggnog, carols, and some good old-fashioned tree trimming, host a tree-trimming party. A lot of single guys don't get their own trees, but they like to enjoy other people's trees. Send out invitations to your friends and ask them to bring more singles—the more the merrier. And be sure to hang plenty of mistletoe.

141. VALENTINE'S DAY NO-DATE PARTY

Valentine's Day is a great day to show your boyfriend or husband how much you care . . . or to wear all-black and party with fellow singles. If you're single, you know how painful holidays can feel. So if you get an invitation to a singles Valentine's Day no-date party, by all means, go. If you don't and you have a few single friends, consider throwing one of these shindigs yourself. Ask all your single friends—both male and female—to bring as many singles as they can gather up for the evening and have a great time.

=Time ⚣=Friends $=Expense

142. "GUY I WASN'T INTERESTED IN" PARTY

They say one man's trash is another man's treasure. This is definitely true when it comes to dating. So to meet some of the guys your friends didn't click with, throw a "guy I wasn't interested in" party and ask them to bring an ex or two (whom they are still friends with, obviously) and see how things pan out.

O PRO *You will know every guy at the party is eligible.*

O CON *There's the chance that a friend will bring a man she still has feelings for (consciously or subconsciously), which could cause major problems in your friendship if you decide to go for him.*

143. RITA'S ITALIAN ICE

Everyone's mood brightens when spring arrives, because of the warmer weather and also because Rita's Italian ice stands all up and down the East Coast open their doors. If you have ever had the pleasure of eating a Rita's Italian ice, custard, or gelati, you know why everyone loves the place. And men especially seem to enjoy Italian ice, possibly because it doesn't seem as feminine as a sundae topped with whipped cream and a cherry. No matter what the reason, on a warm day, the line at Rita's is usually long and constant, which will give you the opportunity to get to know some folks as you wait for your refreshing treat in the form of watermelon, vanilla, mango, or other delicious flavor. Check out *www.ritasice.com*.

O PRO *This is a great place to take the kids and scope for single dads.*

O CON *Although Rita's boasts of being "fat free," this label does not apply to the custard, which has enough fat for the entire week. If you are watching your weight, stick with the ice only.*

144. SCHOOL

If you are an elementary, middle, or high school teacher, you're probably surrounded with lots of drama between students in the hall, in the lunchroom, and in your very own classroom. And if there is a single male teacher who sparks your interest, you may be tempted to slip him a note as well. If you are a teacher, don't rule out your fellow faculty members as potential mates.

O PRO *Teachers are usually patient, smart, and enjoy kids—a great résumé for a man.*

O CON *Some teachers tend to pick up the gossipy nature of their students, so if you start dating a fellow teacher, be prepared for the news to travel around school quickly.*

= Time ♦ = Friends $ = Expense

145.   THAI RESTAURANT

Thai restaurants are wonderful if you are craving a meal that is both hot and sweet . . . and you may find the same combination of men there as well. Thai food tends to attract men with adventurous palates, so if you're looking for a man with whom to try different foods, a Thai restaurant is a good start.

Five great Thai restaurants:
1. Palms Thai Restaurant, Los Angeles, CA: *www.palmsthai.com*
2. Bangkok Thai, Salt Lake City, UT: *www.bangkokthai.com*
3. Sawatdee Thai, Minneapolis, MN: *www.sawatdee.com*
4. Thai House Restaurant, Westchester County, NY: *www.thaihouserestaurant.com*
5. Chantanee Family Thai Restaurant, Bellevue, WA: *www.chantanee.com*

146.   THE VITAMIN SHOPPE

Whether you're in the market for a weight-loss supplement, antioxidant-rich vitamin, calming herb, or a health-conscious man, you can find them all at a Vitamin Shoppe store. For instance, Vitamin Shoppes offer an extensive selection of muscle-building, protein-rich supplements and powders, which draw a lot of men looking to bulk up. So instead of buying your vitamins and supplements at the grocery store or drugstore, pop into a Vitamin Shoppe where you know the selection of products—and men—will be a cut above the rest. Check out *www.vitaminshoppe.com*.

147.   COUNTY COURTHOUSE

If you have no idea where your county courthouse is located, you're missing out on a major hub of activity—and men in the form of lawyers, judges, and local politicians—at your county courthouse. So this year, consider paying your local taxes in person, picking up a few brochures on highway safety, or looking up the history of your property at your county courthouse. There's no telling who you might meet . . . and you'll know he's local.

=Time =Friends $=Expense

148.   HOMETOWN

If you've moved out of your hometown for your career, past relationship, or just bigger and brighter things, you probably only get back there once in a while. But the next time you're there to visit your parents and/or to celebrate a major holiday, don't pass up the chance to pop in to some of the old high school hangouts. Around the holidays, these places usually draw single guys of all ages who want to throw a few back with their old buddies . . . single guys you may have once known and had a crush on. So next time you're home, call up an old girlfriend you've stayed in touch with and head to the local hangout.

O PRO *If nothing more, you will have fun reminiscing with her.*

O CON *Some stones are better left unturned.*

149.   NIGHTCLUB OPENING

Although attending nightclubs on a regular basis might not be the best way to meet Mr. Right, a nightclub-opening party in your area might be worth checking out. These events usually offer discounts on drinks, food, and/or a free cover charge, and people in the neighborhood sometimes go simply to check out a new place. So next time you hear about a new club opening in your city or town, get dressed up and head on over with a girlfriend or two.

O PRO *It's not every day you get to attend a swank event like this.*

O CON *Club hounds, who live for these events, could be prowling for a one-nighter.*

150.   NUDIST COLONY

If you try the beach and love it, you may want to make naked living more of an everyday thing. Nudist colonies offer plenty of activities during which you can meet single men—swimming, tennis, golf, you name it.

O PRO *Men at a nudist colony are probably pretty free-spirited, if that's your thing.*

O CON *Some of them are also weird. Beware.*

151. RAW RESTAURANT

There are health fanatics who swear that 100 percent raw food is the way to go. Doesn't sound bad when you're thinking of carrots or even sushi, but beyond that, raw food may scare folks. But if you have an adventurous attitude and are looking to meet men who feel the same way, a trip to a raw restaurant is in order. The unique nature of the fare itself is a conversation starter, and a lot of these restaurants are great forums for socializing.

Five great raw restaurants:

1. Juliano's Raw Planet, Santa Monica, CA: *www.planetraw.com*
2. Ecopolitan's Minneapolis Restaurant, Minneapolis, MN: *www.ecopolitan.com*
3. Raw Soul Catering and Restaurant, New York, NY: *www.rawsoul.com*
4. Jasper White's Summer Shack, Boston, MA: *www.summershack restaurant.com*
5. Arnold's Way Vegetarian Raw Café, Lansdale, CA: *www.arnoldsway.com*

152. SINGLES SUPPORT GROUP

In a singles support group, you will make friends with new men and women and learn to be more comfortable around members of both sexes. You will learn how members of the opposite sex view you, which can be very helpful when it comes to meeting men. And who knows? You might meet a guy right there in your very own group. You have nothing to lose. To find a singles support group in your area, check out *www.singlesorganizations.com*.

153. SALSA BAR

A lot of Mexican restaurants offer one, where you can expose your tortilla chips to a range of tangy, flavorful salsa creations. As you're at the bar dousing your chips, see who's up there with you. With all the salsas at your disposal, you have the perfect icebreaker—"Have you tried the one with barbecue sauce? It's excellent."

154. UNISEX SHOE STORE

Many shoe stores sell both men's and women's shoes, so next time you're in a shoe store looking for the perfect pair of heels, see if you can find a perfect man, too. You can tell a lot about a man from his shoes, so look for a man who is looking at shoes that fit your style of man, so to speak. If he's shopping for Birkenstocks, he's probably casual and laid-back. If he's looking at Doc Marten's, he's probably a little more rugged.

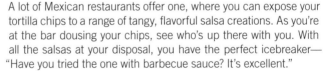

=Time =Friends $=Expense

155. COIN SHOW

🕐
👤
$

Although it may not be your idea of a rocking Saturday afternoon, some men are really into their coin collections. And some of their coin collections may actually be quite valuable. So to find some guys who appreciate a good piece of change, swing by a coin show the next time one comes to your area. You may discover an interest in collectible coins that you never knew you had . . . To find a coin show, go to *www.coinshows.com*.

156. ETHIOPIAN RESTAURANT

🕐

$ $

Ethiopian food is delicious, and you can eat it with your hands! Instead of using a fork, you scoop up the meat, beans, and vegetables with a special spongy bread. And the low-to-the-ground circular tables at an Ethiopian restaurant make them more relaxed; in other words, a great place to meet new people. Men you meet in an Ethiopian restaurant will be adventurous, and they're not afraid to break the rules a little and eat without utensils. To find an Ethiopian restaurant in your area, check out *www.ethiopianrestaurant .com*.

157. LOCK AND KEY PARTY

🕐

$

At a lock and key party, you might literally find the man who holds the key to your heart. It works like this: Women at the party are given padlocks and men are given keys, and the women have to find the man who holds the key for her particular lock. This interactive party is a perfect forum for meeting men. After all, you have a reason to march right up to a man and introduce yourself. If you don't know of any lock and key parties in your area, consider hosting one yourself.

158. MAKE-YOUR-OWN PIZZA PARTY

🕐
👤👤👤
$ $

For a great interactive party where singles can mix and mingle, throw a make-your-own pizza party. Buy a bunch of mini pizza crusts, an array of pizza toppings, from pineapple to sausage to mushrooms, and a few bottles of wine and invite some single friends over for some cooking and great conversation. To make it more interactive, have a "best pizza contest," where all the guests taste the pizza creations and vote for their favorite. To make sure you get a nice mix of singles, ask friends to bring a single friend as a "ticket" in the door.

🕐=Time 👤=Friends $=Expense

159.   A RESTAURANT WHERE YOU HAVE A CRUSH

$ $

If you frequent a favorite restaurant, you may have a favorite waiter who you'd like to get to know better . . . outside of his place of employment. If so, you should let him know how you feel in some subtle ways to give him the green light. For one, you can go to the restaurant often and make sure you give him a wave of acknowledgment. Second, you can request to be seated in his section. And third, you can leave him an extra big tip and if you are feeling particularly bold, a note with your phone number.

160.   SWAP MEET

$ $

At a swap meet, you can get some great stuff at cheap prices . . . and you can meet some nice male vendors and shoppers in the process. Some swap meets follow a theme, selling only sports equipment, computer stuff, or arts and crafts, for example. If you can, go to a themed swap meet that interests you—it will increase your chances of meeting someone you are compatible with. As an icebreaker, try haggling with a handsome vendor—you may get a fabulous bargain and a fabulous date.

161.   BARBER SHOP

$

If you need a trim but don't feel like springing for the price of a full cut and style, or if you have a rather low-maintenance cut, head to your local barber shop—your haircut will be cheaper, and you are guaranteed to be surrounded by men as you get it. And if you want to step it up a notch, look for a barber shop that serves beer to its patrons (some do this). If a guy sees that you are low maintenance enough to get your hair cut at a barber shop and drink a brew at the same time, he may fall in love right there. A lot of places don't advertise their beverage bonuses, so you may have to ask some men friends and find out about booze-serving barber shops through word of mouth.

O PRO *The ratio of men to women is more than guaranteed to be in your favor.*

O CON *You risk a bad or a butch haircut.*

162. | BEER FESTIVAL

$ $

Beer, especially a dark, strong microbrew, is not considered the drink of choice among females. So as a female, you are likely to be (pleasantly) way outnumbered by guys at a beer festival. Many men love to drink—and talk about—beer. At a beer festival, you will have countless ways to break the ice with questions about the Pennsylvania pale ale versus the Seattle stout. For information about beer festivals in your area, do an Internet search on this topic or call your local beer distributor.

> **Five great beer fests:**
> *(According to www.BeerFestivals.org)*
>
> 1. Oktoberfest USA, La Crosse, Wisconsin, annually in October: *www.oktoberfestusa.com*
> 2. Fremont Oktoberfest, Fremont District, Seattle, in September: *www.fremontoktoberfest.com*
> 3. Portland International Beer Festival, Portland, Oregon, annually in July: *www.seattlebeerfest.com*
> 4. Maryland Brewer's Springfest, Frederick, Maryland, in May
> 5. Big Beers, Belgians, and Barleywines Festival, Vail, Colorado, annually in January: *www.bigbeersfestival.com*

163. | HOME REPAIR STORES

$ $

Stores such as Home Depot and Lowe's are crawling with single male homeowners looking for some new fixtures for the bathroom or spackle for the walls . . . homeowners who may have answers to the questions you have about your own home repairs. So don't be shy with your questions about wood stain or how to caulk your tub. Men love to help "damsels in distress." Your icebreaker couldn't be easier than a confused look as you browse the aisles.

❍ PRO *If he's shopping at a home repair store, it means he has some idea how to fix things on his own.*

❍ CON *Not every trip to a home repair store is going to yield available men, so you may have to make a few visits. To keep the spending at bay, plan—and shop for—one home improvement at a time.*

164. POKER TABLE

Poker has fast grown in popularity, and it is typically very male oriented. So if you ante up in a poker game, you are likely to be one of the few women—or maybe even the only woman—at the table. And poker will give you a good window into a guy's behavior—whether he is confident, a bluffer, competitive, or even sexist.

○ PRO *Poker is a fun pastime—you will be happy to know how to play, whether you meet a man or not.*

○ CON *As you learn the ropes, you may lose some dough along the way.*

165. POOL HALL

Playing pool is an excellent way to meet guys, especially if you have some cue skill. Pool halls and bars with pool tables usually attract more men than women. Plus, guys are impressed by and attracted to sharp-shooting women. And even if you are not that good, they will be happy to see you try.

○ PRO *If you don't meet men, you will still have fun playing pool.*

○ CON *Pool halls and bars are not the safest places to patronize alone—this is a good spot to go to with some girlfriends.*

166. BASEBALL GAME

Hot dogs, beer, and baseball—what more could a guy want? Maybe a nice single girl to talk to during the slower parts of the game. One survey showed that 74 percent of women considered a baseball game a good place to meet men. Approach a guy you have your eye on at the concession stand, or take the empty seat next to him if there is one. Just make sure to keep your mouth shut during the action-packed parts of the game.

○ PRO *A baseball game is a pleasant, all-American way to spend an afternoon. If you are having a bad hair day, you will fit right in by wearing a baseball cap.*

○ CON *If you are not a baseball fan, baseball games can be long and torturous. Be prepared to spend more than $10 on a hot dog and a beer.*

167. CAR SHOW

Some men link their cars to their egos, so if you admire a man's prize-winning Austin Healey at a car show, he just might ask you to marry him right then and there. And beyond the extremists, car shows are brimming with guys who, like you, just want to check out some shiny antique cars. In addition to the obvious conversation pieces—the cars—car shows offer some additional opportunities for socialization, such as beer, food, and live music.

168. HOME DEPOT CLASS

Home Depot is a great place to meet men, and a Home Depot class is an even better place. The "How-To Clinics," as Home Depot calls them, are free of charge and present a range of practical home-improvement topics, such as "Applying Wallpaper" or "Tuning Up Your Lawnmower for Spring." The chances that you will be soaking up home-improvement tips next to a guy are pretty good, and you will gain valuable skills at the same time. For classes and times, call your local Home Depot store.

169. SPORTS BAR

Sure, there is a stigma that goes along with meeting a guy in a bar, but the stigma softens if the two of you are there for more than just the booze. So if you have a favorite sports team, head to your local friendly sports bar to watch them play on the big screen. You can rest assured that there will be a multiplicity of single guys watching alongside you. When you see a guy cheering for your team, buy him a beer and strike up a conversation.

○ PRO *Most sports bars have really good wings.*

○ CON *You may have to sift through some sports-obsessed guys who would always rather watch a game than hang out with you.*

170. BEER DISTRIBUTOR

$ $

This is a classic "go where the guys are" place. You don't see too many girls hoisting cases of beer into their trunks at a beer distributor. So if you go to a beer distributor alone, you will not only be among mostly men, you will stand out (in a good way). First, you will appear independent to the guys perusing the beer selections. And second, they will think you're not too uptight to drink a few beers on the weekend. Both are major plusses in a guy's eyes.

O PRO *You can tell a lot about a guy from his choice in beer, so you'll get an instant glimpse into his personality.*

O CON *If a guy seems to know all the store clerks by name and they shout, "see you tomorrow" as he walks out the door, steer clear.*

171. FIREFIGHTING

Few places offer a greater number of guys per square foot than a local firehouse. These places are full of guys willing to donate their time to fight fires. And you don't have to be a guy to volunteer, so to expose yourself to these uniform-wearing do-gooders, volunteer yourself. Firehouses have plenty of things for female volunteers to do, from answering calls to driving the truck to actually fighting the fires.

O PRO *Firehouses usually sponsor a ton of social events for volunteers and members to mingle; sometimes they even have a bar, pool tables, or video games right in the building.*

O CON *Volunteer firefighting is a time commitment and doesn't come without its risks.*

172. FISHING

Traditionally, fishing is not a female recreational sport, so your local fishing spot could offer some great opportunities for meeting an outdoorsy-type guy. So grab a pole and head out. If the fish are biting, you will at least leave with some dinner.

O PRO *You can enjoy the outdoors and relax by the water's edge, and, of course, the fresh fish.*

O CON *If you want to actually catch a fish, you will have to bait your hook . . . with a worm or minnow. You will need to invest in a fishing license and a pole for this activity.*

173. FOOTBALL TAILGATE

$

You can't find much more of a friendly, festive atmosphere than a college football tailgate on a sunny fall afternoon. As long as you have the same team in common, you'll find numerous complete strangers willing to share a drink and/or a sausage sandwich with you, as well as some good conversation. If you are at your alma mater, you will instantly have something to talk about with men you meet—where you lived on campus, your favorite classes, where you hung out on the weekends. The list goes on and on.

174. SHOOTING RANGE

$ $ $

Believe it or not, shooting ranges are becoming an increasingly more popular place for singles to meet. As a female, the guy-to-girl ratio will definitely be in your favor, and learning how to shoot a gun makes for fun conversation. Plus, some guys will find the image of you firing a weapon quite attractive.

○ PRO *In addition to possibly meeting someone, you will learn a valuable self-defense skill.*

○ CON *If you are a hard-core anti-gun activist, the types of guys who hang out at shooting ranges may not be your forte.*

175. SPORTING GOODS STORE

$ $

In the market for some new running shoes or shorts for the gym? Fight the urge to go to a department store or Foot Locker; instead, browse for the items in a good old-fashioned sporting goods store. These stores are frequented by athletic guys, and the men who work at these stores are usually friendly and eager to answer any questions you might have. You will get expert advice on any item you are shopping for, as well as a potential date for the weekend.

176. AUTO PARTS STORE

$ $

If you have a car, you will need to do some maintenance on it once in a while—it just goes with the territory. Be it a new headlight or a new air filter, you can save a few bucks by going into an auto parts store and buying and installing the item yourself. Beyond the savings, a trip to the auto parts store is bound to expose you to some mechanically minded guys, guys who will be happy to help you find the right touch-up paint color and who will be impressed by your choice to "do it yourself."

177. CONSTRUCTION SITE

All right, with the catcalls and whistles that seem to sometimes almost drown out the jackhammers and other noises at some construction sites, these places have gotten a bad rap. But if you're turned on by industrious men who can build, lay tile, or hang drywall, it may be in your best interest to look past the stereotype and stop by a construction site once in a while. A good icebreaker: Stop by a Starbucks or other coffee shop and get a few coffees to go. Take them to the construction site and hand them out.

178. HARDWARE STORE

Need a new faucet for your sink? Oh darn . . . guess you'll have to make a trip to the handy-guy hangout: the hardware store. And who doesn't like a handy guy? So ask a cute one (shopper or employee) which faucet style is best. If things go well, he may help you install it later and then take you to dinner.

O PRO *Any home repair you can do yourself rather than hiring someone will save you some significant cash.*

O CON *Hardware stores tend to draw a lot of married guys, too.*

179. MEN'S CLOTHING STORE

Some of the men you find here will be fashion-conscious with a clear idea of what they are looking for. In most cases, these men enjoy discussing clothes as much as they like to shop for them (you know, the metrosexual type). So if you are shopping for your dad or brother (and even if you're not—you can just fake it), approach one of these guys and ask for some advice. The other type of men you will find are the guys who are clueless about fashion—they just need clothes. These guys will be happy for a little guidance from a cute female shopper, so by all means, offer it up.

180. MONSTER TRUCK RALLY

Here's another event at which you are 100 percent guaranteed to be way outnumbered by men. The men who follow the monster truck rally around the country like the Grateful Dead may not be the best catches, but the normal guys who just look at it as an opportunity to do something different on a Friday night may have some potential. So grab your brother, guy friend, or laid-back girlfriend and check out some demolition. Guys there will see you as open-minded and fun-loving, so they will be happy to meet you.

 =Time =Friends $=Expense

181. OUTDOOR SPORTING GOODS STORE

Some of the best places to meet people are places you enjoy, or places that support one of your hobbies or activities. For the outdoorsy type, an outdoor sporting goods store like Eastern Mountain Sports is an ideal place to meet someone who shares your passion for hiking, kayaking, or whatever your sport of choice. And beyond the shoppers, you may find the guys working at the store interesting as well.

○ PRO *Beyond the potential for meeting a hiking buddy, the more often you frequent stores like this, the more current you will be on their latest sales on Gortex, hiking boots, and all the other gear goodies.*

○ CON *If you are not the outdoorsy type, stay out of these places; chances are someone you meet will ask you to go camping as one of your very first outings together, and they will recognize a true non-camper in a second. Be real.*

182. WOODWORKING COURSE

Woodworking is a very relaxing activity that will get your creative juices flowing . . . and you get to take home an attractive, useful piece of furniture (or a few pieces, depending on the length of your class). These courses also usually attract significantly more guys than girls, so you will have plenty of opportunities to mingle with the opposite sex as you sand and stain. For a woodworking course in your area, check out your local community college or art school.

183. COLLEGE BASKETBALL GAME

If you are attracted to guys who are passionate about basketball and their alma mater, attend a college basketball game. College basketball games are usually filled with enthusiastic male fans, and with all the college bars and eateries in most college towns, there certainly won't be a shortage of places to meet these guys after the game either.

184. COLLEGE WRESTLING MATCH

This is not to say that you should pick up one of the wrestlers at the end of the match. During wrestling season, wrestlers will not be much fun as dinner dates, as they're constantly being asked to put on or take off weight. Plus, they're probably too young for you anyway. But their uncles, older brothers, friends, fathers, or fans watching the match may be of interest to you. And if you enjoy watching sports, a college wrestling match usually promises an entertaining evening. Upon your arrival, scan the room and choose a bleacher seat next to someone you'd like to get to know better. Just make sure to cheer for the same school that he does.

185. HOOTERS

Guys love hooters, both the restaurant and the "hooters" displayed there. Guys also love the pitchers of beer, wings, and big-screen TVs at Hooters, so they flock to the place. Go yourself and not only will you be one of the only female patrons, you will meet guys when they have girls on the brain, which can actually work in your favor. So head to Hooters with a girlfriend and buy a pitcher for a table of cute guys. Check out *www.hooters.com* for locations.

O PRO *The guy to girl ratio and the tasty wings.*

O CON *The brown tights. A Hooters uniform update is in order.*

186. POKER CLUB

Poker is great for women because it is typically very male-oriented. So ask your friends if anyone knows of a poker club in your area or check for an ad in your entertainment paper. Poker is really fun . . . and a great window into your fellow players' behavior in a group.

187. RADIO SHACK

Guys love their gadgets, so they flock to places like Radio Shack, where they can browse the latest in iPods, digital camera equipment, and other electronic devices. Some girls like their gadgets, too. If you are one of them, you can kill two birds with a trip to Radio Shack—an overview of the latest "toys" on the market as well as an overview of the boys who are buying them. Even if you aren't a gadget gal, it won't hurt you to step in a Radio Shack the next time you go to the mall. Between the merchandise, the shoppers, and the employees, you will have lots to look at.

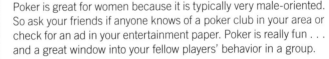

=Time 👤=Friends $=Expense

188. CAMPGROUND (FOR THE NON-CAMPER)

If you are as excited by the thought of sleeping in the wilderness as you are at the prospect of a root canal, you fit into the "non-camper" category. Being a non-camper can be a disadvantage when it comes to meeting men, because lots of men like to camp and engage in camping activities such as fishing, boating, and hiking. To mingle with the campers, you don't have to pitch a tent, however. Grab a friend and head to a campground on a Saturday or Sunday afternoon. Walk through the grounds, sit by the water, watch the boats—observe the camping activities and the men doing them. Then, when a group of guys takes a break, don't be shy!

○ PRO *The outdoors without the risk of raccoons sharing your bed.*

○ CON *You will have to be honest about your non-camper personality from the start; if you pose as the camper type, your relationship with any man you might meet will be based on a lie. Not a good start.*

189. CHRISTMAS SHOPPING ON CHRISTMAS EVE

When it comes to holiday shopping, a lot of guys wait until the last minute . . . literally. To meet some of these well-meaning procrastinators, brave the mall on Christmas Eve. There will be tons of guys scrambling for a good gift for their mothers and sisters. And who better to give these poor guys advice than you? If you spot a guy with a perplexed look, offer to help. He will be more than grateful and may decide to take a shopping break over a coffee with you!

○ PRO *If you need a few last-minute things yourself, you can grab it while you're guy shopping.*

○ CON *The crowds. Christmas Eve is generally a hellish day to shop—steel yourself for the worst.*

190. COLLEGE FOOTBALL GAME

For a fun atmosphere full of men, you cannot beat a college football game on a sunny fall afternoon. Whether it's your own alma mater or a game at a local college or university in your area, grab a fellow football fan or two and crash some tailgates (when it comes to most college football tailgates, people are willing to share a beer or a sandwich with almost anyone, as long as they are wearing the school colors). College football games are full of friendly, successful alums whose first impression of you is that you like to spend a Saturday afternoon at a football game—instant points!

 =Time =Friends **$** =Expense

191.	**COLLEGE APPAREL STORE**

$ $

As part of your visit to your alma mater, you may choose to pick up a new sweatshirt . . . a good idea if you are also looking to pick up a guy who went to the same school. These stores are full of coeds—both alumni and current students—shopping for college apparel and souvenirs. To start a conversation, ask an attractive man whether he thinks you should go for the zip-up hoodie or the pullover. After all, college sweatshirts (and alumni) are a fairly large investment these days—you want to make sure you choose the best one.

192.	**NASCAR RACE**

$ $

Whether it's the cars, the speed, or the beer sponsors, a lot of men love NASCAR. So if you can get yourself to a NASCAR race, you are guaranteed to be surrounded by guys. And those guys will be immediately impressed by your race attendance, so you will be off to a good start, so to speak.

◑ PRO *Even if NASCAR isn't totally your thing, it's exciting to watch.*

◐ CON *Motor heads and rednecks.*

193.	**SPORTS BAR DURING MONDAY NIGHT FOOTBALL**

$ $

Sports bars are a great place to increase your odds of meeting someone purely because of the ratio of men to women. Throw in the Monday Night Football factor, and you may be one of the only females there. So grab a sports-loving girlfriend, throw on some jeans, and check out a Monday Night Football game on the big screen at the sports bar. Watch the guys in the room to see who they cheer for . . . if you like the same team, talk to one of them about the quarterback during a commercial break. Guys love to talk about sports, so it will be the fastest way to get the ball rolling, so to speak.

◑ PRO *Sports bars usually have good specials during Monday Night Football, so you won't go broke if you have to buy your own drinks (and neither will a guy who buys them for you).*

◐ CON *Really big sports fans often don't like to mix women with plays, so to speak. So there may be some guys there who would rather not meet women—if you bump into one of them, don't take it personally.*

194.   SUPER BOWL PARTY

$

If you get an invitation to a Super Bowl party this year, GO! And if you don't, consider hosting one yourself, complete with chili, homemade wings, beer, and other avenues to a guy's heart. Most guys love football and the eating that goes along with it, making a Super Bowl party one of their favorite events of the year. Therefore, unless their team is losing, men you meet at a Super Bowl party will be relaxed and in a great mood—the perfect mode for meeting you!

◑ PRO *If you meet someone who loves the same team you do, you will form an instant bond.*

◑ CON *Timing is tricky here. Don't try to spark a conversation with a guy at the tense end of the second quarter—wait until halftime.*

195.   TAILGATE PARTY

$

Whether it's for a college basketball game or a concert, a tailgate party is a great way to spend a weekend afternoon. And because guys love beer and grill food, they love a good tailgate party to kick off the event. So if you get an invitation to throw down some hot dogs and burgers and enjoy the good company at a tailgate party, by all means, accept. You may meet someone special to sit next to at the sporting event or show . . .

196.   DEEP-SEA FISHING

$

Since deep-sea fishing is not a traditional female recreational sport, a deep sea fishing boat could offer some great opportunities for meeting an outdoorsy type purely because of the male-to-female ratio. And because deep-sea fishing trips usually last at least a few hours, you will have plenty of time to meet your fishing mates. So grab a pole and jump aboard. Even if you don't catch a fish, you will get to enjoy a fun boat ride.

197.   FINAL FOUR PARTY

$

As the March Madness excitement comes to a close, host a Final Four party—not only to gather a group to watch the best teams play, but to meet some new men. Ask your basketball-fan friends to come over and bring a snack and one friend—a male friend, if they can help it. Then mingle between halves and see what happens . . .

198. MINOR LEAGUE BASEBALL GAME

A lot of Minor League Baseball games offer all the perks of a major league game—the stadium, the hot dogs, the soft pretzels, the caps—without the hassles and high prices. So for a fun summer evening, consider heading to one of these games. If you don't spot anyone you're interested in watching the game, you can always check out the players.

199. MOTORCYCLE SHOP

A motorcycle shop is a great example of a place where you are guaranteed to be outnumbered by guys. Men who ride motorcycles really respect women who are interested in motorcycles. (They will respect you even more if you try to drive the motorcycle rather than ride on the back, but one step at a time . . .) Perusing the helmets and chaps at a motorcycle store will be a good start.

200. SALOON

For a different kind of night out, grab a friend or two and head to a good, old-fashioned saloon. If it's a genuine, rough-around-the-edges type of place, you will most likely be way outnumbered by cowboys, so to speak. So put on your most flattering pair of jeans, order beer in a bottle, and kick your feet up.

201. SHOPPING FOR STEREO EQUIPMENT

Once boys get beyond the age of playing video games (all right, some guys in their forties are still playing video games, but that's beside the point), they move on to more adult toys, like the latest in stereo equipment. Go to the stereo section of Best Buy or Circuit City on a Saturday afternoon—the place will be teeming with men. If you spot one you'd like to talk to, walk up to him and ask him which speakers he recommends. He will be flattered that you asked him—a great start!

202. BAR DURING MARCH MADNESS

During the peak of college basketball season, you will find an increase in single, professional, basketball-loving guys at the bars . . . all month long. This is especially true during the last few games (called the Final Four, for those of you not in the know), when the stakes get extra high. So even if it is a Tuesday night, go out where the guys are and get into some games!

⏱=Time 👤=Friends $=Expense

203. BOAT DEALERSHIP

$ $ $

Whether you are seriously in the market for a boat or you're dreaming, a trip to a boat dealership is worth your while. Most guys love boats, and rich guys can afford to buy boats. So naturally, a boat dealership will be full of guys checking them out. Some may just be dreaming too, but they'll be there. And others may be in the market for a Jet Ski—an indication that they are fun-loving. In order to meet these water-sporting men, you will have to be at a boat dealership too.

204. CHILI COOK-OFF

$

Chili cook-offs are fun, festive outdoor events where people show off their chili-cooking skills. Whether you are entering a killer batch yourself or you just want to enjoy the outdoors and some tasty chili recipes, this event is worth checking out—both for the food and for the patrons. Chili is one of those foods—like wings—that tends to appeal to people of the opposite sex.

○ PRO *Chili is a great conversation starter—just ask any guy you see which stand he recommends.*

○ CON *If you meet someone you like, you may want to wait for another day to accept a date. Chili tends to lead to gas.*

205. GRILLING OUT AT THE PARK

$

For a weekend activity, take your portable grill to the park and cook up some burgers and dogs in the sun. Food tastes better outside—it's true! And if you bring enough food to share with some handsome strangers, they are bound to be drawn by the smell of the charcoal grill. Food really is the fastest way to a guy's heart.

206. SOUVENIR SHOP

$ $

Take a day trip to a touristy town and spend a little time in the souvenir shops that attract fellow tourists, including single guys. Your best bet is to go to a town that has an attraction guys are interested in, such as an old brewery or baseball stadium.

Five great souvenir shops:
1. Boston Red Sox Yawkey Way Store, Boston, MA
2. National Baseball Hall of Fame Souvenir Shop, Cooperstown, NY
3. Yankee Stadium Team Store, New York, NY
4. Powell's Souvenir Shop, Portland, OR
5. Souvenir Shop at Anheuser Bush, St. Louis, MO

=Time ♦=Friends $=Expense

207.   WATCHING THE WORLD SERIES AT A BAR

When the World Series games are on, sports bars across the country are packed with guys. So where should you be during the World Series? If you want to meet a baseball fan or two, you should be at these sports bars when the games are on TV. Just wait for a commercial break to strike up a conversation . . . hard-core sports fans will resent being interrupted when the game is on.

208.   ARMY/NAVY SURPLUS STORE

Army/Navy stores have something for everyone. You can find a huge supply of quality sweatshirts, jackets, boots, and shoes. And guys can find guns, ammunition, knives, fishing poles, Carhartts, and numerous other manly items. So after you've finished your shopping, browse the aisles for members of the opposite sex.

○ PRO *To break the ice with an attractive stranger in the fishing section, for example, you can always tell a white lie and say you are shopping for a pole for your father or brother and ask what he recommends.*

○ CON *If the outdoorsy type isn't your type, this may not be your best venue for shopping for men.*

209.   COLOGNE COUNTER

The next time you're doing some department store shopping, take a break and head over to the men's cologne counter, where there may be men sampling brands for a new scent. If a guy is seriously shopping for a new cologne, he's likely shopping for a new lady as well. And he just might appreciate your opinion on which scent smells the best on him.

○ PRO *You can always pretend you are shopping for your dad and ask an attractive stranger what he recommends.*

○ CON *Guys at a cologne counter could be over-dousers.*

210.   DISTILLERY/BREWERY TOUR

If you are a history buff, you will surely enjoy a tour of an old distillery or brewery. On your tour, you may meet fellow history buffs . . . and guys who like tours that involve booze. Either way, the potential for romance is there. Keep your eye out for single men during the tour . . . then sidle up next to one at the tasting following the tour.

211.   L.L.BEAN

With the perfect balance of fashion and function, L.L.Bean stores attract a lot of male shoppers. And better yet, they attract male shoppers who appreciate a well-made army green Adirondack barn coat with plenty of pockets. So as you're shopping for a cozy fleece or a new pair of slipper moccasins, see if you can catch eyes with the guys shopping alone. If things go well, the two of you may merge your initials on an L.L.Bean tote some day.

212.   HORSE RACES

If you enjoy gambling, you've probably attended a horse race or two in your life. If so, you know that it is quite an experience. Beyond the horses, there are a lot of interesting crowds to watch, crowds that may or may not contain an interesting guy. By virtue of drawing a lot of people, horse races can be good places to find men, including men who own horses (rich men). If you are an animal rights activist, this probably is not your venue, however.

O PRO *Horse races are exciting to watch, and you just might win some money.*

O CON *Horse races attract men with gambling problems. Pay attention if you're there midday during the week, and you see the same guy lining up to place his bets.*

213.   INDIANAPOLIS 500 PARTY

A lot of guys love NASCAR. Maybe it's the fast cars, the noise, the beer sponsors . . . or a combination. Whatever the reason, many men flock to watch the Indianapolis 500, and a lot of them will want to keep the party going once the race has ended. So if you get invited to an Indianapolis 500 party, where people gather to watch the race, don't immediately chuckle and toss the idea in the trash. It's an opportunity to meet some guys who never quite let their love for Matchbox cars go . . . So check out the party and keep an open mind.

O PRO *Paired with some snacks and a fun group of people, you may actually find the race entertaining.*

O CON *There could be a few guys at the party who love NASCAR so much that they've turned their basements into a shrine complete with inflatable cars, checkered flags, and beer bottles.*

214.   SNACK AISLE OF A MARKET ON A FOOTBALL SUNDAY

The guys who opt to watch football from their couches instead of at a local bar will need something to munch on. So the guys without the wives and girlfriends to stock the cabinets with chips and pretzels will likely be in the snack aisle of the supermarket picking out snacks and chili con queso. For maximum guy exposure, hit the snack aisle a few hours before game time.

○ **PRO** *You can pick up snacks and throw a football party yourself.*

○ **CON** *You'll miss out on the guys who order out for wings.*

215.   COMIC BOOKSTORE

Yes. Men are kids; this is nothing new. But there are perfectly normal men who enjoy the occasional superhero tale. Plus, you have nothing to lose. You pop in, see who's picking out a vintage Spider-Man comic, and either trap him in your web or move along.

○ **PRO** *While you're there, you can grab a gift for your nephew.*

○ **CON** *Comic book nerds. Some guys are obsessed—beware.*

216.   SPENCER'S GIFTS

Yes, the goofiest place in the mall often has men in it. And depending on your taste, you might find someone you actually like with a sense of humor. Because Spencer's has outrageous and often "edgy" gifts, men often like to go in and browse and have a chuckle or two. They also turn to Spencer's for gag gifts around the holidays or for that big bachelor party. The best part? It's probably just a brisk walk from your favorite shoe store. Pop in and take a look. You have nothing to lose. Check out *www.spencersonline.com.*

217.   ANY EATING CONTEST

They say the way to a man's heart is through his stomach. So, anywhere a man can get food quickly and easily—that's a good start. Now make it a place where he can also get beer. You've just doubled your odds. Now throw in the competitive juices with an eating contest and you have just supersized your chances at finding a man. Remember, you may find an eating-contest voyeur and not an actual participant. Then you've hit the jackpot completely. What kinds of eating contests? Nathan's Hot Dog eating contest or the famous Philadelphia Wing Bowl or many others. Check out *www.ifoce.com* to locate the biggest eating contests in the world. And by all means, dress casual.

 =Time   =Friends $=Expense

218. FISHING LESSONS

For this one, it helps if you have any interest in fishing whatsoever. But, what's important here is that you don't even have to take the lessons. Simply look into it. Many businesses selling fishing equipment offer fishing lessons, so track one down and see what it's all about. Chances are there are men running the shop and giving the lessons. Find out ahead of time who gives the lessons and if you like what you see—go for it.

PRO *Fisherman come in all shapes and sizes. It's quite possible you could land yourself something new and refreshing. Don't forget, Brad Pitt looked pretty good casting his lines in A River Runs Through It. And hey, free dinner.*

CON *If you are a strict vegetarian or an animal rights activist, this one is not for you.*

219. SOAP BOX DERBY RACE

Men like cars. Men like all kinds of cars. In fact, once a year, you'll find the Soap Box Derby Championships on TV and you'll notice a lot of men focused on the performance of these gravity-powered vehicles. The men helping these boys with their cars are not all married. Some are divorced. Some are uncles. Some are scout leaders who are single. And all of them care about kids, which is a huge plus. Check out *www.aasbd.com* to find a race city near you. These events are a lot of fun whether or not you meet Mr. Right, so take a chance!

220. STAR WARS MATINEE

You've probably seen *Star Wars* conventions on television. While those addicted to the futuristic sci-fi films may not be your type, the guys who attend *Star Wars* matinees are the same guys who watch football on Sunday, drive a nice car, and are able to carry on a decent conversation. Before paying ten bucks for a ticket, linger outside the theater and see who strolls inside. You might see something interesting. Then just go and find a seat near him, lean over, and ask him a few questions about the film. May the Force be with you.

PRO *Men of all kinds love* Star Wars.

CON *Some of those men are a little, well, strange and still live with their parents.*

221. ANY PROFESSIONAL SPORTING EVENTS

Grab a few of your girlfriends and go to a baseball, football, hockey, or basketball game in your town. There are tons of men at sporting events, and as long as you can stand some of the men who are a little too forward (and probably inebriated), you just might find one who takes a real interest in you. Plus, it's fun to just get together with your friends and go be flirty for a night while you root for the home team. You might even go home with a souvenir.

222. THE AVN AWARDS

If you're not very inhibited and have no reservations about all things risqué, then this idea could be for you. The AVN Awards are the adult film industry's gala event where people from all around the world come to honor adult films and actors. The convention includes special events, adult novelty demos, autograph sessions, and more. And guess who comes in droves? Men. The surprising thing is that men of all kinds are in attendance. The sex industry just isn't as taboo as it was years ago, which is why you'll find doctors, lawyers, salesmen, and more. For more information, visit *www.avnawards.com*.

○ PRO *It's always held in Vegas, so if you grab a friend and go for a getaway, there's plenty more for you to experience in the town that's already known for its sinful indulgence.*

○ CON *A lot of women want nothing to do with porn, especially men who love it enough to go to an awards show in its honor.*

223. BOWLING ALLEY

Have you noticed the complete transformation of bowling alleys in metropolitan areas across the country? These days, the alleys of old have become the trendy bars of the future. It's true. Alleys began revamping the beer posters and outdated Zaxxon games and replacing them with trendy décor, hip tunes, and a lounge atmosphere that just happens to offer bowling—should the mood strike you. You can now drop in many alleys, grab a drink, and ask any guy to split a game with you. And most any guy would be bowled over by being asked for a game.

224.   HUNTING

Want to kill two birds with one stone? Take hunting lessons. If you're an animal lover, this one will not work for you. But just like there are outdoorsy men, there are outdoorsy women. And this may be for you.

225.   VIDEO GAME STORES

Places like GameStop and Electronics Boutique are now crammed with men—not just boys. Men interested in video games can now be into their fifties! Plus, you'll find all types there. It's true. These days, attractive outgoing men in their twenties, thirties, and forties play video games. Just pop in and pretend you're supposed to find a game for your nephew. Push his buttons a bit. He'll be happy to help.

226.   VOLUNTEER FIRE STATION

This isn't one for a shy girl and is probably best undertaken with friends. Remember, volunteer firemen are not only sexy men in uniform who aren't afraid to put their lives on the line for free, but they legitimately care about the well-being of others. That's an incredible place to start. If you're in the New York City area, you should visit a few fire departments anyway, and thank them for their courage and everything they've done on and since 9/11. However, if you're feeling particularly bold and you're not near New York, go to your local volunteer fire department anyway and thank them for their bravery. Just think about how much they would appreciate that sentiment. Create a large care package filled with groceries and bring it down to your local department. Not only will you feel fantastic about what you're doing, but you will meet some outstanding people.

O PRO *You might meet the handsome, fearless guy you never really thought existed.*

O CON *If you keep hanging around, they might want you to volunteer yourself . . . at least to clean the house or something. This isn't necessarily a bad thing, just something you should be aware of.*

227. GO-CARTING

If you were lucky enough to get behind the wheel of a go-cart before you reached the age of 16, the experience has probably never left you. Before you had a driver's license, you were actually pushing a pedal down, steering, and driving . . . all by yourself! Even though you've been driving for years now, you can recreate the same experience by visiting a go-cart track today. And better yet, you could meet men who are having just as much fun as you are speeding around the turns. Keep your eye out for a handsome driver as you speed through the course . . . then ask him to grab a soda and soft pretzel with you once you've parked.

228. GUN SHOW

By virtue of being men, some members of the opposite sex are fascinated with guns. Handguns, hunting rifles, assault weapons—you name it. So when a gun show comes to town, you may want to hit it up to check out the shoppers. Keep an eye out in your local paper for traveling gun shows coming to town or check out *www.gunshows-usa.com*.

O PRO *Gun shows don't usually draw too many females, so the competition shouldn't be too stiff.*

O CON *If you are a hard-core liberal, you will probably not find the love of your life here.*

229. OUT WITH YOUR BROTHER

He may have been protective when you were growing up, but if you have a brother, he may make for a good wing man now that you are all grown up. Guys are often intimidated by groups of girls, so they may be more likely to approach you when you are hanging with your bro. Just make it clear that you two are not together by being extrafriendly and flirtatious with men you meet when you're out . . . and slip in a "he's my brother" early in the conversation.

O PRO *If you trust your brother, he can give you honest first impressions of men you meet. Plus, he may be more likely to pick up the tab.*

O CON *Some brothers will never get over being protective of their sisters. If this applies to your brother, consider going out with a male cousin or friend instead.*

230.   THE ROSE BOWL

$ $

Next time you are in L.A., swing by the Rose Bowl for a tour. As far as national landmarks are concerned, this one draws a lot of men. Some guys may be drawn by the construction of the Rose Bowl, which holds 92,542 people, and was designed after the Yale Bowl, which was built in New Haven in 1914. Others may want to see the place where Penn State played USC in 1923. But no matter what their reasons for going, a lot of men are guaranteed to be at the Rose Bowl, so it's worth your while to check it out. For more information, go to *www.rosebowlstadium.com*.

231.   SIX-PACK SHOP

$ $

If you are facing yet another night at home with a Blockbuster flick, consider swinging into your local six-pack shop for a good beer to drink while you watch it. Not only will the beer make the movie more entertaining, you might meet someone in the six-pack shop with whom to watch it.

O PRO *The six-pack shop is a place highly frequented by men who don't drink beer fast enough to warrant a case—a good thing!*

O CON *Beer guts (yours and the guy's). Reserve trips to the six-pack shops for special occasions.*

232.   WEIGHT ROOM AT THE GYM

$

Sure, the gym itself is a good place to meet athletic men, but the weight room is like hitting the jackpot. Even the guys who take a spinning class or run on the treadmill for 30 minutes usually lift weights before or after, so at any given time, the weight room is your best bet for testosterone. Guys will admire you for lifting weights for strength and definition, so don't be afraid to participate.

O PRO *Weight training is great for your waistline—the more muscle on your body, the more calories you'll burn.*

O CON *Meatheads. Also, you could cause an injury—to your muscles or your ego—if you try to push it too much.*

233. CAMPGROUND

Metrosexuals aside, a lot of men love the outdoors. And with all the manly outdoor activities it provides—fishing, boating, kayaking, hunting, sleeping in a tent, or drinking beers around a fire—you are bound to find some men at a campground. So grab a few adventurous girlfriends and head to a campground near you. A lot of campgrounds provide cabins and showers for those who want to enjoy nature without giving up too many creature comforts. Outdoorsy men appreciate women who are willing to rough it once in a while, so at a campground, you and your girlfriends will be quite popular. To find a campground near you, check out *www .campground.com*.

234. CRAPS TABLE

Next time you walk into a casino, listen for the cheers. Most likely, they are coming from the craps table—the most exciting gambling spot. Craps moves fast, and the dice can quickly turn in or away from your favor. And it tends to draw quite a crowd. So if you're looking to attract the attention of some handsome gamblers, throw the dice yourself. Or, if you would rather play cheerleader by watching a lucky guy, hang around the table for support. Either way, the interactive, electrifying nature of craps will be a great romantic start.

⊙ PRO *You can place one of a range of bets on a craps table, so it won't get boring.*

⊙ CON *Craps is pretty complicated, so unless you've studied up on the rules, you're best off as an audience member.*

235. RODEO

It does take a certain type of woman to go to a rodeo and to become interested in a cowboy, just as it takes a certain kind of man to ride a bull or bronco. But if you have had a ball riding a mechanical bull, you may not want to rule out a real rodeo to scope for men. Just remember, most cowboys are up at the crack of down and in bed early. Maybe that's a good thing?

236. THE SUPER BOWL

$

$

At the Super Bowl, not only will you get to watch a heated game of football and a rocking half time show, you will get to be among thousands and thousands of men in good moods (at least at the start of the game). So if you enjoy football and can score some tickets to the biggest game of the year, by all means, grab some sports-loving girlfriends and go!

237. STEAKHOUSE

$ $

Aside from vegetarians, men love meat, and a big juicy steak is at the top of most of their meat lists. So if you head to a steakhouse, you are likely to bump into many men, steak knives and forks in hand.

Five great steakhouse chains:
1. The Outback Steakhouse:
   www.outback.com
2. Ruth's Chris Steakhouse:
   www.ruthchris.com
3. Lonestar Steakhouse and Saloon:
   www.lonestarsteakhouse.com
4. Fleming's Prime Steakhouse and Wine Bar:
   www.flemingsteakhouse.com
5. Sullivan's Steakhouse:
   www.sullivanssteakhouse.com

238. BASEBALL CARD SHOW

$

Although you might not personally have any cards to trade, you may be interested in checking out the baseball card owners, sellers, and traders who are all grown up. If you can dig some up, bring a few cards along so you can start a conversation with an attractive trader by asking him how much they're worth. If anything, they may end up being worth a date.

239. THE MILITARY

$

Although it's forbidden for people to date in the military, it's funny how many marriages come out of a shared experience on a ship or base. Of course meeting men is certainly not a reason to join the military, but it is a perk if you are on the fence about the decision. Despite the increasing number of women in the armed forces, the majority are still men, so you will have your pick of men to form friendships with . . . and then maybe date once your duty is finished.

240. THE WORLD SERIES

The World Series is the culmination of the baseball season. If you have baseball fans in your life, you know that pretty much all topics of conversation that don't pertain to the World Series are off during this time. And if you go to the World Series, all those baseball-obsessed men will be there. So if you can get to the World Series, do it—you will be smack-dab in the middle of thousands of excited guys. Check out *www.mlb.com* for more info.

241. BROOKS BROTHERS

If he's shopping at Brooks Brothers, you can tell three things: One, he's got great taste. Two, he's probably a businessman (especially if he's shopping in the suit section). Three, he's got money. If these three things appeal to you, take a jaunt through your local Brooks Brothers store now and then to see what they have to offer . . . both in the form of timeless women's fashions and men.

242. COLLEGE WORLD SERIES

The College World Series takes place in Omaha, Nebraska, in early summer, and college baseball fans come from all across the country. In addition to the potential of meeting single male college baseball fans at the actual games, Omaha offers great restaurants and sports bars where you can find them, including Dub's Pub, Dublinger Pub, and Figby's Lounge. Check out *www.cwsomaha.com.*

243. MOTORCYCLE SHOW

Whether they have their motorcycle licenses or not, most men are fascinated by motorcycles. Maybe it stems from motorcycles they played with as kids, Excitebike on Nintendo, or the Fonz. But for whatever reason, you are guaranteed to find many single men at a motorcycle show. So look for the closest one in your area, throw on a black T-shirt and some chaps (optional), and go!

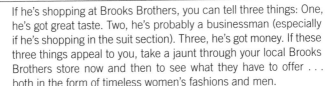

Five great motorcycle shows:
1. The Great American Motorcycle Show, Atlanta, GA: *www.northatlantatradecenter.com*
2. The Toronto International Spring Motorcycle Show: *www.supershowevents.com*
3. Yooper Motorcycle Show and Swap Meet, St. Ignace, MI: *www.yoopermotorcycleshow.com*
4. The Springfield Motorcycle Show, Springfield, MA: *www.osegmotorcycle.com*
5. The Cleveland Motorcycle Show, Cleveland, OH: *www.thekneeslider.com*

 =Time ♦=Friends $=Expense

244. STRIP CLUB

For the more daring at heart, there is the strip club. Contrary to popular belief, unless they are there every week, most guys go to a strip club for a bonding night with their buddies and a different kind of entertainment—not to pick up strippers. In other words, it's not as threatening an environment as many women perceive it to be. In fact, it may present an opportunity. If you go to a strip club with a bunch of friends (mix of guys and girls) on a Friday or Saturday night, you will likely share the edge of the stage with a bachelor party full of single men who are there to support their friend getting married, not to take a stripper home.

O PRO *Because you're not intimidated by the stripper scene, you will appear fun and laid back to the nonstripper obsessed men you meet there.*

O CON *By nature, strip clubs do attract some weirdoes who may project their weirdness onto you when the strippers take a break.*

245. BOATHOUSE ROW

For a non-stop stream of attractive men jogging, boating, and rowing, you cannot beat an afternoon spent at Philadelphia's Boathouse Row. The ten historical boathouses on Philadelphia's Kelly Drive are centers of the rowing community around the United States, and rowers from the boathouses compete at every level, from high school to local clubs to international rowing competitions. As a single woman, a trip to Boathouse Row will be worth your while. Check out *www.boathouserow.org*.

246. CONDOM STORE

You'll find men in condom stores because . . . well . . . men wear condoms. And men shopping in a condom store for varieties with ribs, bright colors, and French ticklers are probably a little more fun than your average Trojan buyer. Plus, extras or not, they practice safe sex.

247.   HOBBY SHOP

With the extensive selection of model rockets, boats, trains, and helicopters, a hobby shop is a haven for a guy who loves to build model versions of transportation. Whether he is there by himself or with his son or nephew, a man will be all smiles at a hobby shop. To meet him, stop in a hobby shop on a Saturday afternoon and do a little browsing. After all, building and launching model rockets can be a fun couple's activity, too.

248.   TOOL SECTION OF A DEPARTMENT STORE

The highest concentration of men in a department store at any given time will be in the tool section. As you browse through jeans and jewelry, they're checking out what Craftsman and Black & Decker have to offer. So once you've found your jeans, check out what the tool section is selling in a friendly, single man. To get the ball rolling, you can always pretend you need some advice on a new power drill (and maybe you really do).

249.   WATCH COUNTER AT A DEPARTMENT STORE

Wristwatches are the most common piece of jewelry worn by men. Even the guys who wouldn't get within six feet of a gold chain or bracelet aren't against wearing a watch, especially if it's waterproof and comes equipped with a compass. So next time you are in a department store, swing by the watch counter to see who's browsing. If nothing more, you can get a nice gift idea for your father or brother.

250.   YANKEE STADIUM

The place where Babe Ruth and other baseball legends made history, Yankee Stadium is a shrine to some baseball fans—some guys are moved to tears. To meet these die-hard fans, you have to be at Yankee Stadium at the same time that they are, either on a tour or at a game. So next time you are in the New York area, swing by Yankee Stadium. Check out *www.yankees.mlb.com*.

251. NUT STORE

Yes, there are still some stores across the country that sell nuts, nut products, and nut butters alone. And men seem to love these nut stores. Maybe because they have them? But seriously, if you are fortunate enough to have a nut store in your city or town, pop into it once in a while for a bag of freshly roasted almonds or some cashew butter . . . and maybe a nice single man who prefers a heart-healthy handful of nuts to a bag of potato chips for a snack.

252. PRO SHOP

Most golf courses include a pro shop, where golfers can go to get fresh balls, shirts, even golf bags, and clubs. In a pro shop, you can find the course's golf pro from time to time, and you can also find a nice steady stream of golfers of all ages. So when the weather gets warm and golfers need to stock up on some new supplies, spend some time in a pro shop . . . you can always pretend you're shopping for your brother or father, and ask the men in there a few questions about golfing supplies.

253. TODAY'S MAN

Where can a man go for a decent suit for a decent price? Today's Man, that's where. So to find a man who'd rather spend his money on dinners out and entertainment than a closet full of expensive suits, take a stroll through Today's Man. On a busy Saturday, you are sure to find something you like in a size 40. To find a Today's Man store in your area, go to *www.todaysman.com*.

254. UNIVERSITY OF LOUISVILLE BASKETBALL GAME

The fans of the University of Louisville Cardinals are some of the most die-hard fans in the country. So if you go to a game, you will be surrounded by excited screaming men. Not such a bad way to spend an afternoon or evening . . . Go to *www.uoflsports.cstv.com*.

255. USED-CAR LOTS

Not all guys are hung up on their wheels, and some used-car lots offer some nice rides these days. So if you are in the market for a used car—and even if you're not—swing by the used-car lot now and then to see who's browsing.

○ PRO *Easy getaway if you don't see anything you like.*

○ CON *Used-car salesmen. In most cases, the stereotype is accurate.*

=Time =Friends $=Expense

256.   WWE WRESTLING MATCH

OK, if you meet a guy at a WWE match and he believes that it is real or is into it in a really intense, weird way, get away from him. But there are some guys at WWE matches who are there purely for the dramatic wrestling entertainment. So for a unique night out—and the potential for meeting a guy who's so bored with the bar scene that he's willing to move on to professional wrestling—consider checking out one of these matches. Visit *www.wwe.com* for more info.

257.   BIKE REPAIR CLASS

As an independent single woman, there are certain things you should know how to do on your own. If you ride a bike, one of those things is how to repair that bike should you run into a problem like a flat or a loose gear on a ride. Another reason you should learn how to repair a bike: Bike repair courses are full of bike-riding men who will be impressed by your desire to learn how to fix your own ride. To find a bike repair course in your area, call your local bike shops.

258.   ARCADE

This doesn't mean you have to head to the local teenage hangout, but there are some adult-style arcades, such as Dave & Busters (*www.daveandbusters.com*), that draw tons of single guys who don't want to grow up (at least when it comes to games). These arcades don't only just provide Golden Tee and vintage Pac Man—they also provide sports and other simulation games such as golf, surf-ing, horseback riding, and many other games that can improve coordination and show you a heck of a good time. And in the center of most of these places, you can also find a bar where you can approach that handsome stranger you saw dunking baskets in the virtual basketball game.

O PRO *You will have a fabulous time and feel like a kid again.*

O CON *Bring your wallet. To get the most out of a trip to one of these places, you need quite a few quarters.*

259. BLACKJACK TABLE

If you enjoy a casino trip now and then, next time you go, spend some time at a blackjack table. Blackjack tends to attract a lot of men. Even if you don't meet someone you're interested in, you might pick up some blackjack tips.

260. ANY LARGE-SCREEN TV ANYWHERE

Does this require any explanation? It's a TV. It's huge. If there isn't a man in front of it now, there will be in 2 minutes. So you should be there too.

261. CIGAR SHOP

For years, cigars were associated with aristocratic, older men who checked the time with a pocket watch. As you probably know, those days are long gone. All kinds of men and now women have become privy to the stogie phenomenon. There are a number of cigar clubs and liquor tastings that promote cigar smoking. The point is, all kinds of men visit cigar shops. Find a busy one near you and just pop in for a few minutes. Not only might there be a handsome, unsuspecting man there, but now you already have a topic of conversation. Simply tell him you enjoy a mild cigar, but you're new to the hobby and would love a few recommendations.

O PRO *If you are into older men, this may be a good place to pick up a nice, handsome one.*

O CON *Addiction to cigars. If you make a purchase, be careful not to pick up the habit.*

262. GOLF COURSE BAR

The best way to approach this is to go in summer. If you time it just right, you can begin your happy hour at a golf course bar and meet guys who spent the day on the links. They're in good spirits and throwing a few back. Not only will this help your budget by receiving free drinks, but if the stigma holds up, you could meet a guy who is successful and active. Find out which courses in your area have upscale bars. Some of the private clubs admit the public.

O PRO *If you like a man with a few bucks in his pocket, this is a nice place to start.*

O CON *A lot of men golf to get away from women.*

 =Time =Friends $=Expense

263.   BODYBUILDING COMPETITION

Like your men with a little muscle? This is the perfect method for meeting a man who cares about his appearance. Here's the most important point to remember: Not all men attending these contests are so jacked-up that you're turned off. Many men who care about having a lean, muscular appearance (without being too jacked up) attend these contests.

O PRO *You'll find a little bit of everything, but guarantees include attractive men, hard bodies, and a lot of baby oil. That's a pretty good day.*

O CON *Some of the guys' heads may be as big as their biceps.*

264.   MEN'S DRESSING ROOM

Have some fun. Cruise the men's department at a large department store and pretend you're shopping for something right near the dressing rooms. See who comes out. If they're still wearing whatever they've tried on, make a comment. "Oh, that's great," should do the trick. From there, it's all easy. But if he asks who you're shopping for, just say your cousin, brother, or father, and then point out something you think would look good on them.

265.   PGA MERCHANDISE SHOW

The PGA merchandise show is the biggest golf trade show around. So naturally, it draws single men of all ages in droves from all over the country. The show takes place annually in Orlando in January. Don't miss it. For more info, check out *www.pgamerchandiseshow. com.*

266.   DEPARTMENT STORE MEN'S SECTION

This one is easy. Cruise around the men's section of any department store, Nordstrom, Macy's, Lord & Taylor, and scan for men. Find something you like and drift into that area of the store. Once you're over there, pick up an item, and ask him what he thinks of it. If he asks you for whom you're shopping, he's interested. Tell him your brother or father, and then see how he feels about a smoothie at the food court.

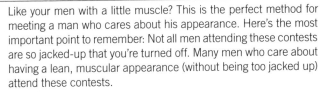

=Time   =Friends $=Expense

267.   FRATERNITY PARTIES

If you're still in college, you already know that you can find men here. But even if you've been out of college for several years, this one can work. Yes, you'll have younger guys drooling over you. That's always a perk. But alumni go back to visit their fraternities all the time. Chances are you can find someone around your age at any fraternity party. Why not give it a shot and enjoy a game of beer pong in the process?

⊙ PRO *It's a fraternity party—so you know you'll have fun.*

⊙ CON *Milwaukee's Best Light may literally be the best beverage on the menu. Plus, fraternity parties are notorious for getting out of hand— wet T-shirt contests, unsolicited dirty dancing—you get the picture.*

268.   SPORTS MEMORABILIA STORE

Most men love sports. It's a fact of life. Therefore, men flock to sports memorabilia stores to ignite their nostalgic love of sports and to find stuff from their favorite teams to put in their living rooms, offices, and cars. So next time you are shopping for a gift for a man in your life . . . or even if you want something for yourself or just feel like browsing, spend a little time in a sports memorabilia store shopping for a man as well.

269.   WING PLACE

From Mr. Wing to Wings to Go, there are plenty of tasty wing places out there . . . and you can bet that guys in your area are frequenting all of them. Whether it's the spicy sauce, the messiness, or the finger-food appeal, guys love wings. Therefore, if a guy spots you chowing down on a plate of wings in his favorite wing place, he may fall in love then and there. So if you can stomach wings, grab a nonvegetarian friend and share a plate of them now and then.

270.   SKEET SHOOTING

When it comes to gun-related activities, skeet shooting is sort of a compromise. It still involves pulling a trigger on a gun, which appeals to men, but the targets are made out of clay. The point is that skeet shooting is a gun-related activity that you as a female might enjoy, and it's great for hand-eye coordination. And even if you don't like doing it yourself, you could attend a skeet-shooting competition, which is guaranteed to be attended by many men. For more info, check out the National Skeet Shooting Association at *www.nssa-nsca.com.*

⏱=Time 👤=Friends $=Expense

271. WAITING IN LINE FOR A NEW VIDEO GAME CONSOLE

These days, video gaming is becoming so popular that people will line up at Best Buy, Circuit City, and other such stores for days to get one of the few precious consoles that come out on the first day. These lines are filled with video game-obsessed teenagers, but they also contain some really dedicated single dads who are willing to take a few vacation days to make their kids happy. These are men you want to meet. So swing by these stores with some hot chocolate and snacks for some of the men waiting in line.

272. SEX SHOP

If you are a little more adventurous and edgy, head to a sex shop with a few fun girlfriends now and then. There is the guaranteed entertainment in the form of toys, games, and adult films . . . and then there may be the adventurous and edgy men shopping there. If you are comfortable with your sexuality, you will have access to more than a few conversation starters.

○ PRO *If nothing more, you could leave with a nice new toy.*

○ CON *Creepy men. Sex shops are chock-full of them—beware.*

273. LANDSCAPING CENTER

Landscaping centers are not only great places to find flowers, plants, herbs, and potted arrangements, but did you ever notice who's helping the customers? Men! It's true. Most landscaping centers require someone with strength, who is also an expert in flora and fauna. Hmm . . . strong yet sensitive? Besides, haven't you been wanting a new pot of flowers?

274. FISHMONGERS

Who doesn't like fish? (OK, well some people don't.) But that doesn't mean you have to enjoy the taste. Just being around fish is fun. Especially in Seattle. The fish-tossing is a sight to behold, until you see the men doing the tossing. Then you'll really be into it. Who knows? He might even help you find a fish you enjoy. If you can't make it to Seattle, stop by your local fishmonger in your supermarket. There are always a few guys back there, and each one of them will swear they can be free of fish-scent before your date.

=Time =Friends $=Expense

d date flea market reunion restaurant tattoo parlor wedding auction ho
ub baby shower casino hibachi ladies night café bake sale brunch river
mbake double date culinary festival smorgasbord tavern church service
mal hospital roommates yacht club school courthouse nudist colony bee
val baseball game car show firefighting fishing tailgating poker campgro
ting contest bowling weight room military cigar shop airport london bri
 eiffel tower vacation hotel cruise mardi gras times square central park
f america mount rushmore hollywood safari smithsonian online animal
e blood drive volunteering special olympics toy drive red cross soup kit
rt gallery book club cooking class library museum college campus orche
ature walk planetarium political rally shakespeare festival disney world
uarium water park caroling parents playground mini-golf county fair co
use laundromat grocery store beach gym subway deli yard sale liquor
post office personal ads company picnic conference water cooler bartend
oncert scavenger hunt karaoke comedy club biking karate softball paint
iling ymca square dancing boardwalk cookout whale watching farmer's
et party friends cafeteria open house singing group bars beach house
ting blind date flea market reunion restaurant tattoo parlor wedding au
ospital club baby shower casino hibachi ladies night café bake sale bru
verboat clambake double date culinary festival smorgasbord tavern chu
ervice spa animal hospital roommates yacht club school courthouse nu
ony beer festival baseball game car show firefighting fishing tailgating
ampground eating contest bowling weight room military cigar shop airp
ndon bridges bus eiffel tower vacation hotel cruise mardi gras times sq
ntral park mall of america mount rushmore hollywood safari smithsonian
e animal rescue blood drive volunteering special olympics toy drive red
p kitchen art gallery book club cooking class library museum college ca
rchestra nature walk planetarium political rally shakespeare festival disn
orld zoo aquarium water park caroling parents playground mini-golf co
ir coffeehouse laundromat grocery store beach gym subway deli yard
quor store post office personal ads company picnic conference water coc
rtending concert scavenger hunt karaoke comedy club biking karate sor
ntball sailing ymca square dancing cookout whale watching farmer's ma
ty friends cafeteria open house singing group bars beach house wine ta
d date flea market reunion restaurant tattoo parlor wedding auction ho
ub baby shower casino hibachi ladies night café bake sale brunch riverl
mbake double date culinary festival smorgasbord tavern church service
mal hospital roommates yacht club school courthouse nudist colony bee
val baseball game car show firefighting fishing tailgating poker campgro
ting contest bowling weight room military cigar shop airport london bri
 eiffel tower vacation hotel cruise mardi gras times square central park
f america mount rushmore hollywood safari smithsonian online animal r
e blood drive volunteering special olympics toy drive red cross soup kit
rt gallery book club cooking class library museum college campus orches
ature walk planetarium political rally shakespeare festival disney world

travelways

275. THE AIRPORT

When traveling by plane, you are bound to be faced with an hour or two of spare time in the airport waiting area. And what better way to speed up a layover than to chat with a nice man? You will never be without a good first line: "Where are you headed?"

O PRO *There are plenty of fascinating, available men in airports.*

O CON *The nice single man you meet could live thousands of miles away.*

276. LONDON'S BRIDGES

Feel free to apply this logic to any busy bridge spot in your area, but for now, think big and dream bigger. London, a city of culture and romance. More than twelve bridges that cross the picturesque Thames River. Think about it. You're walking and sightseeing and like any sightseer, romantic, artist, or a combination of all three, you stop to take in the view from one of London's famous bridges. Men can be found there too. After all, men are romantics. Men walk dogs there. Men enjoy learning about history. Men take photos of the Thames. And most importantly, men know that women love picturesque places. Go make yourself available.

O PRO *A picture-perfect place to meet the man of your dreams.*

O CON *This place is a little more expensive and time consuming than most.*

277. ON A LONG-DISTANCE BUS

Depending on how long you have to be on one, long-distance bus trips can be downright hellish . . . unless you have an eligible guy sitting near you. So use what would ordinarily be a mundane five hours as an opportunity to get to know the person sitting next to you. Even if you don't fall in love, you could meet a nice new friend.

O PRO *He could be riding the bus to spare the environment from one more car on the road. He could be trying to save some money—money that he could spend on you.*

O CON *He could be riding the bus because he has a suspended driver's license. He could be flat broke, living with his parents, and unable to afford a car.*

=Time ♦=Friends $=Expense

278.   THE EIFFEL TOWER

$ $ $

Nothing puts people in the mood for love faster than a trip to the Eiffel Tower. Maybe it's the height, maybe it's the lights, or maybe it's something in the air in Paris; but for whatever reason, the Eiffel Tower is a hot spot for romance. So if you find yourself in the City of Lights, take a trip to la Tour Eiffel and look around for some single gentlemen. If you're there in the winter, try lacing up a pair of skates—entry to the ice-skating rink on one of the observation decks is free with your ticket to the Tower.

Five great French phrases:
1. *Comment vous appelez-vous?* (What's your name?)
2. *Venez-vous souvent ici?* (Do you come here often?)
3. *D'où venez-vous?* (Where are you from?)
4. *Voulez-vous aller boire un verre?* (Would you like to get a drink?)
5. *Je t'aime.* (I love you.)

○ PRO *If it works out, just think about the story you will have to tell your grandchildren.*

○ CON *You could meet someone from the United States or Australia, or anywhere in between . . . either way, long-distance relationships can be a challenge . . .*

279.   GETTING ON A PLANE

$ $ $

Even if you aren't lucky enough to sit next to an interesting man, you may bump into one while boarding. "I met my fiancé while getting on an airplane," says Linda of Spokane, Washington. "We spoke briefly and didn't have a conversation until we were waiting at baggage claim. While waiting for our luggage, we talked and laughed. He asked if I wanted him to be my tour guide while on vacation. I took him up on his offer and had the best first date of my life. We continued a long-distance romance (he in Florida and me in Colorado) for one year before we moved in together. Now we are planning our wedding!"

○ PRO *If you are flying on a 747, you will have hundreds of passengers to choose from.*

○ CON *Because boarding only takes a few minutes and can be a bit chaotic, you will have to act quickly.*

280. ON A PLANE (THE PERSON IN THE NEXT SEAT)

Let's face it—in many cases, we're simply not in the mood to chat with the person sitting two inches from us on a plane, jockeying for the armrest. Sometimes it's just easier to get sucked into a good book or to take a snooze. But if you luck out and the person with whom you are sharing aisle 36 sparks your interest, you have nothing to lose but a few pages of reading. If he doesn't want to talk, you will quickly get the message. If he does, it could be the shortest two-hour flight of your life . . . and the beginning of a beautiful relationship.

PRO *It's just the two of you for the entire flight—no other single ladies vying for his attention.*

CON *The friendly, good-looking man next to you could be from another country.*

281. VACATION

Take a relaxing trip with a few of your favorite girlfriends and there's no telling who you will meet. Go some place that's inexpensive and sunny, like Mexico Springs or Cancun (if you are feeling particularly wild). Even if you don't meet the love of your life, with the mix of sand and margaritas, you are guaranteed to have the time of your life.

PRO *The phrase "relaxing vacation" says it all.*

CON *This one will take a significantly larger investment (time and money) than a typical ladies' night out on the town.*

282. HOTEL LOUNGE

On a business trip, after a busy day, it's tempting to hole up in your cozy hotel room and enjoy the free HBO. But if you are on the lookout for a guy, your hotel lobby lounge is worth checking out. Hotel lounges are often frequented by successful businessmen (who are often there alone) in town for a meeting, men who are just as eager to meet someone to check out the city with as you are. So while you are still dressed nicely from the day, make it a point to stop in for an end-of-the-day drink or coffee to unwind.

283. TRIP TO EUROPE

A great place to meet exciting world travelers is to travel the world with them. Consider a group tour across Europe, for example. You will travel with the same twenty-five to fifty people for ten days or so and share some amazing experiences . . . not to mention lots of hours dining together and riding on a bus. Ask your travel agent if he or she knows of any trips specifically for singles, so you have twenty-five to fifty chances to hit it off with one of your trip mates.

○ PRO *Even if you don't meet someone, you will see some fabulous sites and get a taste of European culture.*

○ CON *You will be with your group a lot, and you run the risk of finding someone, or a few people, in the bunch less than tolerable.*

284. BAGGAGE CLAIM

The 10 or so minutes that you spend waiting for your suitcase to appear on the turnstile can seem like an eternity. So what better way to pass the time than to chat with a handsome stranger? If you have just arrived at your destination, you may meet someone wonderful with whom you can spend a night or two checking out the town.

○ PRO *After a crowded flight, you will have plenty of passengers to choose from.*

○ CON *Weary travelers often don't feel like making conversation or they're rushing to catch a cab or bus—be prepared for rejection.*

285. SINGLES TRAVEL INTERNATIONAL

What better way to get to know an eligible man than while traveling the world with him? Singles Travel International gives singles interested in travel the perfect forum for meeting people who share their passion for exploring the unknown. Traveling in a group of singles to Paris, Monte Carlo, or Rome, you will share many bonding experiences together, and you will be much safer than you would be by yourself. For more information, check out *http://singles travelintl.com.*

 =Time 👤=Friends $=Expense

286. HOTEL POOL

When you are out of town on business by yourself, there's nothing like a relaxing evening at the hotel indoor pool/Jacuzzi. And your evening just might get better if one or two single guys have the same idea. People are often at their friendliest and most open to meeting people when they are on the road on business, and the mood of the day often carries into the night as well. So instead of curling up with a book or the free HBO, grab your bathing suit and a towel and head on down to the pool.

PRO *If the pool is empty, you can always swim a few laps for some end-of-the-day exercise.*

CON *If you are traveling in the middle of winter, you will have to make sure you are . . . er . . . "groomed" for a bathing suit.*

287. ALASKA

As far as states go, you can't beat Alaska for meeting men, where the ratio of young men to women is 114 men for every 100 women. So plan a trip to Alaska with a girlfriend and enjoy the hiking trails, seafood, and Alaskan hotties. Your odds of meeting a nice single man are very, very good. A particularly great place to meet guys in Anchorage, Alaska's biggest city, is one of the eleven bars at Chilkoot Charlies (called "Koots" by the locals).

PRO *There are 24 hours of daylight in the summer, which will give you plenty of time and energy to get out there and meet people.*

CON *Alaska is quite far from "the lower 48," so if you hit it off with an Alaskan guy, you will have to bundle up and move to the coldest state yourself, coerce him to move closer to you, or bear the long-distance relationship.*

288. SECURITY LINE AT THE AIRPORT

If you've flown anywhere post 9/11, you know to expect a long security line. So why not make the best of it? Smile at the people waiting in line with you and strike up a conversation to pass the time. "Where are you headed?" or a simple "hello" are good ice-breakers. If all goes well, you can take your conversation past the security line and into the coffee shop or lounge near your gate.

=Time ▮=Friends $=Expense

289. SINGLES CRUISE

On a singles cruise, you will partake in singles cocktail parties, dinners, live entertainment, theme parties, dancing, beach parties, scuba diving, swimming, and much more . . . all with fun-loving people who just happen to be single. These cruises go all around the world and are usually reasonably priced. So invite a girlfriend or two, sail away, and have a blast meeting and vacationing with a ship full of singles.

○ PRO *A guaranteed fun trip, whether you fall in love or not.*

○ CON *If you suffer from motion sickness, think twice before you climb aboard.*

290. MAGAZINE STAND IN THE AIRPORT

As you browse through the latest issues of *Cosmo* and the *New Yorker* for your flight, look at what (or who) a magazine stand has to offer. A magazine stand in the middle of a crowded airport draws a constant stream of people in search of something to read. So if you have a little time to kill, it might be worth scanning the reading material at a magazine stand as well as the men who are buying it. To start a conversation, you can always ask a guy about his favorite magazine. And who knows—he may end up on your flight.

291. ANHEUSER-BUSCH BREWERY TOUR

One of the oldest breweries in the country and the maker of Michelob, Budweiser, and other brews popular with men, Anheuser-Busch hosts a tour as frequently as every 15 minutes, and the tours are full of men of all ages. In addition to the plant, the tour takes visitors through the brewing process, to the stables that house the Budweiser Clydesdales, and into a hospitality room for beer samples and pretzels (an ideal place to get to know any men from your tour group who sparked your interest during the tour). So next time you find yourself in St. Louis, make it a point to stop at Anheuser-Busch and see what's brewing. For tour schedules, visit *www.busweisertours.com.*

292. AIRPORT BISTRO

Got a few hours to kill before your flight? Put the stress of getting through security behind you and relax at an airport bistro. Airports are crawling with interesting single men from all around the world. Plus, they usually serve some tasty meals. So pull up a seat next to an attractive stranger and see where it goes. If you're lucky, he may be on your plane as well.

O PRO *Men at airport bistros are often alone and just as anxious to talk to someone as you are.*

O CON *The guy you meet may be from a state across the country, or worse, a country across the world. Oh well, if you hit it off, you will have an excuse to take a trip.*

293. MARDI GRAS

If you have never been in the French Quarter during Mardi Gras and you love a good party, it's a scene worth checking out . . . and in the midst of the party, you may just meet a handsome guy to celebrate with. So put on your party shoes and head down to New Orleans!

O PRO *Mardi Gras is teaming with single guys. Some of them may be a little tipsy, but they'll be single.*

O CON *Booze, boobs, and beads are not every girl's idea of a good time.*

294. ATLANTIC CITY, NEW JERSEY

For East Coasters, Atlantic City is sort of a mini-Vegas, offering glitz, gambling, nightlife, and yes, partying. There are singles of all shapes and sizes here. Wealthy businessmen, young college guys, older gents who can't resist a hot game of poker. You name it. It's here. And because the alcohol flows freely, you won't need a conversation starter. They just seem to happen. Especially around an exciting game of craps or at the blackjack table. Although many will tell you that A.C. is great for finding a man for a night or a weekend, rest assured there are fun, outgoing, successful singles in Atlantic City. Plan your trip to match your dating goal. Also, use a dating site to find someone near A.C., and have your friends meet up with his. It could be a weekend you'll never forget!

O PRO *The nightlife never stops and there are singles everywhere.*

O CON *Gamblers—a lot of them are undatable.*

295. THE PLAYBOY MANSION

OK. So getting in the front door isn't the easiest thing in the world. But, if you have connections and can work your way beyond Hef's front door, remember: The mansion is often crawling with single men looking for someone cute and fun. Not all men who visit the Playboy Mansion are out for a fling either. In fact, many successful men are invited because they are leaders in their industry. If you have the right look and attitude, you can be mingling with some of the country's elite. Not a bad way to meet the man of your dreams.

○ PRO *A guaranteed fun time.*

○ CON *The competition is fierce. Enough said.*

296. SPRING BREAK

Spring break is no longer just for teens and college students with raging hormones. A number of single guys and gals get together for an annual ritual consisting of beaches, cocktails, dancing, and socializing. There are a number of Web sites that can point you in the right direction. Concierge.com is a great place to start. This site lists attractive destinations that will appeal to whatever you're seeking. A number of singles Web sites also offer group discounts on spring break trips for adults.

○ PRO *A ton of singles in party mode.*

○ CON *A ton of young college kids in party mode.*

297. YELLOWSTONE NATIONAL PARK

Think in terms of your likes and dislikes. If you love nature and animals, jump online and check out trips to Yellowstone National Park. Not everyone who visits this beautiful site is taken! Plenty of singles visit this breathtaking spot every year—for a number of reasons. Some enjoy the physical activities available in the region. Others prefer wildlife photography, a real wild-west style cookout, or a simple boat cruise. Want to create the ultimate getaway? Find someone on a dating Web site like Match.com from Yellowstone and start communicating. From there, set up your vacation and your first meeting. Get it all in one trip!

○ PRO *You'll see Old Faithful, something everyone should check off their vacation list.*

○ CON *Yellowstone doesn't always draw the youngest crowd, so if you're young, be ready to sift through some cotton heads.*

298.   CLUB MED

$ $ $

Club Med is a spectacular way to combine an exciting vacation with your quest for companionship. Start by visiting *www.clubmed. us* and check out all of the premier vacation destinations Club Med has to offer. Make a note of the countries and resorts you prefer and then do an online search for "Club Med," your destination, and "singles." Immediately you'll find singles trips to exotic places like Turks and Caicos or Cancun. Or, if you want to make the process easier, simply call 1-888-WEBCLUB and ask about singles trips to Club Med destinations. Thanks to the growth of the Internet, the stigma about singles vacations was lifted years ago. People began discussing where to go, when to go, and the benefits and drawbacks of singles vacations across the globe. Club Med vacations are as wild or as laid back as you choose—just do a little homework and your man might be waiting for you with a tropical cocktail in hand!

299.   CONTIKI TOURS

$ $ $

One of the most reputable travel companies for singles between the ages of 18 and 35, Contiki has been organizing travel tours for more than 40 years. Its site (*http://us.contiki.com*) is packed with information, including message boards, photos, and travel logs. In fact, you might be able to meet a man just by logging on their site. But if you prefer something more interactive, check out the list of tours Contiki offers. There is something for everyone, including trips to Australia, Canada, Europe, New Zealand, and even within America. Plus, you'll find destinations that allow you to explore rugged terrain or that let you just lie back and enjoy a tropical breeze with a mai tai.

○ PRO *Whichever trip you choose, there are always men in the group, as Contiki does their best to make the ratio of men to women even.*

○ CON *You will need to shell out some cash and burn some of your precious vacation days, so think this one through.*

300. IBIZA

One of the world's top party destinations, Ibiza is Spain's hottest city. From all-night parties to clothing-optional beaches, this is the place to let it all hang out. You can meet a man and keep him around for your entire trip, just a day, or even just an hour. The relationships you make in Ibiza may be brief, but they can be quite powerful. This trip is highly recommended for women who want to meet Mr. Right, but have a soft spot for Mr. Right Now and any environment even remotely resembling Mardi Gras or Halloween.

O PRO *Even if you don't fall in love, you'll be forever passionate about the excitement Ibiza has to offer.*

O CON *The cost.*

301. THE JERSEY SHORE

This one is reserved for late May through early September, and while those in the Delaware, New Jersey, New York, and Pennsylvania areas are well-aware of the flames the Jersey Shore tends to ignite, it's fast becoming a popular destination for those even farther away. The best part about the Jersey Shore is that you can choose just how wild you want it. There are lazy towns that are more family oriented, but still have bars, clubs, and beaches that are great for singles. And then there are places like Ocean Drive in Seaside Heights where the summer singles sweat away their nights dancing, listening to bands, and looking for their new summer love. Want something classy and fun with just the right amount of wild? Check out Avalon, New Jersey. It's perfect for the single girl looking for successful single men.

302. LAS VEGAS, NEVADA

It's Vegas. Need we say more? Grab a friend—married, gay, straight, single, whatever—and get to Vegas. Gambling, clubs, lounges, and more. It's all here, and there are men everywhere. Not every guy in Vegas wears large gold chains and is there for a one-night stand. But, just to be sure, try seeing the other side of Vegas. You just might find someone worth your while as you peer out across the Grand Canyon or watch the Bellagio light show from a distance. Take a peek at the crowd and see which men are actually watching Cirque de Soleil. They are out there. If you're starved for attention, your best bet is to pull up a stool and try your hand at blackjack. You'll get plenty of attention at the tables. Good luck!

=Time ❕=Friends $=Expense

303. THE RUNNING OF THE BULLS

$ $ $

One of the world's most dangerous parties, the Running of the Bulls isn't for the faint of heart, PETA members, or those against wasting food. But there are plenty of brave men there—many of them Spanish. While it's not suggested that you go to the Running of the Bulls specifically to meet a guy, you can check out all that Spain has to offer and stop by this outrageous tradition along the way. You will meet a lot of people and many of them will be handsome, courageous men. Just try to stay out of the way of the flying tomatoes. Want to learn more about the Running of the Bulls and other fun-filled spots in Spain? Check out *www.spanish-fiestas .com*.

304. TRAVEL COMPANION EXCHANGE

$ $ $

Since 1982, Travel Companion Exchange has been helping single, divorced, and widowed men and women travel more safely and more affordably. Simply, the Travel Companion Exchange finds suitable, respectable travel partners for those who would otherwise be traveling alone. They will help you find a travel companion based on your input and your destination choice. In fact, they will find someone who is perfect for you whether you're traveling within the states or abroad. Check out *www.travelcompanions.com* for more information.

305. WORKING RANCH

$ $ $

Imagine riding a horse across the countryside every day for a week, herding cattle, sleeping underneath the stars after a real cowboy-style cookout just like the old West. Now imagine having this kind of fun with twenty or thirty singles. It happens and it's loads of fun. You might find a guy on your trip who isn't exactly Clint Eastwood. Or, you might find a guy who works on the ranch who becomes your cowboy for a lifetime. Either way, a singles trip to a working ranch would be a completely new experience for many single women. Start with an online search for "working ranch" and "singles." From there, find a location that interests you and see if they offer singles trips and discounts. Before booking your trip, be sure to call the ranch and get an idea for the number of singles going on these excursions and find out what kinds of single men normally participate.

306. CABO SAN LUCAS

Because Cabo is a party in a paradise, there are many singles there who want to get away from it all—except the fun. Lie on powder-laden beaches by day and soak up those pleasant rays before heading over to the swim-up bar at your resort for a fresh tropically sweet concoction. Chat with some of the guys lounging at the bar and ask which of the many bars and dance clubs they'll be visiting that evening. Grab a taxi that night and start scoping! You can walk to many of the local pubs, bars, and discotheques—all teeming with sun-kissed men looking for someone like you.

307. HOTEL LOBBY

Hotel lobbies are crawling with interesting people of all kinds, so this is a great place if you're a voyeur, or if you love striking up a conversation with just about anyone. Some hotels host conventions and parties, and many offer special accommodations to wedding parties. Strolling into a hotel lobby at just the right time can provide you with all kinds of single males—some may be businessmen on the road, some may be there for a convention or a wedding, perhaps some are there on a guys' getaway. Plop yourself on the hotel lobby couch and pick up a newspaper. You'll be shocked at the number of men strolling through—now you just need to start a conversation and see if they're single.

308. IN BED

One of South Beach's hottest clubs, this New Age watering hole offers a bed to lie on, as opposed to the impersonal and uncomfortable barstools of yesteryear. Some say it's just a passing trend. We say, grab a cocktail and lie down with someone new for a change. The guys are certainly there and many of the types who frequent BED will be sure to change the sheets on a regular basis. And that's good news for you.

309. PALMS HOTEL AND CASINO

With the ultimate in luxury salon and spa treatments, trendy people, Rain, the scintillating Ghostbar, and now the all-new Playboy Club, you can see not only why men flock, but why women flock too. Go to *www.palms.com* and check it out. Then book your weekend getaway. Although you may want to keep what happens in Vegas, you'll have no regrets.

 =Time 🕯=Friends $=Expense

310. SEA LION OR OTHER ANIMAL-WATCHING TOUR

If you enjoy whale watching, why not move on to sea lions or another sea species? Some of these tours can be costly, so if meeting a man is your primary goal, then go online and do some extensive hunting for trips for singles. They are out there, but require some searching. A good place to start is with a travel agent specializing in singles travel, such as *www.allsinglestravel.com*.

311. TIMES SQUARE, NEW YORK

You can find it all in Times Square—MTV Studios, great restaurants like John's Pizza, Colony Records (for big music fans seeking hard-to-find albums), the Hershey Store, and even the Museum of Sex. Just get out there and walk around.

○ PRO *This area is crawling with men of all kinds.*

○ CON *Sex and the City—it didn't exactly paint New York as the best place to meet guys. But they did have a lot of fun!*

312. UNIVERSAL STUDIOS

People often associate Universal Studios with kids, when the truth is that Universal Studios is about entertainment—for everyone. There's gourmet casual and fine dining, endless shopping, and their CityWalk row of bars and nightspots offers a Hard Rock Café, Jimmy Buffett's Margaritaville, and much more. Here's the key: The single men are here! Locations are in Florida and California, so visit *www.universalstudios.com*.

313. BOSTON

You will expose yourself to tons of single guys simply by visiting the city of Boston. It seems that Bean Town has the highest percentage of men who have never been married in the country—nearly 54 percent! Plus, it has Harvard, Boston University, Boston College, and other schools full of intelligent students, grad students, and professors. For information on Boston hot spots, check out *www.cityofboston.gov*.

○ PRO *Boston is a great town, so you are guaranteed great restaurants, beautiful historic architecture, and fabulous shopping.*

○ CON *The highest percentage of men who have never been married doesn't mean they don't want to stay that way. You may have to turn on the charm for this stubborn bunch!*

314. DAYTONA BEACH

One of the highest concentrations of men all year takes place at Daytona Beach's Bike Week in March. There are the men with their bikes, and then there are men admiring the bikes. Either way, there are plenty of men for you to meet. And when the sun goes down, you can head to the Daytona Beach Bandshell in Ocean-front Park, where there will be even more men checking out the free concerts, which range from country to jazz. For more info, check out *www.daytonabeach.com*.

315. THE GRAND CANYON

Julie R., 29, from Boise, Idaho, met her husband at the biggest chasm in the United States: the Grand Canyon. "I was in complete awe of the size and beauty of the Canyon . . . then I turned to my right and was even more in awe when I saw Randy, who turned out to be my future husband. It was the most amazing moment of my life," she says. At the Grand Canyon, you can find romance on the roads, hiking the trails, or floating on the current of the Colorado River. For more information, check out *www.nps.gov/grca*.

316. SOUTHWEST AIRLINES

Next time you have to fly, consider flying Southwest. There's a reason this airline is one of the most successful in the country. Not only are the tickets reasonable, the staff is friendly and fun. And when it comes to meeting men, you can't wait for the first-come, first-served seating-style that Southwest practices. Instead of getting a seat number, you sit down in the order you arrive at the terminal. So if you spot a handsome passenger in the seating area, sidle up next to him so you can grab the seat beside him for the duration of the flight. For more information, check out *www.southwest.com*.

317. CENTRAL PARK

For New York City residents, Central Park offers a haven for jogging, walking, barbecuing, and other activities that city living may constrict. So naturally, you can find many city-dwelling men relaxing under the trees at Central Park. Whether you live in the city or you are just visiting, get away from the hustle and bustle for a few hours and take in the Central Park scenery.

=Time ＝Friends $＝Expense

318. CHEESE-STEAK WAR

Love a good cheese steak? You may want to explore for yourself which is the best by trying one at Geno's Steaks in Philadelphia . . . and then heading across the street to try one at Pat's King of Steaks. The two Philadelphia cheese-steak shops have been battling it out on the same block for years, and each place seems to have a loyal following, mostly of men. To meet these men and to get a good conversation going about which steak is best and why, you're best off conducting a sort of "taste test" by going to both shops. So bring your appetite—for cheese steaks and for meeting men!

319. THE FOUR SEASONS

Classy, sophisticated men usually don't stay at the EconoLodge. They stay at the Four Seasons. So to bump into these men, you should stay at the Four Seasons, too. These classy resort hotels are often located in areas full of fun, interactive leisure activities, such as cooking classes, skiing, tennis, and sailing that provide wonderful opportunities to meet fellow guests. And Four Seasons Resorts are very family friendly, so if you're a parent, you can bring the kids. Check out *www.fourseasons.com*.

320. JACKSONVILLE, NORTH CAROLINA

The town of Jacksonville boasts a whopping 175 single males for every 100 single females, so needless to say, in any bar, restaurant, or public place, you are bound to be way outnumbered by men. And better yet, this once-quiet farming community has turned into a bustling business, retail, medical, banking, and cultural center. *www.ci.jacksonville.nc.us*.

321. NASHVILLE, TENNESSEE

Maybe it's the building with Batman ears or the country, blues, and bluegrass music at the bars, but for whatever reason, Nashville tends to attract a lot of men. And in addition to the men, Nashville offers some wonderful live music (there is a good reason it's called Music City), gorgeous southern architecture, and if you're in the mood, an evening at the Grand Ole Opry. Check out *www .nashvillecvb.com*.

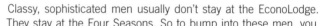

322. NATIONAL BASEBALL HALL OF FAME

Want to see men moved to tears? Take a trip to Cooperstown, New York, to see the Baseball Hall of Fame. Not only does the museum offer numerous baseball-heavy exhibits, such as a ballparks exhibit and 150 years of baseball uniforms, which will draw tons of men; it also features some interesting exhibits from a historical and sociological perspective, such as the women in baseball exhibit and a hall of fame art exhibit. So for a day full of baseball and emotionally moved men, check it out. *www.baseballhalloffame.org*.

323. THE OUTER BANKS

There is a reason so many cars boast that black and white oval-shaped sticker that reads "OBX." For a more peaceful beach experience complete with charming lighthouses, events like oyster feasts, and most importantly, southern surfers, you cannot beat a trip to the Outer Banks, North Carolina. So if you enjoy a more relaxed beach atmosphere as opposed to a town that hosts clubs and wild parties, you will be likely to find a soul mate in the Outer Banks.Plan your trip at *www.outerbanks.org*.

324. PARADISE, NEVADA

Paradise has 118 unmarried men for every 100 unmarried women. So if you take a trip there as a single woman, the odds are in your favor. Another benefit: Paradise contains most of the Las Vegas strip, so you can meet a nice single man and have a ball with him in Sin City. Check out *www.paradisenevada.com*.

325. PUNXSUTAWNEY ON GROUNDHOG DAY

Anxious for spring? You may want to take a trip to Punxsutawney, Pennsylvania, on Groundhog Day to get a glimpse of Punxsutawney Phil in action. Believe it or not, men flock to this event. There is even a Punxsutawney groundhog club that celebrates Phil all year long. So check it out at *www.groundhog.org*.

326.   RIO DE JANEIRO

In addition to some of the world's most beautiful beaches, Rio de Janeiro is home to some of the world's most beautiful men. In addition to the romantic Brazilian guys walking around, there are the men who go to Rio to enjoy the breathtaking natural setting, Carnival celebrations, samba and other music, and many other attractions. Take a trip to Rio with an open heart, and you may come home a changed woman.

⊙ PRO *Carnival is an exciting, lively party that takes place annually in Rio and draws thousands of single men.*

⊙ CON *Rio is certainly not the safest city in the world. Travel with friends and use your street smarts.*

327.   SCOTTSDALE, ARIZONA

In addition to being a hot spot for artists and people who love warm weather, Scottsdale, Arizona, is a great place to go if you are single and older than 55. A lot of single men retire to Scottsdale to enjoy the sunny, laid-back environment. For more info on Scottsdale, check out *www.scottsdaleaz.gov.*

328.   SLOPPY JOE'S BAR

The former hangout of Ernest Hemingway, Sloppy Joe's, in Key West, Florida, gets a blend of tourists, fishermen, and those just passing through. It even gets the occasional intellectual who hopes he may be inspired simply by being in the same surroundings as the famous writer. More importantly, that intellectual might be there when you're there, and the two of you can start a fascinating conversation. For more info, visit *www.sloppyjoes.com.*

329.   WRIGLEY FIELD

Wrigley Field is more than just a baseball field in Chicago, Illinois; it's a true fan stadium, and there is a party at every game. The combination of baseball and a fun party equals a guaranteed high concentration of men . . . which means you should be there to have fun along with them. So next time you are in Chi-Town, throw on a baseball T-shirt and head on down to the field to watch the Cubbies.

330.   CLUB BARCELONA

Love the excitement of a South Beach club but also enjoy a cozy New York bar? You will love Club Barcelona in Hartford, Connecticut, which offers a nice mix of the two—and so do a lot of single men. If you can make it during the week, go to Barcelona on a salsa lesson night (Tuesdays) and snag a guy who can move on the floor. For other events, visit *www.club-barcelona.com*.

331.   THE BREWER'S ART

Set in a grand Mt. Vernon townhouse, the Brewer's Art is a classy alehouse in Baltimore that brews its own beer so, naturally, it attracts many men anxious to try the wheat beers and the porters. And if, like many women, you are not a beer drinker, the Brewer's Art offers raspberry and peach varieties that are popular with the ladies. The relaxed atmosphere at Brewer's Art is ideal for meeting men and getting to know them better over a few brews. For visiting hours, go to *www.belgianbeer.com*.

332.   DEWEY BEACH, DELAWARE

Although it only stretches across a short span of the Atlantic, Dewey Beach has one of the highest concentrations of singles on the East Coast. To meet single guys ranging in age from twenty to fifty who hold occupations from computer programmers to architects to physicians, get a house in Dewey for the summer. In addition to the beach, Dewey features block parties, early bar parties with breakfast bloody marys (yes, the party scene in Dewey is quite lively), and the Starboard, which was recently named one of the top twenty-five bars in the country by *Men's Journal* magazine. Check out *www.deweybeach.com* for more information on Dewey vacations and rentals.

333.   THE GOLDEN DOME

If you've ever seen the movie *Rudy,* you understand the obsession some men have with Notre Dame football. If you haven't seen the movie, you should know that a lot of men love Notre Dame football with such a passion that they could form a new religion. To meet some of these men who bleed gold and blue, take a road trip out to the University of Notre Dame in Indiana for a football game and join in some of the tailgate parties. You, too, may become a die-hard Irish fan. Check out *http://und.cstv.com*.

=Time =Friends $=Expense

334. THE LINCOLN MEMORIAL

If you haven't stood in front of the cement image of President Lincoln—one of the most profound symbols of American Democracy—it is your duty as an American citizen to do so. And if you have, you should probably go back to see it again, because by nature of being a popular tourist destination, the Lincoln Memorial draws a lot of single men in the form of foreigners, out-of-state visitors, school teachers, and single fathers. What better place to strike up a conversation than in front of a national symbol of Americans united as a nation?

335. LAMBEAU FIELD

Since it underwent renovations in 2003, Lambeau Field in Green Bay, Wisconsin, has gone from a stadium that fans used ten days a year to a year-round destination for football fans and families. Lambeau Field hosts a bunch of male-oriented attractions, including the Packers Pro Shop, Packers Hall of Fame, Curly's Pub, and other Atrium dining, event, entertainment, and retail options. So naturally, you will find a lot of men there. Check out *www.lambeau field.com*.

336. SEQUOIA RESTAURANT

As you dine on a delicious meal with a clear view of Washington Harbour, you can do some major man scoping. With the proximity to DC and Georgetown University, the guys are everywhere—rowing, biking, or walking. And many of them stop for a bite to eat at the Sequoia. So if you're in the DC area, bring a girlfriend and some binoculars to the Sequoia and have a fun afternoon.

337. STURGIS, SOUTH DAKOTA

By itself, the town of Sturgis, South Dakota, doesn't sound like much. But when it comes to meeting men, Sturgis's annual Sturgis Rally in August, one of the biggest motorcycle rallies in the world, draws a lot of males. First there are the motorcycle riders themselves (and any ladies with a weakness for the bad boys will be excited about this). Then there are the spectators who come for the beauty contests, food, beer, races, and other manly events. All the information you need to plan your trip is at *www.sturgis.com*.

=Time =Friends $=Expense

338. WASHINGTON MONUMENT

To honor the first president of the United States, crowds of people gather to see the Washington Monument every day. And there are guaranteed to be single men in the form of teachers, out-of-towners, foreigners, single fathers, and so on at the Washington Monument on any given day. So as you go and pay your respects yourself, take your eyes off the giant monument every now and then to see who's standing to your left and your right.

339. WILLIAMSPORT, PENNSYLVANIA

Why should you visit this town in the middle of Pennsylvania, miles from any city or shore? Because Williamsport is the place where Little League Baseball was born, it has a fabulous Little League Baseball museum, and it hosts the Little League World Series each August. So naturally, baseball-loving men will flock to Williamsport in late summer. To increase your chances of meeting these Little League Baseball fans, swing by the Bulldog Brewery, one of the city's most popular hangouts. Check out *www.10best .com/Williamsport*.

340. HENRY'S BAR

Henry's Bar, in the charming city of Charleston, South Carolina, is notorious for its handsome men . . . both in front of and behind the bar. So if you live in the Southeast or will be traveling through Charleston, put Henry's on your list of destinations. If even just for the eye candy, you'll be glad you did.

341. MYRTLE BEACH, SOUTH CAROLINA

With its more than 14 million visitors per year, you are bound to find a man you are compatible with in Myrtle Beach. And with the sixty miles of beaches, restaurants, shopping, and more, there are plenty of fun venues for meeting men. The beach in Myrtle is at its busiest between 2:00 and 4:00 P.M., when hotel guests hit the sand and the sea, so reserve most of your single, attractive guy scoping for this timeframe. Plan your trip by starting at *www .myrtlebeach.com*.

 =Time ♥=Friends $=Expense

342. THE OCEAN HOUSE RESTAURANT

Winner of the Cape Cod View's Best Martini Contest, the Ocean House Restaurant is a popular Cape Cod hot spot full of handsome, single New England men. And with the list of delicious martini concoctions, you will have plenty of drinks to try and discuss with the locals as you check out what the Ocean House has to offer.

343. OLD ORCHARD BEACH, MAINE

When you hear the word beach, you may automatically think Myrtle or Miami, but there are beaches boasting attractive men all over the coast, even as far up as Maine. In addition to handsome, classy New England men, Orchard Beach offers miles of white sand, restaurants, lobster (of course!), water sports, camping, and much more. For more information, visit *www.oldorchardbeachmaine.com*.

344. STEAM ALLEY

If you're in the region of Providence, Rhode Island, don't miss a chance to pop into Steam Alley, a restaurant/bar that attracts tons of attractive and single New England men. Between the big screen TVs, mini arcade, and karaoke bar, Steam Alley is quite the magnet for members of the opposite sex.

345. EMPIRE STATE BUILDING

The backdrop for many romantic scenes in movies, the Empire State Building could be a romantic backdrop for you as well. Each year, more than 3.5 million people climb to the 86th story to get the panoramic view of Manhattan. For optimum chances of meeting Mr. Right, climb to the top on a busy weekend day and let your eyes roam throughout the inside of the building as well as out onto the rooftops of the city. Check out *www.esbnyc.com*.

346. FLATTOP MOUNTAIN

Anchorage, Alaska, is a wonderful place to go to meet men—it has one of the highest ratios of single men to women in the country. A great place to find these guys: the famous hiking trails on Anchorage's Flattop Mountain. You can get some exercise while you check out what the city has to offer. See *www.anchorage.net.*

=Time ♦=Friends $=Expense

347. THE LOUVRE

From the moment you first get a glimpse of the Louvre in the center of Paris, you will be in awe. The museum's architecture and the glass pyramid in its courtyard are worth the visit alone . . . then you get inside. In addition to the Mona Lisa, Venus de Milo, and Madonna of the Rocks, you will be exposed to hundreds of men from all around the world who are intellectual enough to want to explore the world's most famous museum. And the many restaurants and coffee shops in the museum offer plenty of opportunities to meet fellow museum-goers. Find out more at *www.louvre.fr*.

348. MALL OF AMERICA

To see the biggest group of shoppers under one roof, where better to go than the largest mall in the United States, the Mall of America? From its 15 electronics stores, 15 sporting good stores, and more than 35 stores offering men's fashions, there are plenty of reasons for men to go to this mall. And with the nearly 30 restaurants, there are more than enough places to take a break from shopping and strike up a conversation with these men. Check out *www.mallofamerica.com*.

349. MELVIN B'S

One of the largest beer gardens in the country, Melvin B's in Chicago draws an unusually large crowd of men. The patio in the summer is a friendly atmosphere where people hang out casually and meet each other over a few brews. To see what it's all about, check out *www.meetandpotatoes.com*.

350. MILLION DOLLAR COWBOY BAR

For the cowboy fans out there who live in or will be traveling through Wyoming, the Million Dollar Cowboy Bar in Jackson Hole is worth a stop. With manly events like a bike run, pig roast, and motorcycle ride, this place notoriously attracts some of the best-looking cowboys on the West Coast. Check it out at *www.million dollarcowboybar.com*.

 =Time =Friends $=Expense

351.   MONUMENT CIRCLE

For the tourist in you, Monument Circle in Indianapolis is interesting because of the Soldiers and Sailors Monument that sits in its center. For the single woman in you, Monument Circle is interesting because it is full of single men . . . walking the streets and in the pools in the summer or viewing the city's large, decorated Christmas tree in winter. For extra meeting potential, consider taking a walking tour of Monument Circle. For more information, visit *www.historiclandmarks.org/things/heritage.html*.

352.   MOUNT RUSHMORE

Nearly three million people from across the country and around the world travel to Mount Rushmore every year. This large group includes a lot of school trips, including some chaperoned by single male teachers and dads. And then there are the men there to revel at this amazing symbol of American freedom and democracy in the form of giant faces of Washington, Jefferson, Lincoln, and Theodore Roosevelt, carved into the side of the mountain. Check out *www.nps.gov/moru/historyculture/index.htm*.

353.   PESOS KITCHEN AND LOUNGE

Not only does Pesos serve the tastiest tacos and margaritas in Seattle, the place is known to be hopping with attractive singles. The most popular food items are the carnitas (tender sautéed pork cubes in very spicy sauce) and scrumptious grilled prawn fajitas. So have a feast . . . then feast your eyes.

354.   SEARS TOWER

What could make you higher than standing on the 110th floor of the tallest building in North America and the third tallest building in the world? Meeting the man of your dreams there. Located in Chicago, the Sears Tower draws a lot of male tourists who are impressed with its, well, size. And beyond that, there are men working on many of the tall tower's floors. So next time you are in the Windy City, make it a point to check out what the Sears Tower has to offer. For Skydeck hours, visit *www.the-skydeck.com*.

=Time =Friends $=Expense

355. SWISS ALPS

With a unique combination of peace and quiet, hiking, skiing, and breathtaking views, a trip to the Swiss Alps is worth taking. And then, of course, there are the handsome tourists from all over the world and the charming (and neutral) Swiss men. Switzerland is one of the most appealing countries in the world to visit and the perfect atmosphere in which to meet the man of your dreams.

356. SYDNEY, AUSTRALIA

For those of you ladies who have a real weakness for a guy with an accent, there's Sydney, Australia. In addition to breathtaking landscapes, unique wildlife, and lively bars and restaurants, the "land down under" is densely populated with many charming single men. So next time you have some vacation days to burn and a few extra dollars to spend, consider Sydney.

357. AIRPORT BAR

With all the flight delays and layovers involved with flying, if you travel by air, chances are you will have some sort of time to fill. If you know you won't have to drive for the next 12 hours, you may want to relax and enjoy a drink at the airport bar. Not only will a cocktail calm your nerves, you will also open yourself up to meeting the many men who choose to spend their free time in an airport over a few beers. And this crop of men is quite interesting—men of all ages, backgrounds, nationalities, and careers can be found in airport bars, so there's no telling who you might meet.

O PRO *This is one type of bar where it is safe to hang out by yourself.*

O CON *If you meet an interesting man from Ireland or India, you may have to call it quits when it's time to board.*

358. BANKS OF LAKE HARRIET

When the weather turns warm, the banks of Lake Harriet in Minneapolis are filled with handsome men running, rollerblading, and biking. Lake Harriet offers 64 acres of land and 377 acres of water—plenty of acres for men to play on. So for a nice view, sit on the riverbanks. Then hop on the Como-Harriet Streetcar to get back to the center of town and see who's riding.

 =Time =Friends $=Expense

359. BANKS OF THE SEINE

Parisian culture is very outdoorsy—instead of hanging out in bars and clubs on a Friday night, many Parisians throw down a blanket on the banks of the Seine and enjoy a bottle of wine and fresh bread. So if you are lucky enough to take a trip to Paris, once you've scoped out the bank scene by taking a boat ride down the river, take a blanket and a bottle of wine of your own and join the locals. Contrary to rumor, many French people are friendly and eager to meet Americans. And French men are very charming and romantic. Before you go on your trip, learn a few basic French phrases—many French men you meet will be flattered that you are trying to speak their language and anxious to communicate despite the barrier. After all, Paris is the City of Love.

360. BEACH PLACE

At this open-air shopping and dining mall in Ft. Lauderdale, you can find tons of eligible bachelors, both from Ft. Lauderdale and out of town. And with the array of restaurants and shops, there are plenty of opportunities to get to know one of them better. To better your chances, go when it's really busy and offer to share a table with a man who's dining alone. Or take a girlfriend as a wing-woman and see if you can't meet a fun group of men. The open-air layout will give you a nice overview of who's there.

361. BEALE STREET

Beale Street in Memphis, Tennessee—the home of the blues and the birthplace of rock and roll—is a hub of single men. With the booming music and bars, both Memphis men and men from out of town flock to the area. So next time you find yourself in Memphis, throw on a cowgirl hat and have some fun down on Beale Street.

362. FIRST-CLASS LOUNGE IN AN AIRPORT

In addition to the interesting men you may meet on the flight, here's another reason to fly business or first class: Some airports in the United States offer a first-class lounge, where passengers flying business class are invited to spend their time during a delay or layover. These lounges offer a more sophisticated club-type atmosphere than the standard airport bar, and they are full of travelers looking for an entertaining way to spend their airport time. Maybe one of them could spend it talking with you?

🕐 =Time 👤=Friends $=Expense

363. FLYING BUSINESS CLASS

If you travel often for your job and you really want to make the most of your trips (in terms of meeting men, that is), try to bump your ticket up to business class whenever you can. In addition to the more comfortable seats and complimentary champagne and cookies, you will have access to a lot of successful men with whom you can chat.

364. FOUNDRY CAFÉ AND BILLIARDS CLUB

To get a metropolitan-like atmosphere complete with DJs and live music in the heart of Boulder, Colorado—and to meet some men who want a more lively scene than some of the taverns and micro-breweries of Boulder offer—check out the Foundry Café and Billiards Club. The men in the Foundry Café are often the ones most interested in meeting women (taverns don't exactly attract a ton of ladies), and with the eleven pool tables, you can get to know them over a heated competition. Check out *www.foundryboulder.com*.

365. FROG BEAR AND WILD BOAR

With its great drink specials, live bands, and the "longest happy hour," the Frog Bear and Wild Boar is a popular place for the single men in Columbus, Ohio. Plus, every night is ladies' night—no cover for females, all day, every day! For the highest concentration of men, go on Big Ass Beer 'n' BBQ Wednesdays—the men flock to the place. Visit their website at *www.frogbearbar.com*.

366. HOFBRAU HOUSE

The Hofbrau House in Munich, Germany, is one of the largest brew houses in the world. They serve huge mugs of beer and feature a live German musical performance and an all-you-can eat Bavarian buffet . . . so naturally, you can find lots of men from all over the world there. The thing about the Hofbrau House that makes it so ideal for meeting men (in addition to the flowing beer) is the communal seating. Guests sit in mixed groups at long tables, so you will have an opportunity to chat with some strangers as you eat your sausages and kraut. For a complete Munich experience, consider traveling there during Oktoberfest, an event attended by six million people! Just bring your drinking shoes . . .

=Time =Friends $=Expense

367.   HOLLYWOOD, CALIFORNIA

If you've always dreamed of seeing a star in person—or better yet, dating one—consider taking a trip out to the star capital of the world, Hollywood, California. Take a tour of a movie or television studio, make a reservation at one of the restaurants notorious for hosting stars, such as Chasen's or Spago, and do some shopping on Rodeo Drive. Who knows—Mr. Right just may be a famous actor, and you may find yourself strolling down the red carpet with him some day. For more information on how to meet stars in Hollywood, check out *www.seeing-stars.com*.

368.   JOCKEY'S RIDGE STATE PARK

Located in the Outer Banks of North Carolina, Jockey's Ridge is the tallest natural sand dune system on the East Coast. Due to the range of recreational activities the park offers—hiking, nature trails, hang-gliding, kite flying, kayaking, windsurfing, and swimming—the park attracts a lot of athletically inclined men. So if you enjoy these activities (as mentioned before, doing what you love is one of the best ways to meet Mr. Right), or if you'd just like a view of the sand dunes as you walk along the park's 360-foot boardwalk, take a trip to Jockey's Ridge State Park. For information, visit *www.jockeysridgestatepark.com*.

369.   MOTEL BALCONY

For a beach vacation, many people choose a quaint little motel. Most of these motels include balconies, which offer two opportunities for scoping out the men who have chosen the same week for fun in the sun. Balconies will give you a nice view of other balconies, so you can check out men as they come out to enjoy a beer or hang their towels over the railing. Motel balconies also often provide a nice view of the pool, so you can get a good look at the guys as they come off the beach and take a dip. If you like what you see, you can quickly head down to the pool and join them.

370.   MUSCLE BEACH

The name pretty much says it all. Muscle Beach in Venice combines two things that California men love—the outdoors and weight lifting. Yup, Muscle Beach is an outdoor gym where you can watch athletic men work out in the heat of the afternoon. See what it's all about at *www.musclebeach.net*.

371.	ON THE ROCKS PATIO & GRILL

$ $

Men love grill food, and they love beer. And men really love eating grill food and drinking beers outside on a patio with a group of fun ladies, yourself included. So if you live in or near Arkansas or you get a chance to visit, swing by On the Rocks Patio & Grill in Fayetteville, North Carolina, and see what's cooking.

372.	THE SPACE NEEDLE

$ $ $

They say at the Seattle Space Needle, you go from zero to wow in 41 seconds. Sure, that wow will come partially from being propelled 520 feet to the top of the needle in less than a minute . . . but it may also come from the handsome men you see when you get to the top. The view at the top of the Needle is spectacular: you will see snow-capped Mt. Rainier, the Cascade Mountains, the cruise ships gliding across Elliott Bay, and much more. And the Sky City restaurant at the top of the Needle will give you the perfect opportunity to meet Mr. Right as you sip award-winning local wine and dine on freshly caught king salmon as you enjoy the view. Visit *www.spaceneedle.com*.

373.	SUMMERFEST

$ $ $

Being that it is the largest music festival in the world, Summerfest hosts a lot of men. Held annually in Milwaukee, Summerfest features famous musicians and bands, contests, family activities, and food and drinks (45 food vendors!) for 11 days straight. If you are a music lover, the fun, festive atmosphere of Summerfest is the perfect backdrop for meeting a man who appreciates live music as much as you do. To check out what this year's Summerfest will offer, visit *www.summerfest.com*.

374.	SUNSET BEACH

$ $ $

For some wonderful scenery—white sandy beaches, big blue waves, and lots and lots of attractive, tan, and skillful surfers, Sunset Beach in Hawaii is the place. Relax on the beach as you watch the steady stream of surfers come out of the water for a break. As they re-wax, ask them if they could show you a thing or two about surfing. Most surfers are friendly and eager to get more people hooked, so they will gladly give you a quick lesson. Beyond the beach, the surf shops in Sunset Beach are loaded with cute guys.

375.   TOURING A CASTLE IN EUROPE

$ $ $

At some point in your youth, you probably dreamed of meeting Prince Charming in a castle. And on a guided tour of a European castle, your dream just might come true. Your feet walk the very staircases trailed by ancient royalty, and you will get an inside peek at their bedrooms and kitchens, and other intimate details of their lives—plenty of things to discuss with a fellow tour group member at a quaint European café after the tour.

Five great castle tours:
1. Neuschwanstein in Germany (the model for the Disney castle)
2. Edinburgh Castle in Scotland
3. Castel de Monte in Italy
4. Blarney Castle in Ireland
5. Silves Castle in Portugal

376.   DUTY-FREE SHOP

Get a rush from buying something tax-free? Next time you're in an airport, don't miss the opportunity to swing into the duty-free shop, both for some tax-free gin and for a nice mix of men looking to kill time between flights. Duty-free shops offer a range of items of interest to men, particularly the booze—just think about it, if you save the tax on a $40 bottle of whiskey, that's almost $2.50. Not too bad. To get the conversation rolling, you can always say to a man, "Don't you love tax-free shopping?" And then ask him if he has time to grab a coffee or cocktail—plus tax.

O PRO *You can save a few bucks.*

O CON *If he's all jazzed up about the tax-free shopping, he could be cheap.*

377.   NIKKI BEACH

$ $

Beach by day, club by night, Nikki Beach in Miami offers the best of both worlds when it comes to meeting men. Called the "Sexiest Place on Earth" by the *London Observer*, Nikki Beach offers a combination of dining, shopping, music, and handsome men from all over the world. It's a fun, festive forum for meeting new people. To plan a visit, go to *www.nikkibeach.com.*

378. CHICKIE'S AND PETE'S

As the number three sports bar in the country, Chickie's and Pete's in Philadelphia attracts a ton of single guys looking for a place to watch the game and grab some beer and tasty crab fries (a Chickie's and Pete's special). For maximum guy exposure, go when there is a big game and offer to buy a table full of guys a pitcher—they will be anxious to share it with you. Visit *www.chickies andpetes.com.*

○ PRO *Guys galore.*

○ CON *The guys are there primarily to watch the game, and the die-hard sports fans may not be in the mood to meet girls. Reserve your conversation for commercial breaks and halftime.*

379. DAY CRUISE

Set sail on a day cruise with a few friends and you are guaranteed to have a fun day. If you meet a nice guy on the trip, even better . . . With the combination of the water and the booze that comes along with most day-cruise packages, guys, especially single guys, flock to day cruises. So don't miss the opportunity to meet them. Climb aboard. To find a day cruise in your area, type in "day cruise" and your city (provided it is on the coast) in any search engine.

380. REVOLVING RESTAURANT

Looking for a new kind of dining experience? Check out a revolving restaurant. Revolving restaurants are generally high-end, so you will be guaranteed a delicious meal. Plus, the circulating theme of the establishment is a great conversation starter. If you want to approach a guy, you can ask him if he's ever eaten while spinning in circles before. Who knows, all that spinning might make the two of you giddy and in the mood for romance.

Five great revolving restaurants:
1. Sundial Restaurant, Atlanta, GA
2. Sydney Tower Restaurants, Sydney, Australia
3. CK's Revolving Rooftop Restaurant, Tampa, FL
4. Sky City, Seattle, WA
5. The View Restaurant, New York, NY

○ PRO *These restaurants revolve very slowly, so they are motion-sick proof.*

○ CON *Revolving restaurants are rare, so you may have to travel to get to one.*

381. BED AND BREAKFAST

Next time you're traveling alone, be it for work or pleasure, consider staying at a bed and breakfast. With the intimate, interactive setting, you will eat your meals with the other people staying there, other people who may be handsome, single guys. Just watch out—some bed and breakfasts are heavily geared toward couples. Before you book a room, make sure you do some research on the Internet or over the phone concerning the typical clientele.

O PRO *Your meals are included, and the settings at bed and breakfasts are typically very charming—a great place to explore with an interesting fellow guest.*

O CON *Some people don't like the intimate setting. If you are a very private person, it probably won't be to your liking.*

382. FRENCH QUARTER

For a little piece of Europe right here in the United States, consider a trip to the French Quarter of New Orleans. Not only will you get to experience eclectic shops and scrumptious French restaurants, you will get to meet fellow male tourists who love European culture but didn't have the money or time to invest in a trip to France. If you're a little on the wilder side, consider a trip to the French Quarter during Mardi Gras, where men bearing beads abound.

383. HEDONISM

One of the wildest places for singles and couples alike, Hedonism is located in Jamaica, and offers several things many other vacation spots do not: a complete lack of inhibition. Hedonism is now made up of three spots: Hedo I, Hedo II, and Hedo III. Each Hedo is known for its own brand of unadulterated fun, so be sure to research your particular trip. You can find groups of people online and begin communicating before you even make a reservation. There are getaways for couples, singles, and both, so understand where your limits are before you go. Once you've done that prepare to meet a lot of men who will not be the shy type. Start your trip by visiting *www.superclubs.com*.

O PRO *If you are a daring person, this will be right up your alley.*

O CON *If you are, well, less than daring, you may leave with a permanent shocked expression on your face.*

384. ON SAFARI

Check out Web sites like *www.singlestravelintl.com* for starters. You'll see the typical tropical getaways for singles. But if you have your heart set on lions, tigers, and bears, you can find wild safari trips that will get you there. Plus, because it's a trip for singles, you'll find your very own animal magnetism long before you've left the wild.

O PRO *A safari is the experience of a lifetime.*

O CON *The expense.*

385. AMSTERDAM

Amsterdam has become similar to Vegas in that it's a party town, it offers a variety of sinful delights, and it's filled with singles looking to get away for a long weekend and add some serious sizzle to their otherwise standard lives. Depending on your location, airfare to Amsterdam can cost anywhere from $500 to $1000, so it may be in your best interest to plan a trip that will last at least 3 or 4 days. That is, if you want to experience everything Amsterdam has to offer. In fact, while many go for the city's wicked offerings, there is actually a lot of culture in Amsterdam to experience, including the Anne Frank House, the Rijksmuseum, and the Van Gogh Museum, which is the home to 200 of Van Gogh's paintings and 500 of his sketches. If you're up for a fun adventure that happens to include single, international guys, this is the place for you.

O PRO *Single men abound in the city of Amsterdam, and they're from many countries and walks of life.*

O CON *Amsterdam offers some sins that other cities don't legally, so you may encounter some men looking for a, ahem, more impure type of a good time.*

386. PIKES PEAK

Pikes Peak is a mountain in the front range of the Rocky Mountains outside of Colorado Springs, Colorado, and it is a peak place to scope for men. Most guys—at least the outdoorsy ones—dream of climbing a mountain, and breathtaking peaks such as the 14,115-high Pikes really get their juices flowing, so to speak. So if you take a trip to Pikes Peak, look around you for inspired men. You just may be able to harness the good mood and ask one out for coffee. Check out *www.pikespeakcolorado.com* for more info.

387.   SOUND-BAR

If you are looking for a hot night out on the town with exciting men and you are in Chicago, check out Sound-bar, the most popular club in the city. Sound-bar features international DJs, which makes the floor extra exotic . . . and full of adventurous men who love to dance. For more information, check out *www.sound-bar.com*.

388.   SMITHSONIAN INSTITUTE

If you grew up in the eastern part of the country, you probably visited the Smithsonian Institute with a school group. Now that you are older, you might appreciate the treasure in American history that it displays. And in terms of meeting men, the Smithsonian has some exhibits of interest to guys, including a Wright Brothers flying exhibition, a triceratops dinosaur exhibition, a transportation exhibition, and much more. So in between exhibits, keep your eyes open for fellow history buffs you might want to get to know. *www.si.edu*.

389.   TEMPLE BAR

If an Irish accent gets you going and you ever find yourself in Dublin, make sure you swing into Temple Bar, Ireland's most famous pub, for a pint. In Ireland, as is the case everywhere else in the world, where there are pints, there are men. And in addition to Guinness, the Temple Bar "neighborhood" offers a range of amenities, including hotels, hostels, concerts, an art gallery, and more.

390.   LIBERTY BAR & GRILL

With six wide-screen TVs and discounted wings and beer during all football games (called "wingmania"), the Liberty Bar & Grill in Hoboken, New Jersey, is a real hot spot for men. So if you live in the New York City area, grab a few fun girlfriends and head to the Liberty Bar & Grill for a big game. Just make sure to reserve your efforts to meet men for the commercials. Check it out at *www.libertybar.com*.

391.   STAR OF TEXAS FAIR AND RODEO

Want to see some real live cowboys in action, riding bulls and roping cattle? Check out the Star of Texas Fair and Rodeo in Austin. Real cowboys are very respectful toward the ladies, so for a night of line dancing and chivalry, don't miss this opportunity. Plan your visit at *www.rodeoaustin.com*.

 =Time   =Friends $=Expense

392. DESTINATION WEDDING

If a close friend has chosen to get married in Mexico, the Bahamas, or another destination spot, use the trip as an opportunity to meet men. Ask your friend to seat you at the table next to a single man (or men) he or she thinks you will click with, and take every opportunity to mix and mingle with guests at the pool, on the beach, or other common area. Katie Z. of Portland, Oregon, started the relationship with her current boyfriend after a destination wedding. "Mike was a guy I had a brief fling with when I went to visit my friend in college . . . when I saw Mike again at my friend's wedding at the beach ten years later, things immediately sparked up again."

393. CHAPPELL'S RESTAURANT AND SPORTS MUSEUM

Located in Kansas City, Missouri, Chappell's Restaurant and Sports Museum is as close to a haven for men as you can get. It houses sports memorabilia and artifacts, including World Series and Super Bowl trophies, a cozy little bar, and man food from half-pound hamburgers and steaks to fiesta nachos and spicy wings. You will have an easy time finding a man in Chappell's; you just might not have such an easy time getting him to leave! Visit *www .chappellsrestaurant.com.*

394. THE GINGERBREAD MAN (G-MAN)

Between the fraternity brothers, graduate students, alums, and fathers of students, the G-Man in State College, Pennsylvania, is filled with Penn State proud men. The G-Man offers great drink specials, including $3.50 pitchers and $2.50 drinks—a great magnet for men. Did we mention the delicious food? Want to strike up a conversation with one of these men? Do a little research on the Nittany Lions' record and comment on their past or upcoming season. Visit the site at *www.gmanstatecollege.com.*

395. GRAND OLE OPRY

If you find yourself traveling to Nashville on business or just for fun, don't miss a night at the Grand Ole Opry. Even if you're not a huge country-western fan, you will appreciate seeing some of the legends perform live on stage. Plus, the Grand Ole Opry attracts a lot of out-of-towners—guys who are looking to meet someone with whom they can check out the rest of the town!

=Time ♦=Friends $=Expense

396.   TRAVEL CLUB

⊘ ⊘ ⊘
🚹
$ $

Men who join travel clubs tend to be singles looking for fun travel companions. A travel club will not only broaden your horizons by providing you with dozens of ideas for exciting vacations, it will also introduce you to a group of people with whom you can consider planning a trip.

397.   COWBOY WAY ADVENTURES RANCH

⊘ ⊘
🚹 🚹
$ $ $

With the campfires under the stars, stories from local poets, a 100-year-old saloon, and friendly cowboys on this 13,000-acre Montana ranch, you will have plenty of opportunities for romance. You can ride horses and try your hand at herding and branding—no experience is necessary. Just let the cowboys show you the ropes, so to speak.

398.   SOUTH OF THE BORDER

⊘
🚹 🚹
$ $

Located in South Carolina right over the border from North Carolina, South of the Border is a popular destination for people taking road trips down the East Coast. South of the Border offers restaurants, gift shops, and hotels where you can meet fellow road trippers. Road trips are quite popular with single men, so your chances of meeting a few eligible bachelors at South of the Border are pretty good. With the hundreds of billboards announcing the approaching South of the Border on 95 South, there is no way you will miss it. For a funny sneak preview, see *www.pedroland.com*.

399.   40/40 CLUB

⊘
🚹 🚹
$ $

Go where the party is. Whether you're closer to the 40/40 Club in Vegas, Los Angeles, Atlantic City, New York, or even Singapore, you'll find the club is the place to be and to be seen. Filled with a lot of attitude and usually a lot of money, the 40/40 Club is where professional athletes and entertainers go to unwind. And if you have the right look, you can be there too. Find that one outfit that leaves the jaws dropped and give it a shot. You'll find guys there. Just know that they may not be looking beyond that night. Visit *www.the4040club.com*.

⊘=Time 🚹=Friends $=Expense

onlineways

400. ONLINE

As more and more singles meet their true loves with the help of the Internet, the stigma attached to online dating has virtually disappeared. There are more sites than ever that use research-based tools to match people of similar interests and backgrounds. Innovative new tools, like video chat rooms, are taking some of the guesswork out of the process. And sites such as Friendster and MySpace were created for people to hook up with friends—it takes some of the pressure off of the dating aspect, but it still offers the potential for love.

○ PRO *You don't have to beat around the bush—if someone doesn't spark your interest over e-mail, you have no obligation to meet him. You can start the screening process from the comfort and convenience of your own living room.*

○ CON *The blind date factor—it's an inevitable part of the process. And there are people out there who post photos from ten years—and 50 pounds—ago. There are people on dating sites for all the wrong reasons.*

401. MYSPACE

Whether you are looking to meet men from your childhood, your high school, or someone you've recently met in a present life, MySpace is a great forum for meeting friends that could possibly turn into more. MySpace allows you to create your own page where you can express yourself as openly as you'd like. And because other members' pages are so comprehensive, you will get a good sense of their personalities, likes, and dislikes before you decide whether or not you want to contact them. Plus, the service is free! So you have no reason for not getting on it. You'll find all you need—and more—at *www.myspace.com*.

402. THE MUTUAL UFO NETWORK (MUFON)

MUFON is an organization dedicated to the scientific study of UFOs. If you have always had a fascination with outer space—or if you think you yourself have spotted a UFO—consider joining. You are sure to meet an extraordinary group of people (probably some single men included) with an interest in learning about and discussing unidentified flying objects across the country. Visit *www .mufon.com*.

403. CLASSMATES.COM

Many people have re-connected with old friends and old flames on Classmates.com. It's a great forum for a number of reasons. First, it's safe—no one can get your personal information without you putting it out there. Second, it's a risk-free way to contact people. If you are afraid of rejection, you can always mask it with the, "I was just curious to see what you have been up to since high school" excuse. And third, you already have one thing in common with everyone on your high school's site—your home town and your high school. So if things do progress to a date, you will have plenty to talk about.

O PRO *The love you thought you lost may be single or divorced and as anxious to reconnect with you as you are to see him again.*

O CON *To actually contact people on classmates.com, you have to become a "Gold Member" and pay a fee.*

404. MEETUP.COM

"Meetup.com is in its early stages, but I have a feeling it will be as hot as Match.com," says Karen Jones, president of the Heart Matters and author of *Men Are Great*. Meetup.com is an online community that is organized by interest group and by location, so you can find men who share your hobbies as well as your zip code. "I think it is going to be a popular way for people to meet," says Jones.

405. UDATE.COM

Udate is one of the fastest growing dating sites online; people join for a variety of reasons, primarily to meet new people and to become part of an online community. Udate offers matchmaking quizzes and other facilities that will help you meet guys who share the same interests and attitudes about dating as yourself.

406. FACEBOOK

Facebook is an online social network between high school students, college students, some corporations and nonprofit organizations, and military organizations. It's presently the seventh most trafficked site in the United States. People on Facebook chat about current events, politics, music, books, television, and much more. For more information, check out *www.facebook.com*.

O PRO *It's a great screening tool.*

O CON *You need a college e-mail address or an e-mail address from one of the participating companies or organizations.*

=Time ♦=Friends $=Expense

407. MEET MARKET ADVENTURES

$

If you are adventurous and outdoorsy, and you are looking for a companion who is the same way, check out this site, *www.meet marketadventures.com*. You can mingle with singles in fun, no-pressure environments. The group has more than 55,000 members and sponsors events and vacations such as weekend getaways, after-work parties, local day trips, vacations and cruises all over North America.

408. CUPID.COM

$

As an alternative to Match.com, consider Cupid.com, which not only offers free membership, suggestions on places to go on a date, and dating advice, but also provides information on speed dating and other match-making events across the country.

409. FANTASY FOOTBALL

$

Fantasy football leagues provide great opportunities to meet people online, with no dating strings attached. You can get a sense of a person from his player picks, and if you want to get to know him better, you can take your relationship off the virtual field. See *www .fftoday.com*.

◒ PRO *You will probably be one of the only girls in the league, so you will get lots of attention.*

◒ CON *You have to keep up with fantasy football and change your players regularly. It's a bit of a time commitment, so if you hate football, you may not enjoy it. Also, some of the guys online could be married.*

410. FANTASY BASEBALL

$

Fantasy baseball leagues are great for the fun of the competition, the potential to win a few bucks, and the interaction between people in your league. Fantasy baseball leagues offer a no-risk way to get to know the people in your league by the way they pick or trade players. And because many more men than women join these leagues, you are likely to be way outnumbered. Go to *www .fantasybaseball.com*.

411. SINGLEDEMOCRATS.COM

If you are a liberal-minded American who wants to find love in someone who shares your political and cultural views, consider SingleDemocrats.com. They offer all the features of other online dating sites, but with a left-winged theme.

412. SINGLEREPUBLICANS.COM

If you are a conservative American who views similar political opinions as an important part of a successful relationship, consider joining SingleRepublicans.com. The site offers the same features as competitor online dating sites, but with a conservative theme.

413. SILVER SINGLES

If you are older than 50 and looking to meet other mature singles with similar life experiences, check out Silver Singles.com. Silver Singles offers the same format and opportunities as other dating sites, but with a silver theme. For more information, look up "silver singles" in any search engine.

414. YAHOO! PERSONALS

You can use Yahoo! for everything else these days, from e-mail to maps to job searching. So why not try it for dating, too? Yahoo! Personals is worth your while because it splits daters into two categories—people who are looking for a long-term relationship and people who are just looking to meet people and have some fun. That way, there's no confusion. It also provides personality profiles and relationship tests. Plus, you can try out the site for free. For more info, check out *www.personals.yahoo.com.*

415. FLICKR

Flickr is a photo-sharing, community Web site that allows users to post pictures and information about themselves. It's a quick and easy way to learn someone's interests and see what they look like. It's that simple. If you're into hiking, do a search for it. Then review the profiles of men who have posted those pictures and go after them. There's something about hooking up through a site like this that simply feels more natural. Check it out at *www.flickr.com.*

 =Time =Friends $=Expense

416. LAVALIFE

$

Lavalife works for one main reason—you get to choose the kind of relationship you're seeking. As opposed to many dating Web sites, Lavalife allows you to be up front with your intentions and to see others who are seeking the same. You can seek a plutonic friendship if you prefer. Or, you can look for your next date. If you're open to something spicier, you can look for someone who is seeking something more physical and casual in nature. Be open with your intentions and Lavalife will serve you well. There are tons of men here in all of the aforementioned categories. Visit *www.lavalife.com* to learn more.

417. JUSTSAYHI.COM

$

Justsayhi.com is a low-pressure social site, aimed toward singles who are a little skeptical about entering the online dating scene. This site has thousands of members spread all across the country, and as an added bonus, it's 100 percent free to join! If you've ever thought about online dating but have never had the guts to try, this site might be a good start.

418. AIM-HIGHER.COM

$ $ $

Aim-higher.com is a travel Web site completely devoted to fun, sun, and singles! Their Web site is brimming with ideas for the single traveler. For a mellow and more sophisticated trip, try a biking and wine tour through the Pacific Coast and California wine country. A trip like this may help you meet a more distinguished man. Want something wild? Check out Aim-higher's trips to Hedonism! You won't even need a bikini.

419. COWBOYCOWGIRL.COM

$

"Where country meets country," CowboyCowgirl.com is a great place to find men on horseback. The setup is similar to other dating sites, but CowboyCowgirl.com's down-home theme is definitely unique. The site advertises itself as being a place where people come to meet others who share their appreciation for the "country" set of values and way of life. So if this sounds like you, check it out.

 =Time =Friends $=Expense

420. CRAIG'S LIST

$

In terms of dating, some refer to this site as "Craig's Risk," so beware. Not everyone is who he says he is. By all means, meet in a public place and get to know someone before you begin holding hands and exchanging smooches in alleyways or high school dug-outs. A key recommendation is to establish a strong e-mail rela-tionship, then phone relationship before moving on to meeting your mystery man. Just go to *www.craigslist.com* and find the personal ads for your city. You never know what you might find—which is both good and scary. Try to do your best to read between the lines and pay attention to things like grammar, spelling, and punctua-tion. They may help to point you in the right direction.

421. DATEAGOLFER.COM

$

If you love golf and love the idea of dating a golf enthusiast, this could work in your favor. DateAGolfer.com works like any other dating Web site; you post a profile and photos and provide a brief description about yourself and your golf game. Then you begin sifting through the profiles until you find someone you like. From there, you just get in touch, pick a course, and tee off. Not inter-ested in golf but love the idea of dating someone who gives you your space? Golfers can be on the course for 4 hours at a time. Think of all the things you can go do in that time—without him bugging you!

422. REDHEADPASSIONS.COM

$

If you're a natural redhead, a bottle carrottop, or just a "redophile" (someone who loves redheads), Redheadpassions is for you. This free dating and social networking site boasts "lots of freckled fun." Plus, redheads have a reputation for being spunky and uninhib-ited, so if you hit it off with someone, you may find yourself enjoy-ing particularly sassy sack sessions.

423. SECOND LIFE

⏰⏰⏰
👤
$

How many times have you told yourself that you need to "get a life"? Well, now you can. Second Life is an online world that allows you to join a new society. Think of it as life—but all in a virtual world. You can meet people with similar interests, get to know men and women from all walks of life, and even do some flirting. From there, you can exchange actual contact information and see how you connect in person. Check it out at *www.secondlife.com.*

⏰=Time 👤=Friends $=Expense

424. PUBCLUB.COM

If you're looking for a party, this is the site for you. If you're looking for the love of your life, this could be a long shot. PubClub.com is a Web site dedicated to advertising the top parties throughout the United States and the globe! There is a singles section of the site offering singles domestic and international trips for those who lean toward the wild side. There is also an extensive list of activities going on throughout the country. Dive into PubClub.com and see what it's all about.

○ PRO *There will be a man waiting for you—guaranteed.*

○ CON *How long he's around and his level of sobriety could be another story.*

425. YOUTUBE

This is one of the more outrageous ways to meet a guy, but it's been done. Start with your interests. If you love to cook and you are a bit of a voyeur, you're all set. Just go to *http://youtube.com* and type "cooking" into the search field. Then just sift through the videos. Many of them are feeble attempts at humor, but due to the explosion of YouTube, many are now informative and interesting. The best part? You're watching real people. In this case, real men. Watch a snippet, have a cackle, and if you like what you see, you can reach the creator of the video through a link on that page. It's that easy. Imagine people able to send Brad Pitt a quick hello after watching him in *Thelma & Louise*. Now that's modern technology finally providing a useful service.

○ PRO *The risk of rejection is minimal.*

○ CON *There are a few hurdles to jump through with this one.*

426. RODEO SINGLES

The rodeo isn't for everyone. It does take a certain type of woman to go to a rodeo and to become interested in a cowboy, just as it takes a certain kind of man to ride a bull or bronco. So start with *http://rodeosingles.com*—yes, it's true. You can visit this site and find the cowboy of your dreams. Just remember, they're up at the crack of dawn and in bed early. Maybe that's a good thing?

427. RELIGIOUS SINGLES WEB SITES

Web sites now offer dating opportunities for almost anyone's individual tastes, interests, and beliefs. There are Web sites for Jewish people, Muslims, Christians—and all denominations in between. Knowing that right off the bat you'll be searching within the confines of your own beliefs makes your search so much easier. Take a look at sites like *www.christiansingles.com*, *http://jdate.com*, *www.muslimnetwork.com* or just type in a search for "dating" and your particular affiliation. You'll find there are a lot of choices—all with men who could be your future partner for life.

○ **PRO** *You'll know he is the same religion as you, which will make things easier for you and your family if this is a concern.*

○ **CON** *If you are not super religious, think twice about this one— religious singles Web sites usually attract people who are pretty spiritually devoted.*

428. ANY BLOGGING WEB SITE

As you probably know, blogging is a popular way to communicate on the Internet. Whether this medium is being used to express a viewpoint or to simply have an ongoing online conversation, blogging is big—and it's here to stay. So how can you use blogging to meet the man of your dreams? Sites like myspace.com and eTwine.com allow users to quickly and easily join an online community. From there, you can do anything—search for people, discuss specific topics, offer opinions, and more. One minute you'll be on your soapbox about global warming and the next, you might be hugging more than just a tree. Need some more ideas on where to find blog communities? Start with *www.blogsearchengine.com* and type in any interest of yours. For example, you can start by typing "singles" in the search field.

429. FITNESS-SINGLES.COM

Ready to give your love life a workout? This is the perfect place. And don't let the name fool you. Fitness-Singles is for active men and women who want to find a friend, a lover, or a lifetime partner through an array of physical activities. Aerobics, Pilates, hiking, golf, running, biking, and much, much more—it's all here. You just go to the site and post a profile or begin searching first. There are many men with active lifestyles here and you can browse through them all. This one is highly recommended!

＝Time ＝Friends $＝Expense

430. FRIENDFINDER.COM

Want to start out as friends? This could be the perfect place to begin. This Web site has a basic membership that lets you get in touch with men for friendship, love, or something in between. Browse profiles based on geographic location, post your own profile, write a blog, or even join a chat room. Basic membership is free, so why not take a chance? You have nothing to lose!

431. HOTORNOT.COM

It's voyeuristic, ridiculous, cheesy, and fun. Visit *www.hotornot.com* and do some serious scoping! The basic idea is that you rate men based on their photos. But the site also allows you the opportunity to let these men know you'd be interested in meeting them. You can even pay a low monthly fee to contact these men directly.

○ PRO *It can't hurt to just check it out, since it's fun, free, and doesn't require anything other than an Internet connection and an open mind.*

○ CON *The concept—rating a guy on looks alone—is pretty shallow. Plus, if someone qualifies you as "not," it could be a blow to the ego.*

432. LOCAL SINGLES EVENTS ONLINE

Just about every major city has a Web site that connects singles. Simply type in "single" and the name of your town in a search engine and look at the vast array of listings. You'll see everything from trips for singles to local singles events going on in your area. In fact there are probably restaurants and bars that you frequent offering nights just for singles. Some offer speed dating, some offer singles cooking classes, and others simply offer a night for singles to get together. See what the search listings give you and explore some of the singles Web sites.

433. PASSION.COM

As part of the network of sites developed by Friend Finder Network, Passion.com is for women seeking something spicy. Find a guy in your area that meets all your criteria as a lover. It's that simple. Browse profiles carefully and do your man-shopping, but remember, this site is for those seeking something casual and physical—not necessarily a partner for life.

=Time =Friends $=Expense

434.   PLENTYOFFISH.COM

PlentyofFish.com is a community dating Web site that gives users the ability to browse profiles, rate people, and even join dating and relationship forums. Users can speak their minds on almost any dating topic available in their forums and the site is free of charge. Most importantly, this is a Web site that allows you to search through many men in a short amount of time—so start workin' it.

435.   REUNION.COM

You've already accomplished most of your mission if you use this resource. After all, you've already met your connection! It could have been ten years ago or thirty, but the point is that you have an old friend, a former crush, or even a boyfriend from high school who has left you wondering for years. And now, you can reach out to him. Reunion.com makes it easy to sign up and begin searching immediately. Dust off your pompons and get excited about finding that lost love. It could be worth it.

436.   DATE.COM

Date.com is an online dating community that offers a chat room, instant messaging, voice and video greetings, and more. And the keyword search feature allows you to find men who share your interests, such as traveling, reading, or swimming.

437.   EHARMONY.COM

As one of the first online dating sites that used a compatibility test to match people, eHarmony continues to make successful love connections for millions of people. If you feel compatibility is one of the most important elements of a relationship, eHarmony is a good online dating site for you.

O PRO *Since the compatibility test is pretty involved, you will probably have lots to talk about with your dates.*

O CON *Compatibility doesn't always translate to physical attraction. Plus, this site takes all of the searching control away from you. In other words, you have to wait for them to send you compatible matches before you can set up a date.*

438.   ENGAGE.COM

Engage.com is an online dating site that touts itself as a next-generation relationship community where friends collaborate to find love. The site's slogan is "the world's first relationship service where people help each other find love—just like the real world." The site is unique in that you can sign on and play matchmaker or sign up to be matched.

439.   MATCHMAKER.COM

If you're not necessarily ready to settle down but you want to broaden your social circle and open up the possibility for love, Matchmaker.com may be a good dating site for you. Millions of singles from all over the world use this site, so there is certainly no shortage of opportunity.

440.   OODLE.COM

If you are into the online dating scene, oodle.com is an online site worth checking out. Similar to Craig's List, oodle.com is an online search classified ad site. Their personals channel offers an extensive collection of profiles from major dating sites on the Web, along with tools for tailoring one's dating preferences so that you are able to find the perfect profile . . . before you choose a dating site to sign up and pay for.

441.   VOLUNTEERMATCH.ORG

"People volunteer for a number of reasons, and 'meeting people' is always a popular reason," says Jason Willet, director of communications at VolunteerMatch.org. VolunteerMatch is an online site that helps you find volunteer opportunities based on your zip code, interests, and schedule. "You can even find opportunities that are seeking groups, to ensure that you will be meeting fellow, like-minded volunteers," Willet says.

=Time =Friends $=Expense

442. WEALTHYMEN.COM

"I have had an Internet profile on three different big dating sites for three years, and I have had more luck in the last few months on wealthymen.com than I have with any of the other sites combined," says Somer S. from New Brunswick, New Jersey. "I am honestly not a gold digger, but I can really appreciate a man who is intelligent and I am meeting more guys who are on my wavelength," she says. "It is just so refreshing to meet men who are thinkers, have had unique life experiences, have traveled, and have read books," she says. Be advised that, like many dating services, the trial membership is free, but your credit card is automatically charged if you do not end your enrollment.

443. AMERICANSINGLES.COM

AmericanSingles is an online dating Web site that claims to deliver "excitement, love and romance." With the more than 10 million singles in the AmericanSingles database, you are bound to find at least a spark on this portal.

444. BLACKSINGLES.COM

If you are a single black woman, you may be interested in a dating site that features black men only. This site helps you find men of color from all over the world with online chat rooms, message boards, and photo galleries. Plus, membership is free. Even if you don't find love, you may meet some wonderful new friends with whom you share your heritage.

445. CHEMISTRY.COM

Touted as a site that combines elements of both compatibility and chemistry, Chemistry.com is worth checking out if you would like to try online dating for the first time or you have tried other online dating sites without success. To make sure you find a man you are compatible with, Chemistry.com offers a free personality test and guided communication process.

=Time =Friends $=Expense

446.   CHRISTIANCAFE.COM

If you have Christian values and are looking for a man who shares them, check out ChristianCafe.com. The site claims to be different from other religious online dating sites in that it has a "no-nonsense quality that is genuinely appealing to many of today's Christian singles." For a free ten-day trial membership, check out *www.christiancafe.com*.

447.   JDATE.COM

Tired of asking dates if they are Jewish just so you know whether you will be able to take them home to meet Mom and Dad? Stop wondering by finding men on JDate.com, a Jewish online dating service with more than half a million members. You—and your parents—will be happy that you did.

448.   METRODATE.COM

If you live in a major city, you know how hard it can be to make a love connection on a crowded street or in a packed singles bar. So check out Metrodate.com, an online dating site aimed at helping people find dates in their home cities. Even if you don't find love, you may find some fun new friends with whom to paint the town. It's free to create your profile, so what do you have to lose?

449.   PERFECTMATCH.COM

PerfectMatch.com is an online-dating site aimed at helping people find love for the right reasons. There's certainly nothing wrong with that! Whether you are recently divorced, a dating senior, or you've had too many bad dates, it's worth your while to see if you can find Mr. Right at PerfectMatch.com.

450.   FRIENDWISE.COM

Friendwise.com is a social networking site that offers the potential for romance. Friendwise.com is interactive in that you can invite people to join your online community—it is a place to make new friends and reunite with the old . . . and both types of friends may turn out to be "more than friends." And you can express yourself by designing your own site.

451. YAHOO360

Similar to MySpace and other Internet sites that promote meeting people without an overt emphasis on dating, Yahoo360 is worth checking out. On Yahoo360, you can express yourself with blogs, photos, and your interests, and you can constantly update your page. It's a great, safe place to meet people who may turn out to be friends or more. Log on to *http://360.yahoo.com*.

452. MUSTLOVEPETS.COM

Is your dog and/or cat an important part of your life? Is "animal lover" on the top of your list of requirements for a mate? If so, check out MustLovePets.com, a site that helps you meet and/or date fellow animal lovers who are seeking a quality or romantic relationship with someone who understands what it means to accidentally leave the house with your pants covered with pet hair.

453. SINGLESCLUB.ORG

SinglesClub.org consists of singles in the New England area, and it touts itself as the lowest-cost singles club in the country. So if you are a New England resident and are tired of shelling out money for singles groups and getting nothing in return, check it out. Basic membership is free and there are no event fees, so what do you have to lose?

454. SINGLESORGANIZATIONS.COM

To find singles organizations in your area where you can find single men to mix and mingle with, check out SinglesOrganizations.com. You can search the site by state, the type of involvement you are looking for, and by singles themselves.

455. CATHOLICMATCH.COM

If you're in the market for a Catholic guy and you're tired of waiting for just the right moment to ask a man you are dating whether or not he can take communion in a Catholic church, check out CatholicMatch.com, the highest-rated Catholic singles Web site on the Internet.

=Time =Friends $=Expense

456. CONSCIOUS DATING

Founded by marriage and family therapist David Steele, Conscious Dating helps singles form successful relationships. The organization, which has offices in Los Angeles and Atlanta as well as online resources, provides support, resources, and information to singles to help them find life partners. For more information, check out *www.consciousdating.org.*

457. GRADFINDER.COM

If you're looking to reconnect high school and college friends, lost loves, and old friends, consider signing up with GradFinder.com, the largest worldwide online social networking directory on the Internet. Similar to classmates.com, GradFinder allows you to post photos, update your profile regularly, and connect with friends from elementary school through graduate school . . . and potentially rekindle a past fire.

458. LOVEHAPPENS.COM

Formerly Tickle Matchmaking, LoveHappens.com is a social networking site where people meet and introduce each other . . . and a lot of people find romance on it as well.

459. SINGLESNET

More people get married after meeting on SinglesNet than on any other online dating site. That's pretty impressive. Unlike other dating sites out there, SinglesNet doesn't restrict communication to members who pay. If you choose, you can pay and access a larger group of the more than 12 million people who use the site, however. In other words, you get out of the site what you put in, so you have nothing to lose. Log on to *http://www.singlesnet.com*

460. TRUE.COM

If you have hesitated to sign up for an online dating site because you fear your date will turn out to be an ex-con, you are not alone. Many women have this apprehension. Luckily, there is a site that will put those fears to rest. True.com screens all members against one of the largest criminal records databases. So if a man is on the site, chances are good that his record is clean and clear.

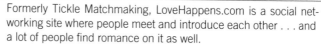 =Time ✚=Friends $=Expense

461. 20FAKIND.COM

If compatibility is important to you in a relationship, check out 2ofakind.com, a dating Web site that makes sure members find dates they click with. You choose the features you're looking for in a man, and then 2ofakind e-mails a list of matches directly to you.

462. DREAMMATES.COM

DreamMates.com has been deemed one of the best online dating sites for women. It's free to place your ad and answer messages, and then you can purchase message "credits" to send messages to both free and paid members.

463. DATING ON DEMAND

Dating on Demand brings online dating to life. Instead of a photo, you get a full video clip of people, so you can get a sense of their mannerisms and personality. To become a part of Dating on Demand, you can submit a dating profile of yourself using a home camcorder, or you can attend one of their dating events where they will videotape you for free. After you submit your video, a Dating on Demand professional will edit it and make it available to viewers within 4 to 6 weeks. At that point, any individual with Cox or Comcast Digital Cable will be able to view your video; if they're interested, they can send you a message through your "Hurrydate" account. For more information, check out *www.datingondemand .com*

464. URBANSOCIAL

If a British accent really turns you on and you're not against meeting men from overseas, check out urbansocial.com, "a stylish online dating service for young urban professionals" in the UK. This site may be a good option for you if your job frequently takes you to the United Kingdom or you have friends or family there. *www.urbansocial.com.*

O PRO *If you are open to moving overseas and you love Europe, this may be your chance—both for love and for a major life change.*

O CON *Meeting a potential mate casually to see if there is chemistry will be hard with thousands of miles between you.*

465.   FANTASY BASKETBALL LEAGUE

This really works if you're working at a company where getting to know people isn't that easy. Eventually, you learn who you're playing and when, and as that time approaches, you can begin playfully harassing your upcoming opponent. Talk a little trash and even throw a side bet into the mix. If you win, he buys the cocktails and vice versa. It's a simple way to get an office romance started. Does it work? You bet it does. And even if it doesn't get you the man of your dreams, it gets you socializing with coworkers. That could lead to a date down the road.

466.   MATCH.COM

The most publicized dating Web site of them all, Match.com allows you to make your search as specific or general as you wish. Search for men near your home or broaden your scope to include your city, state, or even the whole country. Use variables to determine exactly what you're seeking in a man—from height and shape to divorced, with or without kids, eye color, hair color, religious, and political preferences and more. It's a quick and easy way to sift through potential suitors and find the ones who have that certain something you're seeking. You don't have to post a photo of yourself, although it does help men find you quicker. Just be sure to put some effort into your profile and make it stand out from the rest.

467.   NERVE.COM

Consider yourself trendy and opinionated? Think you have it all figured out? Or just cynical about it all? Nerve.com lets you explore every viewpoint under the sun—and it's all with attitude. One of the Internet's hippest locales, Nerve.com takes one subject—*sex*—and covers it from all imaginable angles. Exactly how you like it? Good. Now check out their personal ads. Just imagine, men with brains, opinions, spunk, and charm. This is the place! *www.nerve.com*.

468. CHAT ROOM

Got a topic you are passionate about? Express yourself in a chat room. Not only will you engage in stimulating online conversations with people who share your interest in a topic—politics, dogs, sports, whatever—you could possibly take those conversations/relationships beyond the computer and into real life. As you chat with people in a chat room, get a feel for them through their word choices and opinions. Then, if you connect with someone in particular, ask him if he'd like to meet.

O PRO *A chat room will give you insights into people's personalities.*

O CON *Tread very lightly. Some people in chat rooms are scary. Make sure you meet in a very public place the first few times.*

d date flea market reunion restaurant tattoo parlor wedding auction ho
ub baby shower casino hibachi ladies night café bake sale brunch river
ambake double date culinary festival smorgasbord tavern church service
mal hospital roommates yacht club school courthouse nudist colony bee
val baseball game car show firefighting fishing tailgating poker campgr
ting contest bowling weight room military cigar shop airport london bri
s eiffel tower vacation hotel cruise mardi gras times square central park
f america mount rushmore hollywood safari smithsonian online animal
e blood drive volunteering special olympics toy drive red cross soup kit
rt gallery book club cooking class library museum college campus orche
ature walk planetarium political rally shakespeare festival disney world
uarium water park caroling parents playground mini-golf county fair co
use laundromat grocery store beach gym subway deli yard sale liquor
post office personal ads company picnic conference water cooler bartend
oncert scavenger hunt karaoke comedy club biking karate softball pain
iling ymca square dancing boardwalk cookout whale watching farmer's
et party friends cafeteria open house singing group bars beach house
ting blind date flea market reunion restaurant tattoo parlor wedding au
ospital club baby shower casino hibachi ladies night café bake sale bru
iverboat clambake double date culinary festival smorgasbord tavern chu
ervice spa animal hospital roommates yacht club school courthouse nu
ony beer festival baseball game car show firefighting fishing tailgating
campground eating contest bowling weight room military cigar shop airp
ndon bridges bus eiffel tower vacation hotel cruise mardi gras times sq
ntral park mall of america mount rushmore hollywood safari smithsonian
e animal rescue blood drive volunteering special olympics toy drive red
up kitchen art gallery book club cooking class library museum college ca
rchestra nature walk planetarium political rally shakespeare festival dis
orld zoo aquarium water park caroling parents playground mini-golf co
ir coffeehouse laundromat grocery store beach gym subway deli yard
iquor store post office personal ads company picnic conference water co
rtending concert scavenger hunt karaoke comedy club biking karate so
intball sailing ymca square dancing cookout whale watching farmer's m
ty friends cafeteria open house singing group bars beach house wine ta
d date flea market reunion restaurant tattoo parlor wedding auction ho
ub baby shower casino hibachi ladies night café bake sale brunch river
ambake double date culinary festival smorgasbord tavern church service
mal hospital roommates yacht club school courthouse nudist colony bee
val baseball game car show firefighting fishing tailgating poker campgr
ting contest bowling weight room military cigar shop airport london bri
s eiffel tower vacation hotel cruise mardi gras times square central park
f america mount rushmore hollywood safari smithsonian online animal
e blood drive volunteering special olympics toy drive red cross soup kit
rt gallery book club cooking class library museum college campus orche
ature walk planetarium political rally shakespeare festival disney world

life-enrichingways

469. VOLUNTEERING YOUR TIME

$

Where there is a worthy cause, there are worthy men. So if you find a cause that you truly believe in, put in some time and effort to help it. And choose a position that will expose you to fellow volunteers, which may include philanthropic, available guys. Even if you don't have the time to devote on a regular basis, many charities put together occasional marathons, bike races, and other events that bring together thousands of people.

○ PRO *Men you meet while working for a charity are guaranteed to have a giving nature.*

○ CON *There is a time commitment. You shouldn't volunteer for a charity if your heart isn't in it.*

470. ANIMAL RESCUE

$

Everyone gets lonely sometimes, but nothing cures loneliness faster than the companionship of a pet. It feels particularly rewarding to choose a dog or cat that needs a home. As you browse for your new friend, look around to see if there are any guys doing the same. If they are looking at animals solo, chances are that's how they live too.

○ PRO *Even if there are no handsome guys, you are bound to see some cute animals.*

○ CON *If you aren't an animal lover, you will want to leave immediately and it will be obvious to everyone there. This is one you definitely don't want to fake.*

471. BLOOD DRIVE

$

You have nothing to lose by going to a blood drive . . . except, of course, a pint. It's a good cause and every person who is physically able should donate blood anyway. Plus, if you happen to sit next to a single man, you know that he is a giving person (when it comes to his blood, at least). You will have some time to kill as you give your red blood cells, so you might as well chat. Plus, you will need a snack to boost your blood sugar when you are finished—so ask a handsome fellow donator to join you.

472.   HABITAT FOR HUMANITY

If you have the urge to give back to the community, consider joining a group that embarks on traditionally male-oriented projects, such as building houses. As you are out there building homes for Habitat for Humanity, you are sure to be working alongside men . . . men who want to volunteer their time for a good cause, just like you.

473.   LOCAL ENVIRONMENTAL CLEANUP PROJECT

To keep them clean and welcoming, a lot of communities host environmental cleanup projects, where community members volunteer to clean up trash around their neighborhoods. The next time your community hosts one of these cleanups, volunteer—you will meet single neighbors of the opposite sex you never knew you had, and you will be doing a wonderful service for your community.

○ PRO *You will be able to enjoy the fruits of your labor in the form of a cleaner neighborhood. Plus, any man you meet who is willing to donate his time to pick up trash is probably a giving man overall.*

○ CON *It's a dirty job.*

474.   VOLUNTEERING AT A CHARITY EVENT

You can help make the world a better place and expand your social circle at the same time. And who better to add to your list of friends than fellow do-gooders like yourself? Also, if you volunteer at a one-day event, you can feel good about yourself without filling your already busy schedule—just one day can make a difference! Even better, there are volunteer groups out there just for singles—check out *www.singlevolunteers.org.* Perfect!

475.   VOLUNTEERING AT A FOOD STAND AT A FESTIVAL

Music and food festivals need volunteers to scoop ice cream, pour beer, and serve sausage sandwiches to patrons. If you offer to be one of these volunteers, you will probably serve food and/or beer to thousands of people in a day, which will present you with hundreds of interesting guys to talk to when the line dies down or when it comes time to take your break. So if your company asks for volunteers, don't hesitate to step up—not only will you get the chance to talk to a lot of guys, you will look good to your managers.

○ PRO *Festivals present the perfect social atmosphere.*

○ CON *You will have to give up a day or two of your free time.*

=Time =Friends $=Expense

476. BIG BROTHERS/BIG SISTERS

Not only is becoming a Big Sister a wonderful way to give back to your community, it is also a great place to find a kind, giving Big Brother. As a Big Sister, you will spend time with your Little Sister, but you will also attend meetings with your local Big Brother/Big Sister chapter—meetings that your fellow Big Brothers and Sisters will also attend. Log on to *www.bbbs.org* to find a chapter in your area.

477. PUBLIC BROADCASTING COMPANY FUNDRAISER

"A lot of men show up to local fundraising events because local companies send their workers," says Lori Gorshow, president of Dating Made Simple (*www.makedatingsimple.com*). So if you volunteer at a local public broadcasting company fundraiser that asks people to support Sesame Street and Blues Clues, you will meet these men. And who doesn't want to support public television?

478. AIDS WALK

You've devoted your whole day to walking for a good cause—to raise money for AIDS research. So you might as well make the most of it. As you stroll along, look for different groups to join for a mile or two. At an event like an AIDS walk, almost everyone will be in the mood to meet their fellow walkers. So make it a point to meet as many people as you can. If you meet someone really interesting, you may just want to spend the rest of the walk with him.

479. SALVATION ARMY

Now and then, you can find the coolest item of clothing—be it vintage jeans or an awesome jacket—at the Salvation Army. Not to mention the funky furniture items you may be lucky enough to stumble upon. The secret to Salvation Army shopping is to go often. Not only will you get constant exposure to the best items, you will get constant exposure to the quirky (in a good way), free-spirited guys who appreciate a good Salvation Army find as much as you do.

O PRO *Great deals.*

O CON *These places are very hit or miss—there are "good" Salvos and not so good ones. You may have to make a few stops before you find your favorite.*

 =Time ‖=Friends $=Expense

480. HOMELESS SHELTER

This is a win-win situation, no matter how you look at it. Your time will never be wasted volunteering at a homeless shelter. And you open yourself up to meeting men who also have the heart to volunteer their time to those in need. Consider volunteering for duties such as serving food, where you will stand side-by-side with fellow volunteers and get to know them better.

481. ACS RELAY FOR LIFE

The goal of the American Cancer Society Relay for Life is to keep one member of a team walking or running on a track at all times for 24 hours. It's an inspirational all-night event, complete with a touching illumination ceremony where people walk the track holding candles. Men who participate in the event are usually warm, kind, and philanthropic—a great combination. And many of them have lost a loved one to cancer, so if you have also gone through this ordeal, you will instantly have an important life experience in common. For more information on the Relay for Life, check out *www.cancer.org*.

482. SPECIAL OLYMPICS

As a volunteer for the Special Olympics, you will add joy to the lives of mentally and physically challenged adults and children. As a bonus (and purely as a bonus—you don't want to volunteer unless your heart is truly in it), you might meet men who are willing to offer their time and their encouragement to the same cause. A guy who volunteers for the Special Olympics is almost guaranteed to be sensitive, giving, and sweet. To find out how you can help, visit *www.specialolympics.org*.

483. HOSPITAL VOLUNTEER

By volunteering at a hospital, you will be putting your time to good use to help people. And by volunteering at a hospital, you are also exposing yourself to many single men in the form of doctors, nurses, physicians' assistants, patients, and visiting family members. Hospitals are always looking for qualified volunteers to rock babies, play games with children in the hospital, or push patients around in wheelchairs.

484. NEIGHBORHOOD ASSOCIATION

If your neighborhood has an association (and it is not run solely by people of a certain age group), consider joining it. Not only will you get to help organize some fun neighborhood activities, like a block party or group yard sale, you will meet numerous people (single men included) in your neighborhood who you may have otherwise overlooked in the convenience store or local drugstore.

○ PRO *If you are more involved in your neighborhood, you will feel more neighborhood pride. Plus, you will actually get to know the people who live around you.*

○ CON *This may be a time commitment, and some neighborhood associations are total gossip circles.*

485. VEGETARIAN CO-OP

Vegetarian co-ops are member-owned grocery stores, cafés, or meeting spots that are open to the public. Most co-ops offer vegetarian foods and wellness products, and some also offer yoga classes, cooking classes, community events, and more. And all vegetarian co-ops are excellent places to meet fellow vegetarians—friends, and possibly nice single vegetarian men, as well. The co-op's activities will offer plenty of opportunities for you to get to know your fellow members. So if you are a vegetarian, consider joining a vegetarian co-op for great food and friends.

486. VOLUNTEERING FOR JUNIOR ACHIEVEMENT

Junior Achievement is a nonprofit organization that helps introduce junior high kids to the world of business by teaching them how to create something and make a small profit. By volunteering for Junior Achievement, not only will you be helping to enrich a group of bright youngsters, you will be opening yourself up to meet parents, fellow volunteers, and businessmen in the area who are kind enough to donate their time and advice to a good cause. For more information, check out *www.ja.org*.

487.   CHARITY HAUNTED HOUSE

Join your local community and become a ghoul, goblin, or ghost for charity. You'll meet outgoing men who enjoy holiday shenanigans, plus if the proceeds are going to charity, you know the guy has a heart. In fact, it may mean he is someone who enjoys kids and that's every woman's dream.

○ PRO *Fun atmosphere where you can let yourself go and just enjoy the moment.*

○ CON *You won't be able to see how he normally dresses.*

488.   CHARITY WINE OR FOOD EVENT

These are more popular than ever. Some women go in groups. Some people go as a big group of friends. Regardless, these kinds of events are fabulous for striking up conversation. You're trying to reach the gruyere. He's reaching for the fontina. You're already off to a cheesy start. If you can find these kinds of events in your area, you will be very pleased with not only the number of singles in attendance—but the type of singles there. Every year the Borgata in Atlantic City, New Jersey, holds a "Women in Wine" event to raise money for breast cancer. You can gamble, see celebrity chefs, and movie stars. You can sip your favorite cabernet as you sample something delectable and eye potential new boyfriends. These events are everywhere—just find one near you!

489.   CHARITY GOLF OUTING

Golf outings are an excellent way to meet successful men who enjoy contributing to a cause. Charity golf events are often held to raise money for health-related causes such as breast cancer research and countless others. They are also held for those less fortunate, such as the homeless. You can easily find charity golf events through your community activity board or on your local community cable TV channel. These outings always need volunteers to help set up the event, create gift bags, and greet the golfers. Whether you're playing in the event, greeting golfers before the event kicks off, or if you're having cocktails when the event concludes, there are plenty of chances to meet someone.

○ PRO *A dinner or party normally follows the event.*

○ CON *If you have no idea how to play, it could be a long day for you. Take lessons first.*

=Time =Friends $=Expense

490. AT A TOY DRIVE

Around the holidays, there will most likely be more than one toy drive in the area where you live. In addition to dropping off a toy, why not volunteer to help out for a couple of hours? You can work during the toy drive hours collecting toys, or volunteer to come in afterward to box them up and ship them out or drop them off somewhere. Who knows? In addition to feeling good about yourself, you could meet a fellow do-gooder who has a soft spot for kids. That could pay off in the long run!

491. AS A VOLUNTEER TUTOR

Not only is volunteering to be a tutor a socially responsible thing to do, it also opens you up to meeting men. First, there are fellow socially responsible men in your tutor training class. And then there are your students or the fathers of your students. A lot of foreigners hire tutors to help them brush up on their language skills, so you may form a relationship with a charming man who speaks English as a second language. Most cities have literacy centers that will train you and hook you up with a student in need.

492. RED CROSS

Have you been searching for a way to give back to your community as you search for love? As a volunteer for the American Red Cross, your hunt for both could be over. The American Red Cross, a humanitarian organization led by volunteers, is always looking for volunteers to help with disaster relief efforts, homeless shelters, youth group activities, babysitting, life guarding, and more. As a volunteer, you will likely work alongside some single male good Samaritans. To learn more, check out *www.redcross.org*.

493. MEALS ON WHEELS

Unfortunately, a lot of senior citizens in this country are hungry every day because they do not have the money for food or the ability to go out and get it. To help these people—and to meet some good-hearted citizen volunteers in the process—consider volunteering for Meals on Wheels. You will meet fellow volunteers in meetings and Meals on Wheels events, and you will do a wonderful thing for the community in the process. And after all, men who donate their time to an organization like Meals on Wheels are probably very giving and kindhearted. To learn how you can help, visit *www.mowaa.org*.

 =Time ♦=Friends $=Expense

494.   SOUP KITCHEN

Every city—small and large—and some towns have at least one or two soup kitchens where homeless people can go for a warm place to hang out and a hot meal. These places are constantly in need of people to make and serve the soup at all times of the day, so think about donating a few of your hours a week to the soup kitchen. Not only will you be doing a wonderful thing for your community, you might meet some giving men volunteers serving soup alongside you.

495.   SIERRA CLUB

If clean air, crystal water, and wildlife preservation are important to you, consider becoming a Sierra Club member. There are more than 750,000 Americans in Sierra Club, about half of whom are men. And because this club sponsors quite a few activities that require volunteers, it tends to attract single people who are passionate about preserving a clean environment. For more information on Sierra Club and to find the closest chapter to you, check out *www.sierraclub.org.*

=Time   =Friends $=Expense

d date flea market reunion restaurant tattoo parlor wedding auction ho
ub baby shower casino hibachi ladies night café bake sale brunch river
mbake double date culinary festival smorgasbord tavern church service
mal hospital roommates yacht club school courthouse nudist colony bee
al baseball game car show firefighting fishing tailgating poker campgr
ting contest bowling weight room military cigar shop airport london bri
  eiffel tower vacation hotel cruise mardi gras times square central park
f america mount rushmore hollywood safari smithsonian online animal
e blood drive volunteering special olympics toy drive red cross soup kit
t gallery book club cooking class library museum college campus orche
ature walk planetarium political rally shakespeare festival disney world
uarium water park caroling parents playground mini-golf county fair co
use laundromat grocery store beach gym subway deli yard sale liquor
post office personal ads company picnic conference water cooler bartend
oncert scavenger hunt karaoke comedy club biking karate softball paint
iling ymca square dancing boardwalk cookout whale watching farmer's
et party friends cafeteria open house singing group bars beach house
ting blind date flea market reunion restaurant tattoo parlor wedding au
ospital club baby shower casino hibachi ladies night café bake sale bru
iverboat clambake double date culinary festival smorgasbord tavern chu
ervice spa animal hospital roommates yacht club school courthouse nu
ony beer festival baseball game car show firefighting fishing tailgating
ampground eating contest bowling weight room military cigar shop airp
ndon bridges bus eiffel tower vacation hotel cruise mardi gras times sq
ntral park mall of america mount rushmore hollywood safari smithsonian
e animal rescue blood drive volunteering special olympics toy drive red
p kitchen art gallery book club cooking class library museum college ca
rchestra nature walk planetarium political rally shakespeare festival dis
orld zoo aquarium water park caroling parents playground mini-golf co
ir coffeehouse laundromat grocery store beach gym subway deli yard
quor store post office personal ads company picnic conference water coo
rtending concert scavenger hunt karaoke comedy club biking karate so
intball sailing ymca square dancing cookout whale watching farmer's ma
ty friends cafeteria open house singing group bars beach house wine ta
d date flea market reunion restaurant tattoo parlor wedding auction ho
ub baby shower casino hibachi ladies night café bake sale brunch river
mbake double date culinary festival smorgasbord tavern church service
mal hospital roommates yacht club school courthouse nudist colony bee
al baseball game car show firefighting fishing tailgating poker campgr
ting contest bowling weight room military cigar shop airport london bri
  eiffel tower vacation hotel cruise mardi gras times square central park
f america mount rushmore hollywood safari smithsonian online animal
e blood drive volunteering special olympics toy drive red cross soup kit
t gallery book club cooking class library museum college campus orche
ature walk planetarium political rally shakespeare festival disney world

intellectualways

496.   ART CLASS

If you are looking to expand your mind and your social circle, an art class at a local university or art school is a great way to go. Whether you want to try painting, sculpture, or artistic photography, art classes tend to attract open-minded people who love to try new things and meet new friends . . . or new "more than friends."

497.   ART GALLERY

The wonderful thing about art galleries—aside from the spectacular art, of course—is that it is perfectly acceptable to go to them alone. In fact, even if you don't meet a guy, you are bound to get more out of a trip to a gallery solo than you will with a friend who has a different viewing pace than your own. Art galleries offer a great conversation starter, as well: "What do you think of the exhibit?" or "Which piece do you think is the artist's best?" The perfect time to visit the art gallery: On an exhibit opening night, where there will likely be music, drinks, and a festive atmosphere to accompany the unveiling.

498.   BOOK CLUB

This one is a bit of a long shot, because guys who read and discuss (this second part is the clincher) books are few and far between. So if you are lucky enough to have a few male readers in your book group, get to know them. Even if there are no sparks, you will gain a guy friend who is willing to talk about and analyze things in detail. Plus, you will read books you wouldn't ordinarily choose on your own and meet a whole new group of potential friends, male and female.

○ PRO *You will be inspired to read books on a regular basis.*

○ CON *If he's that into Jane Austen, he might be gay.*

499.   BOOK SIGNING

If you both love a particular book and author enough to brave the line at a book signing, you will have at least one interesting topic to talk about. And with all the great books out there, it could be more than a coincidence that you both loved the same one. If you meet a guy at a book signing, you will probably have a lot more in common than the book. You will be off to a great start.

| 500. | CAR MAINTENANCE SEMINAR |

The fastest and easiest way to expose yourself to men is to entrench yourself in activities they take part in. After all, you won't find many men at a needlepoint or knitting class. A car maintenance seminar is a prime example of a class you can benefit from . . . and that will introduce you to single men.

| 501. | COOKING CLASS |

They say the fastest way to a man's heart is through his stomach, and this cliché may work both ways. Cooking classes attract men who like—or want to learn—to cook. Either way, a guy you meet in a cooking class will likely want to try out his culinary skills on you. And these days, there are cooking classes specifically for singles where people cook together and then sit down and enjoy the fruits of their labor as a group. "Because we were learning and creating as a group, it broke the ice and made it easy to talk to others in the class," says Jaime Jones, who met her husband at a singles cooking class. Companies that organize cooking classes for singles include CookingSchools.com, BestChefs.com, and Serendipity-SF. Other places to find a good cooking class: your local culinary school or community college. Williams-Sonoma, Sur la Table, and similar culinary stores also offer cooking classes.

| 502. | LIBRARY |

If a man is perusing books at the local library on a Saturday afternoon, he is most likely single. And better yet, he is most likely a single guy who reads. At the risk of stereotyping, guys who enjoy passing time with a good book are generally intellectual and sensitive, so if that's your type, you may want to search the stacks for your next date.

◑ PRO *If he's in your local library, chances are, he's local.*

◑ CON *Library quiet rules make it hard to strike up a conversation.*

503. LOCAL COLLEGE CLASSES FOR ADULTS

Whether you're going for an MBA or you simply want to brush up on your European history, local college classes are a great way for you to expand your knowledge base and your dating horizons at the same time. In these classes, you'll meet guys who share your interest of a particular subject. Plus, a guy who is taking college courses in his free time is probably not the lazy type. So the next time it arrives in the mail, don't be so fast to throw that local college class schedule in the trash.

⊙ PRO *Even if you don't meet a handsome classmate, you will probably find classes enriching.*

⊙ CON *If your company doesn't reimburse for education, you'll have to spend a little of your own money to enroll.*

504. MUSEUM

Looking for an intellectual guy who appreciates art and history? A museum is the perfect place for you to find him. And the museum offers much more than exhibit settings—most museums are balancing their educational missions with entertainment these days, offering opportunities for social interaction such as gallery opening parties, tours, performances, lectures, films, and happy hour or cocktail hour events with live music and appetizers. In other words, the perfect scene for mingling.

505. SCOTCH-TASTING SEMINAR

Scotch tastings are becoming more and more popular, and they draw many more men than do wine tastings. In fact, you are likely to be way outnumbered by men at a scotch tasting. Plus, you just might learn something. So open up your mind and your taste buds to some single malts—there's no telling what will happen. Scotch tastings are often done at cigar or martini bars. The next time you find yourself at such a place, ask if they host scotch tastings.

⊙ PRO *You'll be loosened up by the scotch and feeling extra confident and outgoing.*

⊙ CON *Scotch breath and cigar smoke.*

506. BOOKSTORE

Head to your local bookstore, grab a coffee, and enjoy a book in one of your favorite topic areas, be it travel, history, psychology, or cooking. That way, if you notice a guy in your section, it means you have at least one topic of interest in common and can gracefully strike up a conversation. You also have a smooth transition into a date—if you are in the cooking section, ask the guy if he would like to make a meal with you; if you are in the travel section, ask him if he would like to check out a local travel destination you've been meaning to visit; and so on.

507. MENSA

If you are blessed with an abnormally high IQ and you enjoy mingling with fellow intelligent folks, consider becoming a member of Mensa, a society for bright people with high IQs. The Mensa society welcomes people of all political backgrounds and religions— the only qualification is that you have an IQ in the top 2 percent of the population. Most Mensa members are between ages twenty and sixty. For more information, go to *www.mensa.org*.

508. POETRY READING

Where better to find love than where the language of love is spoken? Even if you are not a huge poetry fan, it can't hurt for you to open up your ears and your mind and give it a chance. Poetry readings are usually held in coffee shops, bars, and other venues where art-appreciating single people hang out, so you are guaranteed a coffee or drink and hopefully, some good conversation in between poems.

509. COLLEGE ALUMNI MAGAZINE

It may be to your advantage to start paying attention to the alumni magazine you receive from your alma mater a few times a year. The alumni profiled in these articles are usually successful and sometimes available. The story will offer clues as to whether the featured alumnus is married or single. And with alumni directories and Web sites, it shouldn't be too hard to track him down. If you hit a snag, you can always write a (positive) letter to the editor in response to the story and see where it goes.

510. PHOTOGRAPHY CLASS

Photography is one of those skills that anyone can benefit from learning or improving upon. And unlike other hobbies, it is coed—about half of photographers are women and half are men . . . and who doesn't want to know how to take better pictures? So if you take a photography class at your local art school or college, there are a few things that are almost guaranteed: One, you will have a good mix of men and women in your class, and two, you will learn how to be a better photographer. Photography classes tend to be interactive, with classmates giving suggestions and feedback on each other's photographs and techniques—a bonding experience that could lead to more than just a drink or snack after class.

511. CHESS CLUB

Like poker, chess has become increasingly popular these days . . . especially among men. So join a chess club, and you are bound to be way outnumbered by heady guys who can play a mean game of chess.

○ PRO *Chess is a thought-provoking game that keeps you on your toes.*

○ CON *The men could be somewhat socially challenged, and the games are usually silent.*

512. COLLEGE CAMPUS

If you live near a college campus or, even better, a few different college campuses, consider yourself lucky. Campuses are hot spots for single guys. If you're on the younger side or if you prefer younger guys, you have thousands of students and graduate students to check out. And then, of course, there are the professors and staff members. So next time you want a cup of coffee, consider the campus coffee shop. Or take your jog through campus and keep your eyes open. There's a whole other world of men on campus.

○ PRO *There's a plentitude of smart, educated guys.*

○ CON *Just make sure they are at least 18.*

513.   LECTURE AT A LOCAL COLLEGE OR UNIVERSITY

Most colleges and universities sponsor lectures given by famous people, such as authors, politicians, and philosophers. These lectures are often open to the public (and free) and are likely to attract intelligent, single men in your area who are open to new ideas. To scan the audience members, get to a lecture a little early and sit in the very back. That way, you can change your seat and move closer to anyone who looks interesting.

○ PRO *You just might learn something.*

○ CON *Unless you are in the market for a much younger man, you will have to be careful to discern the college students from the community audience.*

514.   POLITICAL CAMPAIGN

If you are passionate about politics, a local political campaign could be a great place to meet your match. You're guaranteed to meet men who belong to the same political party as you do, and the cooperation required to successfully work on a political campaign will be a wonderful bonding experience. So after an afternoon of hanging campaign posters, ask one of the single guys to grab something to eat.

○ PRO *You will be politically like-minded.*

○ CON *Political campaigns demand a lot of your time; if you are not passionate about the cause, this one is probably not the best for you.*

515.   ORCHESTRA

For musicians so talented they can actually make money playing an instrument, an orchestra can be a wonderful place to make social connections as well as musical ones. Hey, if you can make beautiful music together in theaters and at outdoor venues, just think of your potential in other places. . . . So if you possess a marketable musical talent, try out for an orchestra in your area. If nothing else, you will make some wonderful friends.

516. USED BOOKSTORE

If you love books, chances are you have discovered the best used bookstore in your area. Many used bookstores are more than places to get cheap books: They sponsor poetry readings, serve coffee and other snacks, and offer a wonderful place to meet a man who loves reading as much as you do. So keep your eyes open for attractive guys browsing the used books and be prepared to approach him and recommend the best book you've read lately. Even if he's attached or not interested, as a reader, he will appreciate your recommendation.

517. HISTORICAL HOUSE TOUR

If you love history and historical architecture, you'll love a historical house tour. Most historic towns sponsor house tours where you can walk through the oldest mansions and homes in the area. They are usually done in medium-sized groups, and they draw people with a similar interest in history, including history-loving guys.

518. POLITICAL SPEECH

If you are really into politics, make it a point to attend a speech by a local politician or national politician who comes to your area. And if you are only sort of into politics, you should make an effort to attend political speeches . . . for the single politically minded men who will be there. Political speeches are forums for people who are passionate about—or interested in—politics. Just make sure the politician you're going to see is in the political party you support. Be aware that if the speech is touted as a fundraising event, it is expected that you make a donation, and many make large donations at that.

519. SCRABBLE NIGHT

Scrabble can be a really fun (and competitive) game. So fun, in fact, that some people host Scrabble nights. If you don't know of a Scrabble group you can join, consider starting one yourself. Scrabble will spark some great conversation and interaction between group members . . . which could lead to a relationship beyond the game. While it's only a game, be aware that people who are into Scrabble enough to attend a Scrabble night may be exceptionally good (maybe even better than you!) at the game.

520.   TYPING CLASS

$ $ $

If you are like a lot of people, you spent your high school typing class talking and daydreaming, thinking you'd never need to use typing anyway, right? Well, you've surely had a rude awakening over the last ten or so years that the Internet has been popular. So to brush up on your skills, you may want to consider taking a typing refresher course to speed up your typing and to expose you to guys around your age who also blew off typing in high school. To find a typing class in your area, contact your local community college.

O PRO *Instead of a typewriter, word processor, or Commodore with a black screen with green type, you will get to practice typing on a real computer this time.*

O CON *If you are already an expert typist, you won't get too much out of this class.*

521.   PAINTING CLASS

$ $ $

Whether you are gifted artistically or just love to try, a painting class will be perfect for you. Because it leaves so much open to abstraction, painting appeals to artists of all skill levels. The typical painting class lasts about six weeks and draws people of all ages and backgrounds . . . including some single guys looking to expand their artistic and social horizons. The class will attract open-minded men who want to try something new or improve on an existing skill in a class of similarly open-minded adults. These classes often lead to social gatherings at restaurants and other events outside of the gallery . . . plus, you will have a few paintings to show for your efforts when the class comes to a close. For watercolor classes in your area, check local community colleges, art schools, and high schools.

O PRO *You will learn a creative new skill, and the men you meet in a painting class will probably be intelligent and sensitive.*

O CON *Depending on where you take the class, it could be pricey. Community colleges usually offer the best prices.*

522.   BUDDHIST RETREAT

There are spiritual people out there who would rather meditate for hours on end than attend a church sermon on a Sunday morning. If you fit this mold and identify with Buddhist principles, you will get a lot out of a Buddhist retreat. These retreats, which last anywhere from a weekend to ten days, consist of a lot of meditation, but they also provide an opportunity for Buddhist followers to meet each other. Men you meet at a Buddhist retreat will share some of your core spiritual beliefs, so you will feel an instant connection. Mary P. of Allentown, Pennsylvania, met her current boyfriend at a Buddhist weekend retreat. "We bonded immediately," she says. "We started attending other Buddhist events together as friends, but our friendship blossomed into something more. It turns out we have a lot more in common than a respect for the teachings of the Awakened One."

523.   COMPUTER CLASS

Computers are upgrading so fast these days that you may periodically need a refresher course. Whether you're taking it to learn a new program or to brush up on your skills in an existing one, a computer class can do wonders for your résumé. If you work on a computer, as so many of us do, your company may be willing to pick up the cost of enrollment. Plus, most computer classes are full of ambitious young professionals you can rub elbows with . . . and if things go well, maybe more. So look beyond your computer screen and at your classmates now and then.

524.   NATURE WALK

Love the outdoors? Why not go for a nature walk? Whether you go with a friend or sign up to go with a group, nature walks are a great way to get fresh air, and to find out more about the plants and animals that exist in or around your area. You may also find out more about a cute outdoorsy guy also on the walk. Contact a conservation center in your area for recommendations on where to walk or just hit a local trail on a time that's likely to be busy, like Saturday afternoons.

○ PRO *A guy on a nature walk is likely to be environmentally minded and an animal lover.*

○ CON *It could be dangerous to walk in the woods by yourself. Bring along a friend.*

 =Time =Friends $=Expense

525. SINGLES TRIVIA NIGHT

Love trivia and want to put your skills to good use? Consider joining or hosting a singles trivia night. Only invite singles and play Trivial Pursuit or another popular trivia game. Trivia is a great window into a guy's general knowledge base (is he a Sports & Leisure pro, or is he well-versed in Arts & Literature?), and it will help you decide if you want to take your relationship beyond the game.

526. SPANISH CLASS

Considering that more than one in ten Americans older than age five speak Spanish, most people can benefit from a Spanish class, whether it's necessary for business or communicating with people in public places. Sign up for a class at a local college or university and not only will you learn Spanish, you'll likely meet male class-mates as well. And why not get together with one of your class-mates "after class" for coffee to practice your Spanish skills?

O PRO *Spanish speaking skills.*

O CON *With the tests and the homework, you'll feel like you're back in school again (this is a plus for some and a negative for others).*

527. STRESS-MANAGEMENT SEMINAR

We've all got stress in our lives; it's how we deal with it that counts. A stress-management seminar is an excellent way to get some suggestions on how to deal with stress in a positive manner. And a stress-management seminar can be an excellent way to get acquainted with men who are also trying to deal with stress in a positive manner. To better your chances of meeting the type of guy who sparks your fancy, look for specific stress-management seminars, such as Stress Management for Professionals or Stress Management for Entrepreneurs, etc., rather than Stress and Anger Management for Guys Who Are About to Lose It.

528. SYMPHONY

If you're looking for something new to do—and some new people to check out—get tickets for the symphony on a Friday night. Concerts often include an intermission where food and drinks are served—an opportunity to get to know the refined men at the concert.

O PRO *It's a great excuse to pull out your most fabulous dress.*

O CON *Depending on where you live and the size of the symphony, tickets may be pricey.*

 =Time =Friends $=Expense

529.   CIVIL WAR REENACTMENT

For history buffs, a civil war reenactment can be very exciting and fun. These reenactments are usually held on actual battle grounds or at national parks. To meet guys who share your passion for American history, or maybe male school teachers taking their students on an educational trip, you can't beat one of these reenactments. Some of the most popular Civil War reenactments in the country include the annual Gettysburg reenactment, which takes place in the summertime in Gettysburg, Pennsylvania, the Civil War Reenactment in Fresno, California, and the reenactment in Statesville, North Carolina, which takes place in early fall.

530.   TATTOO CONVENTION

If you have a tattoo, are considering getting a tattoo, or are just interested in learning more about body art, a tattoo convention can be a great place to scope for some single, inked guys. No longer just found on muscle heads and sailors, tattoos can be a sign that a guy doesn't mind risk-taking—which can be a great trait in a date.

531.   FIRST-AID CLASS

Everyone can benefit from learning first aid, so a class will be composed of people from all walks of life who want to know how to treat injuries in the event of an emergency. If you are lucky, there will be a guy or two you're interested in on whom you can practice dressing wounds.

532.   ARCHAEOLOGICAL DIG

Archaeological digs are conducted by universities, historical societies, and museums year-round, all over the world. So if you have an interest in historical artifacts—and an interest in guys who are interested in historical artifacts—consider joining one of these group digs. Some digs are limited to archaeologists and professionals, but others take interested volunteers (unless you are an archaeologist, this volunteer-type is the one you want). Not only will you have the potential to uncover valuable pieces of history, you might be side-by-side with attractive guys with the same goal.

=Time =Friends $=Expense

533. CPR CLASS

Whether you have children, you take care of children, or you just want to know how to save someone's life in the event of an emergency, you can benefit from a CPR class. And these courses are usually composed of people of all ages and backgrounds, including single men. And although you normally practice CPR on a dummy in the class, you may want to practice on one of your classmates later if you two get along. And beyond your classmates, your CPR skills may come in handy if you ever need to perform CPR on an attractive stranger . . .

534. SINGLES LECTURE

This is an easy one. Any guy who attends a lecture on how to meet potential mates is ripe for the picking. So check the paper for singles lectures in your area. Even if you don't meet the man of your dreams, you may pick up some pointers on how to better your chances.

535. SCULPTING CLASS

If you are looking to expand your mind and your social circle, a sculpting class at a local university or art school is a great way to go. Not only will you get to test your skills in working with clay, sculpting classes tend to attract open-minded people who love to try new things. So you will meet some creative new friends, possibly some who turn out to be more than friends.

536. SPIRITUAL OR NEW AGE BOOKSTORE

If you love books and you are a spiritual person, chances are you have discovered the best spiritual bookstore in your area. Many used bookstores are more than places to get spiritual books these days . . . some of them serve coffee and other snacks, and offer a wonderful place to meet a spiritual man who loves reading as much as you do. So keep your eyes open for attractive guys browsing the books and be prepared to approach one of them and recommend the best spiritual book you've read lately. Even if he's attached or not interested, as a reader, he will appreciate your recommendation.

537.   RESTAURANT NEAR A COLLEGE

There is a lot more to be found here than guys wearing Greek letters bragging about the keg stand they did the night before. There are graduate students focused on becoming successful. There are teachers' assistants and there are a number of single professors. Drop in and scan the place to find that one studious and friendly looking gent, then just say hello. It's that easy!

538.   SEX EDUCATION COURSE

This one requires some research, but you can find sex education courses that appeal to singles. This is a very direct way to learn what you're both into right away. Courses like these begin with online research, since many singles seeking sex education like to start anonymously. Community colleges often provide courses in sex education. Give the professor a call and find out what the course is all about and what kind of people attend.

539.   TAX PREPARATION CLASS

Right off the bat you know that any guy who wants to learn to do his own taxes is responsible and something of a do-it-yourself person. You'll also know that he's not afraid to ask for help. All very good things. Additionally, you'll learn how to do your taxes on your own. That could save you anywhere from $75 to $300 and maybe more! You have nothing to lose. Get to class!

540.   WRITER'S WORKSHOP

You're getting the skills you've always wanted to improve your writing. And the guy next to you is an aspiring screenplay writer. You can't beat those benefits. Many community colleges offer writing courses, from business writing to poetry to playwriting. Contact the professors to learn how many people are normally in the class and the ratio of men to women in the class. Then just grab a pencil and go.

541. ART SUPPLY STORE

Like the brooding, complex artistic type? Head over to the local art supply store and do some "shopping." You'll find artists, painters, graphic designers, and more. Walk right up to someone who catches your eye and tell them you want to create a portfolio of your work and you're not sure how to begin. He'll ask what you do and you can just say you do sketches or you're a graphic designer. As he's pointing out a few possible options, tell him you actually saw him walk in and you just wanted to meet him. Flattery works. Go find your masterpiece.

542. PLANETARIUM

Planetariums offer visitors a fascinating view into the solar system. Plus, many people go to planetariums to simply get away from it all and relax. While they may not be teeming with Brad Pitt look-alikes, you will find single men there unwinding and taking in a little science education lesson. Although it may seem a little "far out," you have nothing to lose on this one.

○ PRO *If you have children, planetariums can be wonderful places to meet fellow single parents.*

○ CON *Nerds . . . but that can be a good thing.*

543. COLLEGE ALUMNI GROUP

You may have been more in the frame of mind to do keg stands with your girlfriends than to try to date in college, but now that you are older and wiser, you may wish you had looked more closely at the guy sitting next to you in accounting. So what better way to meet the guys you missed out on in college than to join your alma mater's alumni group? A lot of these groups have interactive sites online now, so you can chat with fellow alums in between the in-person social events.

○ PRO *The tailgates, mixers, and other social events sponsored by alumni groups are excellent places to get to know some of your fellow alums better.*

○ CON *If you live thousands of miles from your college or university, this one may be tough.*

544.   WEB SITE DESIGN CLASS

Getting out of your routine and trying hobbies is always a great way to meet new people. Whether you find the man of your dreams or friends for a lifetime, find something that you'd be interested in learning. Many community colleges offer Web site design classes, which are not only beneficial for building your own Web page, but there are often men in these classes looking to pick up the skill.

545.   FRENCH CLASS

Want to learn the language of love? Take a French class. French is a beautiful language, and it will make a trip to Paris go much more smoothly. (Although French people will still laugh at your accent, they will appreciate your trying to order a crepe in their language.) In your class, you will meet romantic men who also appreciate French culture . . . and they may make wonderful travel companions once your class is over. To find a French class, look at colleges, community colleges, and universities in your area.

546.   GUBERNATORIAL CAMPAIGN

If you are a politically minded person, you are no doubt anxious to get involved in a full-fledged political campaign . . . but it can be tough to hook up with a presidential candidate. So why not aim a little more locally with a gubernatorial or senatorial campaign. Many of these local campaigns are male-dominated, so you will most likely be way outnumbered by politically passionate men. Not a bad position to be in. Plus, at the end of the day, you will rest assured that you did all you could for your candidate and your party. For more information, check out *www.electionprojection.com* for a list of the candidates in your area.

547.   MARK TWAIN HOUSE

For literature and/or history buffs, a trip to the Mark Twain House in Hartford, Connecticut, is an enjoyable experience. Guided tours take you through the 19-room Tiffany-decorated mansion that belonged to the author of classics like *Tom Sawyer* and *Huckleberry Finn*. Most tours are done in groups, so you will have the opportunity to mingle with your fellow tour members (hopefully, some will be single guys interested in Mark Twain or single male teachers doing research for their classes), both in the house itself and in the museum. For information, check out *www.marktwainhouse.org*.

=Time =Friends $=Expense

---

548. POLITICAL RALLY

To increase your chances of meeting a passionate politically minded man and to contribute to a good cause, you can't go wrong by taking part in a political rally. *Cosmopolitan* magazine points out that the hottest political organization these days is the Save Darfur Coalition, dedicated to ending genocide in Darfur, Sudan. The number of members—including intelligent male members—is fast increasing. So if you personally feel passionate about the cause, check out upcoming roundtables, concerts, and other events at *www.savedarfur.org*.

---

549. SELF-HELP SEMINAR

We can all use a little self-reflection and self-improvement, so a self-help seminar can only bring good things into your life . . . and perhaps, new men who aren't afraid to explore their softer sides. Look for seminars in your area that feature a subject you are interested in that include groups—the more interaction, the better your chances of finding love.

---

550. SHAKESPEARE FESTIVAL

If you love Shakespeare or just enjoy a well-acted performance, check out a Shakespeare festival. In addition to Shakespearian plays (acted as they used to be—outdoors), Shakespeare festivals include actors dressed in Shakespearian clothing, good food, souvenirs, and more. This is a great place to meet intellectual men who are entertained by more than just sports.

Five great Shakespeare festivals:
1. The Oregon Shakespeare Festival: *www.orshakes.org*
2. Alabama Shakespeare Festival: *www.asf.net/index.aspx*
3. Colorado Shakespeare Festival: *www.coloradoshakes.org*
4. The San Francisco Shakespeare Festival: *www.sfshakes.org*
5. The Cincinnati Shakespeare Festival: *www.cincyshakes.com*

---

551. ITALIAN CLASSES

In the mood for romance? What better way to celebrate it than to learn the most romantic language: Italian. Not only will you leave the class better able to interpret the menu at your favorite Italian bistro, you may meet a romantic man with whom to share your meal. To find an Italian class, check the colleges, universities, or community colleges in your area.

 =Time   =Friends $=Expense

552.   GRADUATE SCHOOL

If you have been toying around with the idea of getting an MBA, Master of Science, or other graduate degree, think about the intelligent, tenacious single men you could meet in class—it might be the motivation you need to finally sign up. For a major career change, you may want to quit your job and go back full time, completely immersing yourself in the intellectual lifestyle of a grad student. Or, you could go back to evening and weekend classes—a fabulous way to meet professional single men.

○ PRO *This is a win-win. You will meet new people and gain educational credits at the same time.*

○ CON *The cost. Unless your company pays for you to go back to school, graduate school can take a heavy toll on your wallet.*

553.   PHILADELPHIA ART MUSEUM

Sure, the Philadelphia Art Museum has some great exhibits, including a knights' armor exhibit that surely draws men interested in ancient weaponry. But above all, you will find the highest concentration of men on the steps of the museum, living out their Rocky fantasies by mimicking Sly's famous ascent. So for best results, head to the Philly Art Museum on a nice day so you can see who makes it up the stairs with the fewest huffs and puffs. For hours and events, visit *www.philamuseum.org.*

554.   EMBRY-RIDDLE AERONAUTICAL UNIVERSITY

This university in Daytona Beach, Florida, is a hot spot for aspiring pilots, most of whom are men. And because Embry-Riddle is one of the best aeronautical schools in the country, these men are guaranteed to be smart. They can be found in coffee shops and bars around the university, and they are eager to talk about planes and flying. If you find yourself meeting one of these pilots, be sure to steer the conversation up to the sky, so to speak.

555.   POWELL'S BOOKS

If you are an avid reader or you just appreciate men who read, make sure you stop into Powell's Books the next time you find yourself in Portland, Oregon. Powell's offers more than 200,000 used and new books and regularly hosts author readings that draw men (depending on the author). It also has a fabulous coffee shop, where handsome men can often be found. Check out *www.powells.com.*

=Time =Friends $=Expense

556. THE UNIVERSITY OF VIRGINIA

Abercrombie and Fitch's first catalog featured only students from the University of Virginia. Considering that the A&F catalog features some of the most attractive faces in the country, it's a nice advertisement for the student body of UVA. To meet these hunky undergraduate and graduate students, you have to go where they hang out. So if you take a road trip to Charlottesville, Virginia, stop in Clemons Library and browse the stacks. Then swing by "The Corner," a collection of shops, restaurants, and bars down University Avenue, UVA's main drag.

O PRO *UVA is a very good school, just a hair below Ivy League status, so in addition to being good looking, its men are also quite smart.*

O CON *If you're in your late thirties or forties, you may be beyond college men . . . but there are always the parents, professors, and staff members.*

557. FRANK LLOYD WRIGHT HOUSES

The architect Frank Lloyd Wright was famous for constructing buildings that intertwined indoors and outdoors and included unique geometrical blocks. Two of his most famous houses are Taliesin West in Scottsdale, Arizona, and Fallingwater in Bear Run, Pennsylvania. These houses are interesting in terms of their historical and aesthetic value (after all, Frank Lloyd Wright was the most famous architect in U.S. history), but they are also worth visiting because they attract a lot of men. Like George Costanza, many men dream of being architects. And in addition to the dreamers, these famous houses may draw actual architects who want to see the work of a genius in their field. So be sure to hop in a group tour.

558. GUITAR LESSONS

Taking guitar lessons is a great way to expand your horizons, both musically and socially. You will learn a new skill you can have fun with alone or with friends and meet new people in the form of your teacher and fellow students. For best results, look for a group lesson.

=Time ☀=Friends $=Expense

559.   HISTORIC MANSION TOUR

$ $

To get an inside look at how people lived in centuries prior . . . and to meet some fellow appreciators of historic architecture in your guided tour group, spend a Saturday afternoon on a historic mansion tour. The interactive nature of this kind of tour will allow you to get to know your group members a little better . . . so see if you'd like to take the relationship off mansion grounds and into modern day. Some of the country's most impressive mansions can be found in Newport, Rhode Island.

560.   COLLEGE OR UNIVERSITY DINING HALL

$ $

Even if you're not a student or a professor, you might want to pop into a college or university near your home or place of employment for lunch or dinner now and then. Most dining halls take cash and are open to the public . . . and they offer a nice selection of foods. But more importantly, college dining halls are a hub for intellectual men in the form of staff members, professors and instructors, graduate students, and (if you're young enough or like younger men) students. For best results, go at prime dining hours, like noon or 6 P.M., when you will be more likely to have to share a table with an interesting stranger.

561.   THE MCAT, GMAT, OR OTHER ENTRANCE EXAM

$ $

If you're planning to attend graduate school and have to take an entrance exam to apply, you probably have to schedule the test at a busy testing center . . . a busy testing center full of future graduate students who, like you, want to further their education. During a test is certainly not the best time to approach someone, but as you take breaks to stretch or crack your knuckles, take a scan around the room. If someone catches your eye, approach him on the way out and ask if he'd like to get some coffee to unwind.

562.   COFFEE SHOP NEAR A GRAD SCHOOL

$

If you live near a college or university with a grad school, there are guaranteed to be dozens of cool coffee shops—filled with cool, intellectual students and professors—within a few blocks radius of it. *Cosmopolitan* revealed that 60 percent of grad school coffee shop clientele are men, so the odds are in your favor. So don't miss out on this killer combination of stimulating coffee and conversation.

kid-friendly**ways**

563. DISNEYWORLD

If you have kids, Disney is a wonderful place to take them and possibly, to meet single dads. And if you don't have kids, with the movies, games, rides, live events, and more that Disney now offers, there is definitely plenty for adults who are young at heart to do. So take a fun girlfriend with you on a trip to Disney and have a ball. You know the men you meet there will be fun-loving and free-spirited. Check out *http://disneyworld.disney.go.com*.

564. THE FRANKLIN INSTITUTE SCIENCE MUSEUM

The Franklin Institute is a magnet for smart men and single fathers. The permanent exhibits include a huge beating heart that patrons can walk through, a sports challenge exhibit, and an electricity exhibit. Plus, the Franklin Institute hosts cool international traveling exhibits that bring people in from all around the tri-state area. The interactive nature of the institute makes for great conversation starters, and it is close to restaurants and coffee shops where you can take your science discussion further. The only problem may be a long drive if you don't live near Philadelphia, where the museum is located. *www.fi.edu*.

565. THUNDER ROAD

Most guys are big kids, so they love a day that exposes them to some of the activities they loved before puberty—go-carting, adventure golf, water wars, and so on. And at Thunder Road in Sioux Falls, South Dakota, these big kids can engage in all these activities. So if you are a single parent, take your kids to Thunder Road and keep your eyes out for single dads and men there with their friends for some fun. And if you're not a parent but you're still a big kid at heart yourself, you will have just as much fun. Plan your trip at *www.thunderroad.info*

566. COLONIAL WILLIAMSBURG

For history buffs or parents who are looking for an educational—yet fun—place to take the kids, Colonial Williamsburg in Virginia is a wonderful choice. Williamsburg attracts a lot of men in the form of single dads, teachers, and men who are simply interested in American history. And because Williamsburg offers museums, restaurants, and shops, there will be plenty of places for you to meet men who share your interest in the Revolutionary War. For information, log on to *www.history.org*.

567.   BRONX ZOO

The Bronx Zoo is one of the largest zoos in the country, offering more than 4,000 animals for your viewing pleasure. Even better: The Bronx Zoo is the heart of the Wildlife Conservation Society, so your entry fee and other money spent there will go toward saving wildlife around the world. At the zoo, you are likely to walk the grounds with environmentally conscious, animal-loving men, so be sure to check out the two-legged mammals as well as the four-legged ones. Find out more at *www.bronxzoo.com*.

O PRO *If you have children, the Bronx Zoo makes a wonderful day trip, and it is a haven for single dads.*

O CON *The Bronx isn't the safest area of New York. Stay on zoo grounds.*

568.   GRACELAND

Maybe it's the music, maybe it's the hip gyrations, and maybe it's the screaming women he attracted, but regardless of the reasons, a lot of men have a borderline unhealthy obsession with Elvis Presley. So Graceland, Elvis's abode, is a great place to go to meet men. And beyond the guys, you'll find touring Graceland to be a one-of-a-kind experience that takes you deep into the life of the King. After you're through with the tour, you can check out what Heartbreak Hotel has to offer . . . both in terms of the heart-shaped pools and the men who plan on soaking in them. Check out *www.elvis.com*.

O PRO *Graceland is a fun place to take the kids if you are a single mom.*

O CON *Some diehard Elvis fans are downright weird. Be prepared.*

569.   FERRY TO THE STATUE OF LIBERTY

Next time you're in New York City, consider hopping on a ferry to get an up-close view of Lady Liberty. There are a few different types of ferries that travel to Ellis Island—speedy ones, slow ones, and ones that serve dinner and drinks. Even if you are a native New Yorker, you will get a kick out of riding out to the statue now and then . . . and you may meet a fellow city man taking his kids or out-of-town friends or relatives for a tour.

O PRO *This is a great cultural activity to do with the kids if you are a single mom.*

O CON *Get ready for a lot of tourists.*

=Time =Friends $=Expense

570. BAPTISM OR CHRISTENING

At a baptism, you know you have a special infant in common with everyone in the room, including any eligible men. And if a guy is at a baptism by himself, the chances are good that he is single—men generally don't attend religious ceremonies or occasions involving infants without their significant others, at least if they can help it. And the chances will also be good that the two of you are of the same religious background.

571. PARENT/TEACHER MEETING

If you're a single mom and your child's teacher just happens to be a single guy, don't pass up the opportunity to get to know him better. This doesn't mean you should show up to a parent/teacher confer-ence in a low-cut top and flirt—it just means that you shouldn't rule him out just because he's teaching your son or daughter how to read. After all, next year he will no longer be your child's teacher. So bring an apple and a smile to the meeting and hand him your phone number. You can say it's just in case there is an emergency with your child, but he'll probably read between the lines.

O PRO *You have an excuse to have a face-to-face meeting with him, so you will get a sense of his personality through that and through the stories from your child.*

O CON *This one has the potential for awkwardness. Tread lightly.*

572. SOCCER FIELD

Grab a girlfriend, niece, or nephew (or your own child, if you are a single mom) and head to the games at your local fields. Soccer fields are becoming increasingly more popular meeting spots, with some people even going as far as to call them "the new singles bars for single fathers." Plop down next to the single father or uncle who catches your eye and strike up a conversation. There's an easy and obvious first line: "Which one's yours?"

O PRO *You will be appropriately dressed in jeans and sneakers— no heels or excessive primping required.*

O CON *Not all the fathers who are there with their kids will be single. To avoid an awkward situation, check for wedding rings before you make the first move.*

---

573. **THE ZOO**

$ $

If you like animals, take an afternoon stroll through your local zoo. If you spot a guy staring at the monkey cage solo, chances are good that he is single. And watching animals could be a great conversation starter for the two of you.

---

574. **AQUARIUM**

$ $

A city aquarium can be a fascinating way to spend an afternoon. As you gaze at the tanks, you are bound to see creatures you've never seen before. And you might see some interesting men you've never seen before as well—men who enjoy learning about sea animals as much as you do. Smart, ambitious single guys generally don't spend an afternoon alone at home in front of the TV—instead, they head to a place like the city aquarium. So in between tanks, keep your eyes open for guys walking around solo; you may find someone just as captivating as the tiger shark.

---

575. **WATER PARK**

$ $

Nothing will throw you back to the carefree, joyous days of your childhood quicker than a fast ride down a twisting waterslide. So grab a younger family member or a fun girlfriend and head to the water park on a summer Saturday. Guys you meet there are guaranteed to be fun-loving. Just make sure you hold on to your bathing suit. Water slides are notorious for accidental wardrobe malfunctions.

---

576. **CHRISTMAS TREE FARM**

$ $

Just because you live alone doesn't mean you can't enjoy a large, natural Christmas tree during the holidays. And to ensure you get a fresh tree for a reasonable price, your best bet is to head to your local Christmas tree farm. As a single female, you may need some help picking out the perfect tree and getting that tree onto your car to take home . . . help from one of the strapping tree guys at the farm. Beyond the farm employees, you may also find your single male Christmas-spirited counterpart browsing for the ideal tree for his house or apartment.

577. ONE-YEAR-OLD'S BIRTHDAY PARTY

If you've got friends with kids, you are guaranteed to get some invitations to a one-year-old's birthday parties. You may resist, thinking it will be like a scene out of *Romper Room*, but think again. At age one, kids don't even know what a birthday is, so the majority of the guests will be the parents' friends . . . some of whom may be single. In fact, these parties are perfect—usually during the day, so there's no obligation to stay all night. And if you meet a guy you find interesting, the two of you can make plans for dinner.

○ PRO *These parties will attract single guys who aren't threatened or turned off by parties involving children.*

○ CON *There will be some kids, and a few of them might cry. If you are not a baby person, bring your patience.*

578. ORCHARD

Whether it's to pick apples in the fall or peaches in the summer, a trip to an orchard is a pleasant one. If you have a young niece or nephew, grab him or her, or go with a friend or by yourself. On a nice weekend day, some orchards are hopping, especially in the fall. As you search for the perfect fruit, keep an eye out for the perfect fruit picker, too, in the form of a guy without a female counterpart.

579. DANCE RECITAL

If you've been invited to go to your niece's or friend's daughter's dance recital, go. Not just for the joy of watching little girls perform . . . but potentially to meet proud uncles, godfathers, or male family friends. Only a sweet and sensitive guy would give up a Friday night to watch a dance recital. So in between songs, keep your eye out for solo guys in the audience.

580. TAKING YOUR FATHER OUT ON FATHER'S DAY

On Father's Day, most restaurants are packed with sons and daughters who, in addition to or instead of the standard tie, have decided to take Dad out for a nice meal. Granted, your attention should primarily be on your dad on this day, but if you spot a nice son and his dad waiting for a table, don't hesitate to be friendly. If you hit it off with the son, you will already have met one or both of his parents! And hey, if you are close to your dad, maybe he could make a great wing man.

=Time =Friends $=Expense

581. HALLOWEEN PARADE

For some wholesome fun with your neighbors, grab a few friends and a chair and hit the curbside for your annual Halloween parade. While you're there, check out what your town has to offer—both in Halloween creativity and single guys. Pay particular attention to the volunteer firefighters and other local volunteer organization floats. That way, if you spot someone who catches your eye, you will know where to track him down.

582. THE NUTCRACKER SUITE

OK, most of the men you see at a production of the *Nutcracker* are either on the ballet board of directors or they were dragged there by a woman in their lives. For your sake, let's hope they were dragged by a mother or sister, not a wife. Either way, most *Nutcracker* productions offer an intermission where the audience can mingle over food and drinks—the perfect opportunity to get to know a guy better who caught your eye during the "Dance of the Sugarplum Fairy."

O PRO *Men or no men, the Nutcracker will put you in the holiday spirit.*

O CON *This isn't the most guy-filled event, but there will probably be at least a few. Plus, around the holidays (which is when this show is usually put on), tickets can be pricey.*

583. PIANO RECITAL

If you've been invited to go to a musically gifted child's piano recital, go. Not just for the joy of watching young musicians perform . . . but potentially to meet proud uncles, godfathers, or male family friends as well. In between songs, keep your eye out for solo guys in the audience and talk to them over punch and cookies afterward.

584. CHRISTMAS CAROLING

Nothing will put you into the holiday spirit faster than an evening full of Christmas caroling. And when it comes to meeting men, caroling offers multiple possibilities: There are your fellow carolers, and then there are the guys who open the door to hear you sing (which can be embarrassing if your voice isn't exactly American Idol worthy). Either way, don't overlook Christmas caroling as an opportunity for some romance . . . just in time for Christmas.

=Time ✦=Friends $=Expense

585. SCOUTS MEETINGS

While being a scout leader is a time-consuming commitment that can be considered less-than-fun by even the most caring mothers, aunts, or family friends, scout troops are often looking for extra help for a meeting because of a field trip or a particular arts and crafts project that may require more than one person older than the age of ten. So the next time your daughter, son, niece, or nephew is looking for an adult to help out at a scout meeting, consider going. You could find yourself making a birdcage out of popsicle sticks with a handsome single father or uncle.

586. PLAY DATE

If you have children or if you have a friend who has children, don't underestimate the power of the play date for meeting single dads. While your kids frolic on the playground, you can get to know the single dads better and decide if you would like to schedule a date of your own.

O PRO *You will know he has experience with children.*

O CON *Not all men who go on play dates with their kids are single. The Mr. Mom thing has become increasingly popular.*

587. THEME PARK

Whether it's Disney, where you can feel like a kid again, or Six Flags, where you can enjoy the rides, a trip to a theme park puts everyone in a good mood. For a fun day, grab a friend or a niece or nephew and head to the theme park closest to you. On a Saturday in the summer, theme parks are packed with people of all ages, including some single guys with their friends or nieces or nephews. If you are with an odd number of people, try to get in line for the roller coaster near an attractive theme-park goer. You may just get to sit with him . . .

O PRO *If you meet someone, your relationship will be off to a very fun start.*

O CON *Motion sickness. No matter how cute he is, if you get motion sick, don't follow him onto any rides that spin.*

588. LITTLE LEAGUE GAMES

They're not just for parents anymore. Single relatives often attend Little League games. The entertainment is on the field, but there's nothing wrong with making some new friends in the stands. Often, there are young, single coaches who still get involved for the love of the game. If you know from the beginning that they enjoy both kids and sports, you're already ahead in the count.

589. TOY STORES

Chances are you've had to run to the toy store to buy gifts for nieces, nephews, and friends. Or if you're a single parent, you've been there for your kids. But if you want to meet a man, visit a toy store around the holidays. All kinds of people are browsing the aisles looking for the right gift. Just because someone's buying a toy, it doesn't mean he's a parent—and even if he is, he could be divorced. This is yet another way to bump into someone in a fun way. Pick up a toy and play with it. See if the guy in your aisle reacts.

○ PRO *A fun flashback to your youth.*

○ CON *Toy stores can be a hideout for immature guys.*

590. CHUCK E. CHEESE

It's all about kids having fun. But just think of all the single dads out there who have their son or daughter for the weekend and want to make sure they have the time of their lives. They're at Chuck E. Cheese! Grab your niece, nephew, or your friend and her little one and go! Or, if you have a child of your own, even better. You will find single men who know how to spoil their son or daughter (those quarters for the arcade games add up). Just think, they could be spoiling you next! To find one near you, visit *www.chuckecheese.com*.

591. YOUR PARENTS

Your mom and/or dad know more people than you realize. And they know *you* better than you realize. Maybe Dad's golfing buddy or Mom's friend from work really are good catches. Talk to your parents and tell them not to go overboard, but that you're just wondering who they know—and if any of their connections are attractive, successful men. You never know unless you ask.

○ PRO *You won't have to worry about them approving.*

○ CON *This one, in principle, may bother you.*

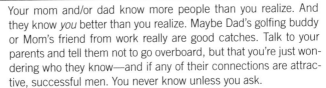
=Time ♦=Friends $=Expense

592. BAT MITZVAH

If you are Jewish or have Jewish friends, you have probably celebrated a few 13-year-old female birthday parties in the form of bat mitzvahs. Because they draw such a broad mix of friends, relatives, and acquaintances, these events provide an opportunity to mix and mingle with men of all ages and backgrounds. So the next time you receive an invitation to a bat mitzvah, don't pass it up. Put on your most stylish dress and go.

593. CHAPERONING A SCHOOL EVENT

If you have children, you will kill two birds with one stone by chaperoning a field trip. One, by participating in the event, you will make your son or daughter very happy. And two, you could meet a handsome single male teacher or a nice single dad who also offered his time to join the trip to Washington, DC, a natural history museum, or the petting zoo.

594. COLD STONE CREAMERY

Almost everyone loves ice cream, and when you can mix up your own creations, even better. That's why so many people—men included—are flocking to the more than 1,300 Cold Stone Creameries around the country. You can choose one of the original creations, such as Cheesecake Fantasy or Birthday Cake Re-mix, or you can create your own using the mix of tasty toppings, sauces, and ice cream flavors. As a conversation starter, ask the cutie behind you in line what he plans to mix up . . . then ask him if he'd like to sit down and chat while you enjoy your delicious creations. To find your nearest Cold Stone Creamery, go to *www.coldstonecreamery.com*.

595. NEIGHBORHOOD BLOCK PARTY

Considering our hectic lifestyles, most of us don't get to know our neighbors as well as we should. Neighbors are worth getting to know—you might hit it off with one, or a friendly neighbor may introduce you to his friend, brother, or uncle. And you never know when you may run out of flour or milk in the middle of a snowstorm. Either way, if your neighborhood sponsors block parties, by all means, get involved. And if it doesn't, consider organizing one yourself. To get started, type up a flyer asking for people's interest and drop one on every doorstep in your block. Even if the party never comes together, you might meet some nice new acquaintances.

=Time =Friends $=Expense

596.	**PLAYGROUND**

If you have children, your local playground is the perfect place to meet people for potential play dates . . . and to meet single dads for potential real dates. So as you play with your children, nieces, or nephews, keep your eyes peeled for dads without partners. At the playground, it's perfectly socially acceptable to be just as bold as you were when you were little—just walk right up and introduce yourself.

O PRO *If nothing more, you could meet a nice friend who also has children.*

O CON *Sketchy men. If you spot a man hanging around the playground without children of his own, steer clear.*

597.	**BAR MITZVAH**

If you are Jewish or have Jewish friends, you will no doubt attend a few bar mitzvahs. Although these events celebrate the coming of age of a 13-year-old boy (way too young for you!), they provide an opportunity to mix and mingle with brothers, uncles, dads, and friends of all ages.

O PRO *Bar mitzvahs usually include dinner, dancing, and an open bar—great forums for meeting men.*

O CON *If you are Catholic and looking for a man of the same faith, a bar mitzvah will be a crap shoot.*

598.	**CORN MAZE**

As fall sets in and Halloween approaches, corn mazes start popping up in rural areas. Not only do these mazes offer a challenging, fun, and sometimes spooky outdoor experience, they also attract men with their kids, nieces, or nephews, and if they are extra young-at-heart, just themselves.

O PRO *Corn mazes are a wonderful activity to share with your children if you are a single parent.*

O CON *If you live in New York City or a similar metropolitan area, you may have to drive a few hours to get to one.*

599.   MINIATURE GOLF

$

If you're not so great on 18 long holes, why not go for 18 shorties . . . complete with clowns and windmills to aim your ball at? No matter what your age, mini golf is a fun outing, and it tends to draw an equal mix of both men and women. If you have kids (and even if you don't), this is a great place to go scope for single dads and guys who aren't afraid to throw a little fun into their golf.

600.   PICK-YOUR-OWN STRAWBERRY PATCH

$

While you might not find too many single men alone or with their buddies at a pick-your-own strawberry patch, you may find some single dads or men who have volunteered to take a niece or nephew for the day. So if you have children, take them for a nice sunny afternoon of strawberry picking and make sure you look past the leaves to see who's picking around you. If you don't have children, take a girlfriend and catch up as the two of you fill your baskets with berries. Even if you don't leave with any phone numbers, you'll have a tasty and healthy addition to your next few bowls of cereal.

601.   CHOCOLATE FACTORY

$ $

There's a reason Casanova used chocolate in place of champagne to woo his women . . . it contains compounds that mimic the physiological response we get when we're in love. So at a chocolate factory, where the aroma of chocolate and the little samples are plentiful, you may just catch a man at the perfect moment. Chocolate factories are a great place to take your kids (they will feel like they've jumped into Willy Wonka's factory), and therefore they are a hot spot for single dads. Or, you might find a guy who loves chocolate so much he wants to explore how it's made. Either way, this is a guaranteed fun trip.

Five great chocolate factories:
1. Hershey's Chocolate World, Hershey, PA: *www.hersheys.com*
2. Ghirardelli Square, San Francisco, CA: *www.ghirardellisq.com*
3. Scharffen Berger, Berkeley, CA: *www.scharffenberger.com*
4. Whetstone Chocolates, St. Augustine, FL: *www.whetstone chocolates.com*
5. Lake Champlain Chocolates, Burlington, VT: *www.lake champlainchocolates.com*

602. KIDS' LEMONADE STAND

The next time you pass by kids selling lemonade, buy a cup. It will only set you back a few cents, and it will probably be refreshing on a hot day. Beyond that, it will make the kids happy. And if they have a single father, it will make him happy. Plus, you may happen to pull up to the stand for a glass at the same time as a nice single man . . . and you will know right away that he has a sensitive nature.

603. BOTANICAL GARDENS

Did you know that vanilla comes from an orchid plant? If you take a trip to the New York Botanical Garden or other botanical garden in the country you can learn many other fascinating factoids about flowering plants. And along with the gorgeous flowers, you can check out the single men who are there with their children, moms, sisters, or by themselves.

Five great botanical gardens:
1. The New York Botanical Garden: *www.nybg.org*
2. The Missouri Botanical Garden: *www.mobot.org*
3. Denver Botanic Garden: *www.botanicgardens.org*
4. Atlanta Botanical Garden: *www.atlantabotanicalgarden.org*
5. San Antonio Botanical Garden: *www.sabot.org*

604. EASTER EGG HUNT

Unless you don't celebrate Easter, surely you remember the days of charging into an open field with your basket in hand and scooping up as many dyed eggs as possible in order to win the chocolate bunny or other Easter prize. As an adult, you may get as much fun out of an egg hunt by watching kids go for it. So if you have kids of your own or nieces and nephews, head out to the local egg hunt on Easter morning. You never know what good sport is hiding under the bunny costume or how many single dads have volunteered for the egg hunt this year.

605. THROUGH YOUR KIDS

If you have grown children and have found yourself single again in your middle-aged years, consider using your children as a means to meet men. After all, your kids can be a window to their friends' parents, their teachers, their professors, their coworkers . . . the list goes on and on. Casually mention to your son and/or daughter that you are looking to meet someone special and he or she will probably get going on a search. After all, kids want their parents to be happy.

=Time =Friends $=Expense

606. CANDY STORE

It may seem a little old fashioned, but there is just something really sweet (no pun intended) about a couple meeting in a candy shop. And although they are fairly few in number, there are still some quaint candy shops in smaller towns and cities across the country. If you have a sweet tooth, pop into the candy shop in your area now and then for some fresh candy and potentially, a fresh man. A thoughtful guy will think of candy when it comes time to buy a gift for his mother, sister, friend, secretary, or other women in his life and therefore, head to a candy shop.

O PRO *In addition to gaining a tasty treat, you will support a mom-and-pop shop in your neighborhood.*

O CON *Men also shop for candy for their wives—check for rings.*

607. DAYCARE

If you are a single working mom, a great daycare center can be a lifesaver. And there are probably a few single dads who feel exactly the same way about your particular daycare. So instead of rushing in the morning and dropping your kids off at the last minute, give yourself some extra time to leisurely walk into the daycare and see the parents of the children your kids share toys with on a daily basis. And if you don't spot any single dads on your own, ask the people working at the daycare if they know of any available dads in the bunch—most people love to play matchmaker.

608. PETTING ZOO

If you have children in your life—either your own, nieces and nephews, or friends' kids—take them to a petting zoo for the day. With the pony rides, and up close and personal views of sheep, llamas, and other pettable animals, the kids will have a memorable day. And with the single dads strolling around on a busy summer Sunday, so might you.

O PRO *The interactive nature of the petting zoo makes it easy to meet the fellow adults in the ring.*

O CON *E coli: Make sure you and the kids scrub your hands upon your departure.*

609. DISNEY ON ICE

If you have young children in your life—your own, a sibling's, or a friend's—you know how much they love Disney. Nothing will make kids more excited than a trip to Disney on Ice. And with all the uncles and single dads in the arena, you may get some entertainment of your own. Hang out for a few minutes in the lobby and at the snack stand to see what the event has to offer in the way of audience members. To find a show near you, visit *http://disney .go.com/disneyonice*.

610. MAKE YOUR OWN SUNDAE BAR

Audrey B. from New York, New York, met her husband at a make-your-own sundae bar at a wedding. "As we went through the line, I noticed we were putting all the same toppings on our ice cream. I turned and introduced myself to him and we ended up hanging out for the rest of the night . . . and the rest of our lives." Although make-your-own sundae bars aren't on every corner, you can find them in some buffet-style restaurants and as Audrey proved, they are great icebreakers.

611. BABYSITTING

If your sister, brother, or friend asks you to take their kids for the day, jump on it. After all, it is an opportunity. Make it a full day of fun for the kids and take them to places you would never normally go—the playground, the kiddie pool, or the amusement park, for instance—and you will expose yourself to a whole new batch of men in the form of uncles and single fathers.

612. DINOSAUR EXHIBIT

At some point in their lives, most men were fascinated by dinosaurs. Whether they're young enough to have watched *Jurassic Park* as children, or they simply lived out their dinosaur fantasy with rubber figurines, in between Nintendo, G.I. Joe, and/or riding bikes, dinosaurs probably made their way in. So naturally, you will find many men at a dinosaur exhibit at a museum—either by themselves, with a few friends, or with their children. So for your children, for your own education, and to potentially meet a man interested in science and prehistoric creatures, check out a dinosaur exhibit. A lot of dinosaur exhibits are traveling, so type "dinosaur exhibit" into any search engine to find the closest one to you.

=Time =Friends $=Expense

613.   ICE CREAM PARLOR

There is something innocent and romantic about an ice cream parlor, and the delicious ice cream is an added bonus! It's not the most obvious place to meet people, but it is possible. Take it from Lisa, age 31, "I was at the boardwalk in New Jersey doing a little late summer shopping, and I got a craving for some ice cream. Waiting in line behind me was the last person I expected to see—a cute single guy! I went with the custard cone with sprinkles and he went for one without sprinkles. We started talking and 45 minutes later, we had exchanged phone numbers. I was happy that I had an ice cream craving that day!"

O PRO *It is socially acceptable to go to an ice cream parlor alone.*

O CON *Unless you want to gain a few pounds or love nonfat yogurt, you should probably limit your trips to the ice cream parlor.*

614.   COUNTY FAIR

If you live in a rural area, there is bound to be a county fair once a year that offers a showcase of farm animals, quilts, prize-winning vegetables, food, and music. So you might as well grab a girlfriend—or heck, go alone—for an afternoon full of county fair fun. You may snag yourself a nice, single farm boy, or you may meet someone who, like yourself, was just looking to check out some blue-ribbon sheep. Just beware: These fairs tend to bring the strangest of the strange out of the woodwork, but at least you will get a chance to do some quality people-watching.

615.   PUMPKIN PATCH

When the air starts to chill in the first days of fall, you can't help but get that nostalgic urge to eat candy corn and carve a pumpkin. So why not do both? Grab a girlfriend, or a niece or nephew, and head to your local pumpkin patch to pick out your gourd of choice. You just might find a like-minded guy there with one of his friends, nieces, or nephews who loves fall just as much as you do.

616. FAMILY REUNION

$

Some family reunions draw huge groups of people, including friends of family members—potential guys for you to meet and hit it off with.

O PRO *Family reunions usually involve a lot of interactive games that get people talking and mingling, such as horseshoes, volleyball, etc.*

O CON *There is always the danger that you will be related to someone you potentially could be interested in and not know it—make sure you research the family tree before things go too far.*

617. MINIATURE BOWLING

$ $

For a different activity, grab a niece, a nephew, or a fun friend and do some miniature bowling (also called duck bowling). Miniature bowling alleys are increasing in popularity and provide fun for all ages. Scan the alley for nice guys who've offered to take a child or two in their lives out for an afternoon or evening of miniature bowling fun. If you can, sit near one of them and see what happens—if you're feeling bold, offer up a friendly match.

618. SINGLE PARENTS SUPPORT GROUP

$

Those of you with children know, number one, how hard it is to be a single parent, and, number two, how hard it is to balance kids and a dating life. If you meet a guy in a single parents' support group, you'll know he has children and understands this juggling act. Plus, there will be no guessing—both of you are there because you are single and you have kids.

619. FLYING A REMOTE CONTROL PLANE

If single dads are your thing (or you're not intimidated by a man with a son), head to the remote control plane flying area with a nephew or friend's son on a weekend afternoon. You will see many dad/son combinations living out their dreams of flying with a small joystick and a miniature plane . . . and some of those dads are bound to be single.

620. PARENTS WITHOUT PARTNERS

Whether you are divorced or have never been married, if you are a single parent, you will find comfort, support, and maybe, a single dad with whom you can spend the rest of your life at Parents Without Partners. Parents Without Partners prides itself on providing single parents with an opportunity to make friends and share parenting techniques. There are thousands of Parents Without Partners members in the approximately 200 chapters in the United States and Canada, and ages range from eighteen to eighty. For more information, check out *www.parentswithoutpartners.org.*

 =Time ♦=Friends $=Expense

everydayways

621. THE BANK

The bank can be a fabulous place to meet men. In most cases, you have to stand in line—the perfect opportunity to make friends with someone who banks at your branch. And most people who go to the bank have at least a few bucks to their name, so you won't have to worry about whether the guys you meet there are totally broke.

⊙ PRO *If you go to the bank at a busy time, like after work on Friday, you will have plenty of chances to meet people in line.*

⊙ CON *The icebreaker line in this situation could be tough. Guys are very wary of gold diggers, so saying something like, "What brings you here?" or "Come here often?" could be a fast crash and burn.*

622. COFFEEHOUSE

These days, people go to coffeehouses for many different reasons—to study, to read, to get a nice espresso buzz, and to meet fellow coffee lovers. The caffeine makes you chatty and the atmosphere makes you relaxed—the perfect combination for approaching the handsome guy a few tables away. And some coffeehouses are adding props to their venues as well, including games, used books, live music, or even poetry readings. All of which draw nice, sensitive, coffee-sipping men.

⊙ PRO *Coffeehouses are on nearly every corner these days, and they are frequented by single guys.*

⊙ CON *Coffee breath can be a turnoff. Be sure to spring for the curiously strong mint tin if you're planning on flirting.*

623. PLACE OF WORSHIP

Your local place of worship can be a good, safe place to meet men. There is one important rule with this one, however: It's fine if you were a member of the church before, or if you joined because of spiritual reasons. It is not so fine, however, if you joined the church with the sole purpose of meeting a man. Church is one place that is not acceptable—morally or socially—to attend purely for the purpose of widening your social circle or dating possibilities.

⊙ PRO *You will know for sure that a man you meet in church has the same religious beliefs as yourself.*

⊙ CON *If the church is strict, any casual dates you have with fellow members may be frowned upon.*

624. AT THE CONDIMENT BAR AT A COFFEE PLACE

Real men aren't afraid to order a latte, and they're not afraid to put a little extra cream and sugar in it. So sidle up to the guy at the condiment bar and ask him what his coffee drink of choice is—maybe he will want to share his next one with you!

○ **PRO** *A lot of coffeehouses attract regulars so if you don't work up the nerve to talk to him the first time, you can return at the same time a different day and hope to bump into him.*

○ **CON** *Many guys take their coffee black, so they might not be at the condiment bar any longer than it takes to grab a coffee cozy.*

625. DOCTOR'S OFFICE

OK, you may not be feeling your most outgoing when you are sitting in your doctor's waiting room with the flu or after throwing up all night, but if you're just there for a routine visit or a relatively innocuous condition, your doctor's office waiting room could be an ideal place to meet a man. First, unless your doctor is unusually efficient, you are bound to be stuck in the waiting room with fellow patients for a minimum of 30 minutes—a great opportunity to put down the *Glamour* and strike up a conversation. Second, a guy in a doctor's office waiting room is less likely to be wary of doctors (in other words, less likely to be a stubborn tough guy).

○ **PRO** *If a man is at a doctor's office, it means he is conscious about his health and not above or afraid of going to the doctor, as some men are.*

○ **CON** *He could be there for something contagious, such as herpes, lice, or a genital fungus.*

626. THE GROCERY STORE

As you shop for your groceries for the upcoming week, you can also take a look around for a man. Among the seafood and frozen foods, there are single guys attempting to plan meals for themselves, often single men who cook! A great conversation starter at the grocery store is the food itself. So if you spot a single guy perusing the tropical fruits, for example, say something like, "Excuse me, I'm looking for plantains—have you seen them?"

627.   LAUNDROMAT

There is a natural cycle that goes along with washing your colors and whites, a cycle that involves about an hour and a half of down time for you to fill with a good book, work . . . or socializing with the handsome fellow laundry-doer a few orange plastic chairs down. If you live in a city, the Laundromats are full of single men washing their sheets and boxers. So even if you have a washer and dryer in your home or building, take your laundry out for a spin once in a while and see who you bump into.

○ PRO *Laundromats lend themselves to striking up conversations with strangers because everyone is killing time between loads.*

○ CON *If you realize mid-conversation that the handsome stranger is not so interesting to talk to, you're stuck there for at least 30 to 60 minutes.*

628.   THE MALL

Whether you are in the market for some new stuff or you just feel like taking an indoor stroll while doing some good, old-fashioned people-watching, the mall can be a great place to meet men. Even the guys who hate shopping have to suck it up and do it once in a while, and they will be appreciative of any help they can get from a friendly, fellow single shopper. So in addition to bargains and the latest fads, keep your eyes peeled for guys the next time you walk the mall. And if you spot a guy who appears stumped in front of a shirt rack, politely offer to help him make a decision.

○ PRO *At the mall, you can combine exercise, shopping, and man searching.*

○ CON *If you frequent the mall, you may end up spending too much money. Keep your mall man-shopping to a frequency level you can afford.*

629.   OUT ALONE

It may sound crazy and scary, but your chances of meeting a guy may be better if you leave your girlfriends at home. For one reason, some men are intimidated by groups of women, and your dream guy may be less likely to approach you if you are surrounded by your friends. Plus, because you are solo, you will be more likely to be at your most outgoing. You don't have to go out by yourself every night, but every once in a while, head out to your favorite restaurant or martini bar by yourself . . . you will be surprised at how many single guys are doing the same.

○ PRO *You can make your own itinerary—go home whenever you feel tired, eat when you are hungry, and so on.*

○ CON *Going out alone isn't without its risks, so street smarts are in order. Never leave with someone you've just met, and stay in public, visible places.*

630.   RENTING A MOVIE

If you see a guy perusing the aisles at Blockbuster or Hollywood Video on a Friday night, he might as well have the word "dateless" stamped across his forehead . . . or maybe he is just happily independent. Either way, he is most likely available. To break the ice, join him in the aisle of his choice (unless it is the adult aisle—too much too soon) and ask him what he's seen lately that he liked. Who knows—the two of you may be enjoying a rented flick together.

631.   THE BEACH

The relaxed, carefree atmosphere at the beach is perfect for approaching a guy who catches your eye . . . and there are plenty that will. Lifeguards, surfers, sunbathers—the beach is teeming with tan, good-looking men.

○ PRO *If you are a beach lover, you will have a wonderful day whether or not it includes a new guy.*

○ CON *If you are uncomfortable showing your skin, you will have to get over it and put on a swimming suit.*

632. CHANGING A TIRE

Ever see a guy standing next to his car with a flat tire on the highway . . . looking helpless? Surprisingly (because they would never admit it), there are a number of men out there who have never changed a tire. So if you do know how to do it, you can lend the poor guy a hand. Just be cautious with this one—only stop to help if the guy in distress is in a well-lit, public place.

633. CONVENIENCE STORE

If there is a convenience store close to where you live, you probably frequent it more often than you'd like. Somehow it seems worth it to spend an extra dollar on each item when the store is within walking distance . . . and it's likely that your neighbors feel the same way. So if you don't have the nerve to approach the attractive guy standing in front of the ice cream pints one day, you may see him again soon. And if you don't, convenience store employees are clued in on more about their customers than you'd think. Slip the girl at the register your phone number or business card and ask her to give it to your ice cream guy the next time he comes in.

634. FAVORITE RESTAURANT

If you head to your favorite restaurant by yourself on a Friday night, you will be guaranteed at least one important thing: A really good meal. Glance around for men who are dining alone as well. It may be more than a coincidence that you both love the same cuisine and decided to indulge in it on the same evening. Take a chance: Flag his server and send him a whatever-he's-having on you.

635. THE GYM

Gyms are full of fit, friendly, driven, and successful people; and in most gyms, at least half of them are men. In general, guys like girls who are in good shape. (Healthy good shape, not pin-up good shape.) Plus, gyms are social gathering places where people make friends, meet exercise partners, and sometimes head out for a drink or a bite to eat after a tough session.

○ **PRO** *Even if you don't meet a guy at the gym, your self-esteem will probably improve as your physique does, upping your chances of meeting men in all situations.*

○ **CON** *Gym memberships can be expensive. Shop around your area to find the best deal.*

=Time =Friends $=Expense

636.	IN THE RICE AISLE AT THE SUPERMARKET

You are shopping for rice. He is shopping for rice. You both like rice—it could be the beginning of a beautiful relationship. So as you are deciding between a long-grain wild and a hearty brown rice to accompany the dish you are planning to cook that night, be friendly to the fellow rice shopper in your aisle. You may end up ditching the meal altogether and going out for a bite . . . with your rice man. Andrea met her boyfriend, Jonny, this way. "He called me out on the fact that I was checking him out when I was picking up some rice for dinner. We joked about it, and two years later, we own a house together!"

637.	STARBUCKS

A recent survey showed that Starbucks is the new bar scene. And the coffee drinks at Starbucks are worth the extra few bucks. Starbucks is brimming with single men looking for a caffeine buzz, and the relaxed yet upbeat atmosphere is bound to lead to some great conversation. To improve your chances of meeting someone, plop down at one of the tall bistro tables at a busy time and keep an eye out for an attractive man who needs a seat. Another opportunity? At the pickup stand as you wait for your latte—it will give a whole new meaning to "pick up."

638.	ON THE SUBWAY

You're already smushed up against the passenger next to you, so if he seems like he might be a nice, eligible bachelor, why not strike up a conversation? For one, from your proximity, you know he is free of body odor, and for two, some chitchat will be a refreshing change from the typical solemn atmosphere.

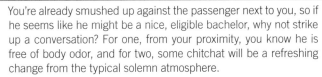

PRO *If he's riding the subway, there's a good chance he lives in your city.*

CON *If you want to get to know each other better, your conversation will have to be brief and to the point.*

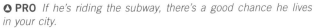

=Time =Friends $=Expense

639. IN TRAFFIC

Ever glanced over at the car next to you at a stoplight and been instantly attracted to the guy behind the wheel . . . only to have him drive forward while you make a left, never to see each other again? Well thanks to a new Web site, you may be able to hook up with those elusive traffic hunks after all. At *http://flirtingintraffic. com,* you can obtain a flirtingintraffic sticker and ID number, so the next time you hit it off with someone through a windshield or window, your ID number will be available to him so he can hook up with you online. And if you are lucky enough to spot an ID on his car, you can do the same.

○ PRO *It's a brilliant concept! And if you have ever experienced a sunken heart as you watched the potential love of your life drive away, you can have better luck next time.*

○ CON *This is a relatively new concept and will only be effective if more and more flirtatious drivers catch on.*

640. ON A TRAIN

Whether it's a commuter train that you ride daily for 30 minutes or an overnight car on which you have your own cabin for the night, a train can be the perfect starting point for romance. For one, you and the potential single man of your dreams are both stuck on the same moving vessel for a period of time, so you might as well chat. On a commuter train, you are likely to see the same men repeatedly day after day; so in case you don't have the nerve right away, you will have multiple chances to make your move. And on an overnight train, there is the notorious food and bar car where you can enjoy a snack and scope the scene.

641. WALKING YOUR DOG

If you have a dog, you know all too well that man's best friend loves to meet other dogs. So instead of dreading the leash bracing and scolding that sometimes goes along with a walk down a heavily dog-populated street, embrace your dog's outgoing nature and use him or her as a means to break the ice with a dog-walking single man. You will know you have at least one (important) thing in common—a love of animals.

642. THE VET'S OFFICE

If "animal lover" is one of your requirements for a mate, the waiting room at your veterinarian's office is an ideal place to meet him. And at the vet's office, you can determine whether he is a cat person or a dog person even before you exchange your first words.

○ PRO *If he's at the vet's office, he obviously has a pet, which indicates patience and sensitivity.*

○ CON *He could be there with the "family" pet—check for wedding rings or references to wives or girlfriends.*

643. BAKERY

Now and then, it's delightful to get something fresh from your local bakery—be it a cinnamon bun or cheese Danish on a Sunday morning, or a half-dozen cream cheese cupcakes just for the heck of it. Because they are so good, these bakeries are often swarmed by people with the same idea as you—to satisfy their sweet tooth. So instead of rolling your eyes in annoyance at the line as you wait, use it as an opportunity to chat with the guy next to you. You have the perfect question to break the ice: "What's your favorite here?"

○ PRO *Guys with a sweet tooth are usually on the sweet and sensitive side themselves. Plus, if he's in your neighborhood bakery, chances are he's in your neighborhood.*

○ CON *Regular trips to the bakery could take a toll on your waistline and your health. Keep this one to a minimum of once every few weeks or so.*

644. PHYSICAL THERAPIST'S OFFICE

No one's advocating that you go out and hurt yourself in order to get physical therapy to meet a man. However, if you have a chronic or acute injury, and you find yourself at the physical therapist's rehab room riding a stationary bike or practicing stretching exercises on an exam table or stability ball, take a look around. There are a lot of athletic guys who require some physical therapy now and then. And most sessions in the rehab room take at least an hour—plenty of time for you to get to know some of your fellow recoverees.

645. BUS STOP

You are waiting for the bus. He is waiting for the bus. You are both planning on boarding the bus. Sure, you can keep your nose safely in a book. But you can also be friendly and meet someone you could potentially go out with later that week. So don't be shy as you sit under the protective plastic awning if the person sitting next to you catches your eye.

O PRO *Depending on the length of your bus trip, you can sit next to your bus stop buddy and continue the conversation for a while as you travel . . . and maybe even hang out together at your destination as well.*

O CON *There are always those travelers who prefer not to talk. Don't be hurt if you get the cold shoulder.*

646. CAR WASH

In general, men prefer the do-it-yourself car wash to the drive-thru. So one afternoon when you have a little extra time to spend washing your wheels, opt for the do-it-yourself and take a look around you as you pull into the bay. You'll see men with their cars, which, if you believe that cars reflect a person's personality, will give you an instant indication of whether the two of you will hit it off. So smile at your car-washing neighbors in between the wax and vacuum. There's no telling where it will go.

647. DEPARTMENT OF MOTOR VEHICLES

All drivers have to make the dreaded trip to the DMV for a new driver's license every four years. If you think about it as an opportunity to meet people, it may seem a lot less hellish. So use the long line as a chance to be friendly with the folks standing around you.

O PRO *You can rest assured that someone you meet at the DMV probably has a driver's license.*

O CON *As Seinfeld said, the DMV isn't exactly full of the most beautiful people. In fact, he uttered the term leper colony. Enough said.*

648.   FURNITURE STORE

If you are in the market for a new love seat or dining room table, you may find more than what you are looking for at a furniture store. On a busy Saturday afternoon, furniture stores are brimming with single people—guys included!—looking for a new piece to make their house or apartment feel more like home. If a guy is shopping for furniture solo, it's a near guarantee that he sleeps alone on a regular basis. So strike up a conversation and see if you can put an end to the lonely nights for both of you.

O PRO *New furniture.*

O CON *Nice furniture is a major investment. But you can always just browse . . .*

649.   HEALTH FOOD STORE

This one is a win-win situation. Worst case scenario is that you make a trip to the health food store and leave with a few bags full of nutritious food. Best case scenario is that you also leave with the phone number of a nice man who enjoys amaranth cookies as much as you do. Health food stores are generally not that crowded, so it will feel natural for you to approach a fellow shopper. And you can always break the ice with a question—ask him what his favorite brand of organic pasta is. Or, if an employee catches your eye, ask him what he recommends for a healthful, mid-afternoon snack.

O PRO *Men who carefully watch what they eat are generally responsible and together in other facets of their lives as well.*

O CON *You are going to have to shell out a little more money to fill your cart than you would at your standard grocery store.*

650.   PUMPING GAS

Unless you live in a full-serve-only state like New Jersey, pump your own gas whenever you get the chance. Not only will you save a little per gallon, you will be outside among the other people who prefer to pump their own. As your gas tank fills, you have a few minutes—but only a few minutes—to catch eyes or strike up a conversation with any nearby pumpers who look interesting.

 =Time =Friends $=Expense

651.   ON THE STREET

This doesn't mean you should walk the street, which could be taken the wrong way by some guys. It means that as you walk down the sidewalk, whether you're walking your dog or rushing to get a cup of coffee before you go to work, keep your eyes open. Attempt to make eye contact with the people you pass who look interesting to you . . . you never know who you might "catch eyes" with long enough to stop and talk.

◑ PRO *You will have an unlimited supply of street-walking guys to choose from.*

◑ CON *If you live in a really busy city like New York, you may have trouble getting anyone to make eye contact with you.*

652.   PET SUPPLY STORE

As a proud pooch, kitty, fish, or reptile owner, you most likely hit your local pet store often for gourmet food, new collars, or toys for your pet to enjoy. As you browse for pet items, take a look around. If you spot a single male pet owner doing the same, the two of you may have more than a pet in common; chances are good he spent his last Saturday night next to a furry creature just like you did. To break the ice, ask him what his favorite pet food, pet shampoo, or other pet item is. A conversation about your pets will easily lead to other facets of your life.

◑ PRO *Single guys who own animals tend to be caring and sensitive by nature.*

◑ CON *There's always the chance his girlfriend or wife is at home with the pet, but you never know until you ask.*

653.   SHARING A TAXI

If you find yourself waiting at the same corner with a guy you find interesting, ask him where he is going; if you two are headed in the same direction, offer to share the cab with him. (Even if he's not headed in your direction, you could create a "diversion" to go his way.) There's no telling where it will go . . . even after you two part ways.

◑ PRO *Since the two of you cooperated right off the bat, your relationship (if it goes beyond the cab ride) will be off to a great start.*

◑ CON *If you don't hit it off, this new stranger knows which neighborhood you live in, if not the exact building.*

=Time   =Friends $=Expense

654. STEAK AND SUB SHOP

Men love a good steak sandwich, so naturally, they will flock to the places that make the best ones. And most guys like a low-maintenance girl who enjoys a greasy cheese steak once and a while. If you notice a guy you are interested in, ask him if he'd like to sit down and eat with you.

O PRO *You will probably be way outnumbered by men.*

O CON *You and the men will be chowing down on cheese steaks and subs—not the most romantic atmosphere . . .*

655. WEIGHT WATCHERS

Losing weight with someone is an instant bonding experience. Weight Watchers has been touted as one of the best weight-loss programs out there, both because of the easy-to-follow point system and because of the supportive nature of the Weight Watchers groups. The classes are coed, and people offer lots of support and encouragement to each other. During the weight-loss process, you may meet someone who you have more in common with than a few extra pounds. To celebrate making your goals, ask him to grab a cup of coffee with you after the session. There's no telling where it will go.

O PRO *Your relationship will be based on support and positive reinforcement.*

O CON *There's the potential to fall into a bad-eating pattern together. Make sure you keep up the calorie counting.*

656. SALAD BAR

There are many perks to a salad bar, the two biggest being the selection of make-your-own tasty salad ingredients and the interactive nature of the make-your-own setup. As you piece together a healthful concoction of ingredients, look to your right, left, and in front of you for any health-conscious men doing the same. If you spot someone you'd like to get to know better, comment on his choice of artichokes or feta (whatever the topping may be) as a salad topper and see where it goes.

657. YOUR CHILD'S SCHOOL

If you are a single parent, you certainly aren't alone these days. There are plenty of single dads out there, too. And where better to find a single dad with a child who is the same age as yours than at your son or daughter's school? Unless they are Mr. Moms, the single dads aren't too hard to spot. If you consistently see a father dropping off his daughter or son and attending parents' events alone, he's probably raising the kids alone or Monday through Friday. So (after the kids are safely in the classroom), don't be afraid to introduce yourself.

○ PRO *You have a major lifestyle factor in common.*

○ CON *You will have to take your time when it comes to introducing your kids—kids tend to get attached quickly (especially when there are other kids involved), and if things don't work out, it could be harder on you and on them.*

658. DELI AT THE GROCERY STORE

A great place to find guys who are grabbing something quick for dinner on the way home from work is the grocery store deli. So grab a number and pay attention to the people who are a few digits before you and a few digits behind you. If you can strike up a good conversation in line, the two of you may decide to ditch the cold cuts and go out for something altogether different.

659. CAR DEALERSHIP

Even if you are not seriously shopping for a car, you can stop by a car dealership now and then and check out the new body styles . . . and the guys who actually are seriously shopping for them. There are a lot of successful single guys who choose to spend some of their disposable income on a nice car, and as they browse, they may be attracted to a girl who appears to like the same make of car.

○ PRO *Beyond the car shoppers, there are also the dealers and the finance guys.*

○ CON *If you stop in the same dealership a few times and express no interest in buying, you may get some cold shoulders. Make sure you vary your stops.*

660.   DENTIST'S OFFICE

People who are religious about professional cleanings usually visit the dentist twice a year, spending an estimated hour per year in the waiting room. You could spend that hour with your nose in a *Good Housekeeping* or *Parents* magazine (even though you don't have kids) or you could take a look around you and chat with the fellow religious dental-cleaning clientele waiting their turn.

661.   TANNING SALON

This one cannot be advocated wholeheartedly because of the potential effects on your skin and your health, but if you are the tanning type, you may bump into your male counterpart one Saturday morning as you step out of your booth. Some guys—usually, metrosexual guys or guys who are into bodybuilding—like to stay tan. If either of these types turns you on, you may do well to find one of them at the tanning salon.

○ PRO *These guys will be guaranteed not to be pasty white.*

○ CON *Tanning, especially in tanning beds, has been proven to cause skin cancer. If skin cancer is something you'd like to try to avoid, steer clear of the tanning salon.*

662.   WAL-MART

Wal-Mart provides some great one-stop shopping: You can grab a CD, a case of soda, and some night cream all in the same store. And you can also find single guys roaming the aisles for their own random array of items. For maximum male exposure, hit Wal-Mart after work or on a Saturday or Sunday afternoon.

663.   WAITING FOR TAKEOUT FOOD

Don't feel like cooking? Head to your neighborhood restaurant/bar and peruse the menu for something that sounds good. Be it a veggie pizza, Caesar salad with chicken, or a grilled eggplant sandwich, most restaurant/bars offers some healthful dinner choices. Plus, you will have twenty minutes or so to kill waiting for your food to enjoy a soda, cocktail, or beer at the bar . . . where you are likely to meet successful single guys who decided to do the same.

○ PRO *This is a nice excuse not to cook.*

○ CON *As a single woman sitting at a bar, you could be approached by some weirdos. Be prepared.*

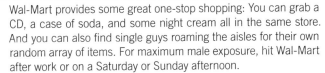

---

664. ELEVATOR

They don't call it an "elevator pitch" for nothing. You have only a few precious moments to get any conversation accomplished in an elevator, so if someone catches your eye, you both have to move quickly. The elevator is a good "safe" spot because, if you are in a building or hotel you hardly ever go to, you have nothing to lose. If you get rejected, you'll never see the person again. If, however, you are in the elevator in your work building, you may risk an uncomfortable elevator ride some time in the future. But hey—you only live once. So don't be afraid to hand your card to a handsome stranger as you approach your destination floor.

---

665. WHOLE FOODS (OR SIMILAR SUPERMARKET)

"Where would a successful single man go at the end of a workday if he was too tired to cook and had no one to cook dinner with?" asks Karen Jones, president of the Heart Matters. "He would go to the prepared food section of a nice grocery store." So on your way home from work, grab a cup of coffee, sit down, watch the guys pick out their dinner, and pick out the one you like.

○ PRO *While you are there, you can get a nice prepared meal for yourself . . . and maybe you can sit down with someone and eat together.*

○ CON *Timing is crucial with this one. As Jones mentioned, if you don't hit the grocery store at the end of the workday, it may not be worth your time.*

---

666. NAIL SALON

There are more and more guys out there who care about the details of their appearance. These "metrosexual" guys are waxing their backs and eyebrows, getting their nails done, and more. If you like a well-groomed guy, you just might spot him the next time your feet are soaking pre-pedicure. So instead of burying your nose in the latest *Marie Claire*, look around you and get to know the guys there. You just might end up with a boyfriend you can take to the spa with you on a Saturday afternoon—talk about the best of both worlds!

667.   CAR REPAIR WAITING ROOM

$ $

Sometimes, when you just need an oil change and tire rotation, it's better to just wait it out instead of getting a loaner car or a ride. And even if you are having more done, you may want to spend some time in the waiting room to see who you meet. If you are in the market for a man with a 9 to 5 job, schedule your repair or maintenance for a Saturday morning.

○ PRO *You'll save the expense of a loner car; plus, some of these waiting rooms today are equipped with TVs, computers, and magazines, so you won't be bored.*

○ CON *If you're having extensive work done, you may have to kill six hours or more. In the event that you don't meet a great guy, bring a book.*

668.   GREETING CARD STORE

You may spend 20 minutes or more in a card store on the hunt for a card that reflects what you are trying to say. While you are there, look around you for any men doing the same . . . and pay attention to the section they are in. For example, if a guy is struggling to find an anniversary or romantic birthday card, move on—he's attached. But if he's looking in the father, mother, brother, sister, or other section, the chances are better that he's single. And if he's taking his time to find a good card, that's a good clue that he is sensitive and caring. To break the ice, you can say, "It's so hard to find a good card, isn't it?"

669.   DELI

$ $

If you work near a deli, particularly a deli that serves sandwiches notoriously packed with ham or turkey, it is in your best interest to patronize that deli at least once a week for lunch. Why? Most men love a sandwich packed full of meat, so this establishment is bound to be a lunchtime hot spot for guys—whether they work in a nearby office or are painting a building in the area. And because of the crowd, you may be forced (oh darn!) to share a table with an attractive stranger. Michelle P. from Allentown, Pennsylvania, is living proof that delis can be hot spots for romance: She met her man in a deli known for its "Hog" sandwiches stuffed with meat and cheese.

○ PRO *If you are a vegetarian, most delis offer veggie sandwiches.*

○ CON *Lunch hours don't leave you with much time to get to know someone—you will just have to quickly exchange phone numbers.*

=Time   **†**=Friends $=Expense

670. ESCALATOR AT THE MALL

As you ride to the second floor of shops, you have 60 seconds or so to smile at the handsome stranger a few steps up or down from you and see where it goes. If he is carrying a bag, you can comment on the store name written on it by asking him "Are they having any good sales there?" or "Do they have some good stuff now?" If all goes well, you may find yourself sharing a coffee or a Cinnabon with him before you finish your shopping.

○ PRO *If you get the cold shoulder, you can make yourself feel better instantly with a new blouse.*

○ CON *Due to the mobile nature of the escalator, you have to act very quickly.*

671. MASSAGE PARLOR

Despite all the rumors about massage parlors and "alternative" services offered there (and yes, some of these rumors are true), there are plenty of legitimate massage parlors. And these massage parlors can be good places to meet men in the form of fellow customers in the waiting room and the massage therapists themselves (the male ones) as well. Don't get too friendly with your massage therapist during the massage, however, which may make him uncomfortable. But after you're completely relaxed and feeling thankful for his services, go ahead and be friendly.

672. HERB SHOP

If you are into alternative medicine, you probably frequent the herb shop in your area for ginseng, gingko, or other natural remedies for what ails you. And you are sure to spot a guy or two browsing the aisles for alternative products as well . . . guys who are into natural medicine, just like you. By virtue of being in the herb shop, you and any men you see there will have something important in common—a respect for alternative cures.

○ PRO *Most herb shops sell products advertised to improve sexual enhancement; even if they don't actually work, if you get to know your fellow herb shopper better, you can have fun trying it out.*

○ CON *Herbal products tend to be expensive and many have not been proven to work.*

673. OUTDOOR CAFÉ

On a sunny afternoon, you simply cannot beat a trip to an outdoor café for lunch or a refreshing drink. What's so great about these cafés, particularly the ones in big cities, is that the seating is often sort of haphazard. You may be at a table with your friend, but feel like you are part of the groups at the tables to your right and left as well . . . which can be a very good thing if either of those tables contains friendly single men. To meet men, make the most of your time. "We all have those times when we feel overwhelmed or down and we don't know what to do with ourselves," says Karen Jones, president of the Heart Matters and author of *Men Are Great*. She recommends you use those times as opportunities to meet men. "When you have 15 minutes or 45 minutes of free time, thumb through this book and look for a place where you can go. If you're in an interactive mood, for instance, choose a restaurant or café. If you have something to mail, go to the post office and see who's there. Go down the list and pick the winner for the moment," she says.

674. HOT-DOG CART AT LUNCH

A lot of men, especially bachelors, prefer a quick, pre-prepared lunch they can load with toppings and take with them as they walk down the street. So the hot-dog cart is a natural fit. Now and then, if you work in a city, forego the salad at your desk or the lunch in the cafeteria with coworkers and head to the street for a good, old-fashioned cart hot dog.

O PRO *The place is guaranteed to be swarming with all sorts of guys—suits, working men, and everyone in between.*

O CON *Some of these carts haven't exactly gotten glowing reviews from the Board of Health.*

675. DINER COUNTER OR BAR . . . WITH PUZZLE IN HAND

Sit at the counter of a diner or bar and bring a crossword puzzle. Ask the cute bartender or the interesting solo patron sitting next to you if he knows a six-letter word for "show dog." [p-o-o-d-l-e]

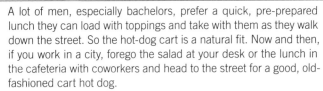

676. PANCAKE HOUSE ON A SUNDAY MORNING

Nothing gets a lazy Sunday started better than a plate of syrup-soaked pancakes from a pancake house. If you live in a small city or town, these places tend to draw a lot of regulars, single men included. So go enjoy some pancakes solo or grab a friend and head to the pancake house at the same time every Sunday for a few weeks—you are bound to see some familiar faces.

❍ PRO *If you go later in the morning, a big plate of pancakes will probably hold you over until dinner.*

❍ CON *If you get a side of breakfast meat week after week, your health may suffer.*

677. SHOVELING SNOW

Snow is beautiful and all, but the shoveling part really sucks, especially if you live alone and are responsible for your own sidewalk and/or steps. The good thing about shoveling snow, however, is that it gets all the neighbors out on the street at the same time—a great opportunity to get to know the people (and hopefully, the single guys) who live near you. So put on your cutest hat and scarf, grab that shovel, and get going. You may find yourself sipping hot chocolate by the fireplace with one of your cutest neighbors a few hours later.

678. PARKING GARAGE

If you work in the city . . . or just go there to shop now and then . . . you've no doubt had to navigate your way through a parking garage. Next time you find yourself weaving through the levels to find a spot, pay attention to who's around you once you park and get out. Parking garages are full of single guys parking their cars for work or for a jaunt through the city. So pay attention. And if there is an elevator, try to hop on with someone interesting and get acquainted on the ride down to the street.

❍ PRO *You can check out his car, which could give you a glimpse into his personality.*

❍ CON *You have to exercise extreme caution and never approach a man in a garage alone at night.*

679. BREAKFAST PLACE DURING THE WEEK

"Women usually prefer to have their business meetings over lunch, but a lot of men like to do them over breakfast, early in the morning," says Lori Gorshow, president of Dating Made Simple (*www .makedatingsimple.com*). Also, men who are going to spend their day laboring need to have a hearty breakfast to start the day. So stop at a breakfast place that's close to numerous office buildings in your area on the way to work and scope out the diners.

O PRO *Even if you don't see anyone you're interested in, you can at least grab a coffee and a muffin before work.*

O CON *You'll have to get up a little earlier than usual to make time for the stop.*

680. GARAGE SALE

Need a few items to supplement your home or apartment? Spend a Saturday in the spring or summer checking out some garage sales in your area. You're likely to get some great deals and if you're really lucky, to meet a few men looking to unload some stuff. To maximize your single guy exposure, look for certain clues: If there are toys or baby equipment for sale, move on—it's probably a married couple. If you see old dart boards, golf clubs, and other "guy" stuff only, you may have hit the jackpot—check it out.

681. LIQUOR STORE

The liquor store may not be the best place to pick up regulars, but if you go at the right time you may bump into a guy you want to get to know better. To catch the people shopping for some wine or booze for a weekend party, head to the liquor store at about 6 P.M. on a Thursday or Friday evening—prime time for professionals to stock up on their liquor.

O PRO *You may get a glimpse of a guy's personality based on his liquor of choice. If he's fisting two bottles of Mad Dog, he may not have grown up yet. A fine Chianti? Quite the contrary . . . .*

O CON *Alcoholics.*

682. SATURDAY BRUNCH

$ $

Guys love breakfast foods. Period. So you will find men chowing down happily on breakfast foods—mixed in with some lunch foods—at a Saturday brunch. Investigate which restaurants in your area serve Saturday brunch and head over between 10 and 12 on the next Saturday morning you are free. Worst case scenario: You will leave only with a full stomach.

683. SUNGLASSES STORE

$ $

The next time you are in the market for a new pair of shades, use it as an opportunity to meet someone. Go to the store at a time when you think a lot of men might be shopping—after work during the week, or on a Saturday morning or afternoon. As you try on pairs of shades, ask an attractive guy you spot what he thinks of them on you. If he is patient and honest, you can take your relationship out for coffee. If he is more interested in finding his own glasses, move on.

O PRO *No commitment. If you scan the store and don't see anything you like, either in a shade or a man, you can save your shopping for a better day.*

O CON *You don't need new sunglasses more than once a year, on average, so this isn't one you can use too often.*

684. COZY COUNTRY CAFÉ

$ $

Nothing to do on a Saturday afternoon? Invite a girlfriend to take a ride out to the country with you and enjoy lunch at a cozy café. Try to find a café that is located near a golf course—as the guys get done with their 18 holes, they will be ready to relax over some lunch and some good conversation with you!

685. DRIVING IN A CONVERTIBLE

$

"Traffic is an awesome place to meet guys," says Lori Gorshow, president of Dating Made Simple (*www.makedatingsimple.com*). And this is particularly true if you are driving a convertible, out in the open. So next time you're stuck in traffic or at a light, make the most of it—look to your left and your right and see what the road has to offer. Or, if you don't own a convertible, rent a candy-apple red '66 Mustang or that sky blue Mini Cooper and take it out for a spin one Saturday afternoon—either solo or with a boisterous girlfriend who can take the wheel and let you do the flirting.

⏱=Time ♦=Friends $=Expense

686.   OUTLET MALL

Not only does an outlet mall provide some great bargains, it may also provide some great bargain shoppers in the form of frugal, fashion-conscious guys. If a guy is shopping by himself, chances are good he's single. And he may appreciate some advice from you. So make a few runs through the men's and unisex stores (J. Crew, Eddie Bauer, The Gap) and scan for guys with perplexed expressions. Or take a break at the food court and see who is dining alone.

687.   RAKING LEAVES

While raking leaves in your back yard, you can kill two birds with one stone. For one, you'll get your leaves raked . . . at least for the time being. And two, you will open yourself up to meeting more of your neighbors, since most of them will also be out raking. If you spot a neighbor you'd like to get to know better, go beyond the wave. Don't be afraid to put the rake down for a few minutes and make a little conversation.

O PRO *A good excuse to enjoy a beautiful fall afternoon.*

O CON *Unless you just moved in or just acquired a new neighbor, you may have already scoped out everyone in your neighborhood. And raking can cause blisters!*

688.   ASIAN FOOD MARKET

If you love Asian food, you will love an Asian food market. From wasabi to teriyaki to soy, these markets offer the best in precooked Asian food as well as the ingredients to make fabulous Asian dishes at home. At an Asian market, you will also find people who share your passion for cuisine from the Far East, perhaps some guys who would like to share some sushi with you some time.

O PRO *If you are too hungry and impatient to wait to cook your own meal, some markets offer tables where you can sit down and enjoy some precooked food—a great place to meet fellow diners.*

O CON *Unless you live in a metropolitan area, you may not have one of these markets near your home.*

689. COFFEE SHOP, EARLY IN THE MORNING

At the crack of dawn, coffee shops are filled with men. Whether they're on their way to a construction site where work can start as early as 6 in the morning or holding a business meeting so they can fit more into their 9 to 5 day, it's worth your while to wake up a little bit early and head out for joe to go. You'll be surprised to see how many guys are caffeinating while much of the world is still asleep. Talk about the early bird getting the worm.

690. DAIRY QUEEN

When an ice cream craving hits, nothing will satisfy it faster than a good old Blizzard at Dairy Queen. Chocolate or vanilla, Snickers or Butterfinger . . . the list of choices goes on and on. And while you're pondering what will satisfy you as you wait in line, take a look around you. Guys enjoy ice cream too. And if a guy is waiting in line at Dairy Queen by himself on a Friday or Saturday night, the chances are good that he has no one waiting for him at home.

691. DOUGHNUT SHOP

Even guys who don't really like sweets usually like doughnuts, so you are likely to see quite a few men at a doughnut shop on a weekday morning, particularly if the shop is located in a business district. Head to the nearest doughnut shop between 7 and 8:30 in the morning and you are likely to get the freshest selection of doughnuts . . . and men. If you go at a regular time each day, you might start to notice other regulars—be they in business suits, police uniforms, or construction gear.

692. FOOD COURT AT LUNCH

If you work close to a mall, consider heading over to the food court on your lunch break. Not only will you have a wide selection of foods to choose from, from salads to burgers to burritos, you will probably have a wide selection of men on their lunch break to choose from as well. And the grab-a-seat-at-any-table type of seating arrangement could work in your favor if you just have to sit with the cute guy eating his chicken chow mein.

=Time =Friends $=Expense

693. TARGET

Whether you are in the market for new shoes, a new bookshelf, or a soccer ball, you'll find them all at Target. No matter how random your list of needs, you're bound to fulfill most of them at the store with the bull's-eye. And because Target sells so many items, it attracts many different shoppers. To find the shoppers that interest you most—the single, attractive male ones—go to the sections where they shop. The electronics section, sporting goods, food, and men's clothing sections are a good start.

○ PRO *Target offers some quality stuff at a decent price, so it probably draws some quality male shoppers as well.*

○ CON *It's difficult to leave Target without buying at least a few impulse items (those picture frames with the little bows are just so darn cute!).*

694. APPLIANCE SHOPPING

If you've recently moved into a new condo, apartment, or house, you're probably in the market for a few new appliances. Instead of browsing for these items online at home, head out to the appliance store and take advantage of both the floor sales and the single guys who are also shopping for new appliances. If you spot a guy checking out a fridge or dishwasher by himself, you can be pretty confident that he lives alone (or has a very trusting girlfriend or wife). So saunter on up to him and ask him which brand he thinks is the best.

695. BAGEL SHOP

To get your day started on the right foot, head to a bagel shop for a freshly made bagel and cup of coffee. To add a man to the mix, head to the shop early in the morning, when lots of men stop by on their way to work.

○ PRO *If the shop is crowded, you'll have the perfect excuse to share a table with a cute stranger.*

○ CON *A bagel in the morning may make you sleepy; to avoid a carbo crash, get a wheat bagel and eat only half.*

696.   CARPOOL

If you have to deal with a longer commute to work, you might as well make the best of it with a carpool. For one, a carpool will save wear and tear on your car. Two, it will save you money on gas and will give you the right to drive in the fast "carpool lane" on the highway. And third and most importantly, it will open up your group of friends. Not only will the people in the carpool themselves be potential dates (if they are single guys), the men and women in the car will know people who know people. And any one of those people could be single and available.

697.   GETTING MEXICAN TAKEOUT

This may seem like a bad place to meet men because you usually just pick up your food and drive quickly home to enjoy it. But instead of waiting until the end of the fifteen to twenty minutes to pick up your order of fajitas or enchiladas, head over a little early and see who else is waiting for their tasty Mexican feast. If there's a bar, grab a margarita or soda. Single men get takeout food a lot, and they love Mexican food, so you are likely to see a few guys waiting for their meals. And then there are the guys who just stopped for a Corona after work.

698.   IN LINE AT THE GROCERY STORE

Even if you don't mind grocery shopping, you probably hate the dreaded line at the end of your trip. But this line can actually be a positive—it may contain single male shoppers with carts full of food, meaning that if you are lucky enough to pull in behind one of them, he will be next to you in line for at least 5 to 10 minutes. To maximize your guy exposure in the grocery store line, try to think like a guy and go when you think the men will be there. Good times include after work, on a Saturday afternoon, or right before a big game (although in this case, he may just grab a few bags of chips and some salsa).

699.   JURY DUTY

Being called for jury duty can actually be a blessing in disguise. First, there's the $12 per day stipend. Second, it opens you up to witnesses, lawyers, and fellow jurors you wouldn't meet otherwise. So make the most of the situation and be friendly. Who knows—after the trial is over, a "friendly" lunch could lead to much more.

=Time   =Friends $=Expense

700.   WAITING IN LINE FOR A FLU SHOT

When the weather starts to cool and the leaves change color, people begin to think and worry more about the dreaded flu season. And now that flu shots are no longer reserved for pregnant women and people older than 65, there will be people of all ages waiting for them. Take advantage of what could be a boring situation by getting to know the people standing next to you in line. Even if you don't meet the man of your dreams, you might make friends with someone who will introduce you to him. Go during lunch or after work, when other working singles are likely to go.

O PRO *You'll be protected from at least one strain of the flu and if things work out with someone you meet in line, you'll know he's protected too!*

O CON *The potentially long (and boring) wait if there are no cute prospects.*

701.   BUTCHER SHOP

I'm not necessarily talking about the guy behind the counter. But don't discount him either! Free filet mignon could be a welcome addition to your diet and your budget. Regardless, drop into your local butcher shop. Sometimes you'll find chefs looking for the right main course. Or, you might just find that single professional male who happens to love to cook. Wouldn't that be appetizing?

O PRO *Lots of meat, both behind and in front of the counter.*

O CON *Not the best place for you if you are a vegetarian.*

702.   JIFFY LUBE

It may not seem like the most glamorous place for a romantic first encounter, but if you begin planning your day the way a single man might, you could end up in the driver's seat. Set up your oil change for around lunchtime during the week. Make sure it's a Jiffy Lube that is in the middle of a busy area. You're guaranteed to end up waiting for your car as you sit next to some unsuspecting businessman who's doing the same. Strike up a conversation and off you go—purring like a kitten.

703.   MCDONALD'S DRIVE-THRU

$ $

The next time you have a tough day at work and would rather plop down in front of the TV than spend time cooking dinner, consider the McDonald's drive-thru, where there will be cars full of single guys ordering double quarter pounders with cheese. To see these men, look in your rear-view mirror as you wait to place your order. If you spot someone you like, smile and wave . . . then pull over once you've gotten your meal and see if he stops. You have nothing to lose.

○ PRO *Between the salads and grilled sandwiches, there are many "good" things on the menu at McDonald's these days.*

○ CON *If you have a problem with willpower, you may find it difficult to forego the chicken nuggets for a grilled chicken salad.*

704.   NEIGHBORHOOD DRY CLEANER

$

If you have a job where you have to dress up everyday, you have probably discovered that $1.00 per shirt is a small price to pay to be able to open your closet and choose from a line-up of clean, pressed tops. And, because they fear the iron like a bad case of food poisoning, most guys drop their shirts off at the cleaners weekly as well. Point being that if you frequent the cleaners in your neighborhood, you are bound to bump into some male professional neighbors.

○ PRO *The dry cleaner provides you with the opportunity to check something off your to-do list and scope for guys at the same time— a nice combination.*

○ CON *If you live in a small neighborhood, your dry cleaner could be slightly more expensive than one located right downtown. But it could be a small price to pay for the neighbor exposure . . .*

705.   NEWSSTAND

$

There is a certain romance about the newsstand. You both are busy at successful careers. You're on the go. He's on the go. And, you're both the type to stop at a newsstand, grab a pack of gum, pick up the latest newspaper for work, check out your favorite magazine briefly, all before returning for your big meeting. It's your perfect opportunity to slip in a quick "hello" or even slip him a business card. Maybe it will turn into a business relationship . . . maybe a lot more!

706. SOFT PRETZEL CART

In some regions, the soft pretzel is the lunchtime (and sometimes breakfast-time) treat for movers and shakers in the business world. It's quick, easy, and filling. That's why you'll find many businessmen grabbing one on the go. Just ask them where the mustard is for an easy way to get cooking.

707. STAPLES

Yes, Staples. Businessmen are constantly streaming in and out of stores where office products are sold. The last-minute presentation, ink cartridges, copy paper—you name it, they're in need of these kinds of supplies. The key is finding the right one near you. If you know where all the offices are, then you know where the men will be seeking office supplies. Just drop in and browse. And if you don't see someone you like, you can always get that fancy paper for your résumé or a new date book.

708. SUSHI BAR AT LUNCH

You like sushi. He likes sushi. And magically, you are both at a sushi bar on your lunch break. So get yourself to a sushi bar solo (coworkers will distract you with gossip and/or work talk) and stay open to meeting your fellow diners. At the bar, you won't feel awkward eating alone and if no one sparks your interest, you can always strike up a conversation with the guy rolling the sushi.

709. AUTO DETAILING COMPANY

Schedule an appointment to have your car detailed during a time when you know a lot of single men might be having their car done. One thing is for sure, men like cars. And a man who takes care of his car is probably a man who will be mature, thorough, and responsible. If you're feeling fearless, call an auto detailing place near you and ask if any single men are coming to pick up their cars that day. Perhaps the employees know of someone who might be right for you. Who knows, the guy who runs the place might be interested.

○ PRO *You will make yourself noticed, and get your car detailed in the process!*

○ CON *If you trade your car in every two years or drive a company car, you may not want to shell out the cash to get it detailed . . . but you can at least get an estimate.*

=Time ☻=Friends $=Expense

710. FLOWER SHOP

$ $

This one works much better in cities and places where there's a lot of hustle and bustle, especially when the flowers are sitting outside for passersby to admire. There's something irresistible about a woman taking in the scent of fresh flowers. Men are drawn to it. So see if you can't pop in a flower shop where you can be easily noticed. If your timing is right, a guy will see you and inquire why a beautiful woman needs to be buying herself flowers. Feeling really bold? See if the manager of the flower shop knows any single men. Remember, flower shop people know a lot of people's personal stories.

711. IKEA

For women in their twenties, thirties, and forties, IKEA is an absolute must if you want to shop for single men. Let's face it, you're going to find a cute new bathroom rug, trendy glassware, or a funky new lamp anyway, so this trip will serve you well regardless of whether you meet the man of your dreams. But keep this in mind. IKEA offers reasonably priced furniture and home accessories, and single men are all about keeping their homes somewhat affordable. Quite frankly, IKEA should offer singles nights, since their stores seem to be crawling with available men. If you want to meet a man at IKEA, the best way to approach him is to just walk up to him and ask him where something is. IKEAs are so big that everyone gets lost at some point. See if "he" can show you the way.

712. THE GEEK SQUAD

Having computer troubles? Consider calling the Geek Squad. These tech wizards, known as "Geek Squad Agents," will come to your house and fix your hard drive, upgrade your software, or anything else you can think of when it comes to your PC or Mac. While they all know what they're doing, they're not all geeks. Who knows? Maybe there will be some chemistry between you and a cute Geek, and you can exchange e-mail addresses. Just remember, they're not miracle workers. So don't even think about messing up your laptop just so you can have an excuse to call in the Geeks. You'll be sorry if he can't fix your problem . . . even more sorry if *she* can't fix your problem. Find a geek at *www.geeksquad.com*.

713. RESTROOMS

The rules have changed when it comes to restrooms. Club and lounge owners understand the flirtation factor when it comes to having members of the opposite sex sharing coed bathrooms, or at least sharing the point of entry. It allows men and women to have a more subdued conversation and a chance to get closer. Trendy bathrooms have become the thing in lounges, and because the idea is to increase the flirt factor, singles benefit the most. The next time you head out with friends, be sure to check out the bathroom and don't be afraid to linger outside the entrance—you'll discover that it's the place to be if you want to strike up a conversation.

○ PRO *A lot of trendy bathrooms are well-decorated and comfortable these days.*

○ CON *Guys (and girls) can do some pretty gross things in bathrooms, so you may not want to hang out there long, no matter how nice the sinks and countertops are.*

714. RENT A HUSBAND

No, I'm not suggesting anything illegal here. These "husbands for hire" don't perform all husband duties, but they might be able to put in your storm windows, fix a leaky sink, or clean out your gutters. There are lots of handymen who offer their services around the house for those of us who may not be so handy. So next time you need an odd job done that you can't do on your own, look in the phone book under "handyman services" or something similar, and keep an eye out for places with a catchy name. Often, these guys work for themselves, and their prices are usually more reasonable than large companies. So if you can save money, get your showerhead fixed, and get a date, what else can you ask for?

715. PIZZA PARLOR

Men love pizza. They love Dominos, Papa John's, Pizza Hut, and authentic Greek and Italian pizza. So therefore if you go to a pizza parlor, you are likely to find men of all ages . . . especially if the place also serves beer. So grab a girlfriend and head to your local pizza place to throw down a few slices now and then. Compared to other "junk" foods, pizza is pretty good for you . . . and it's cheap.

716. DINER

Not only are diners great for long menus that offer everything from chicken croquettes to Western omelets to cheesecake—24 hours a day—they are also great for scoping out men. First, diner meals are usually quick, so you can get in and out in a jiffy if no one catches your eye. Second, diners are usually decorated heavily with mirrors, so you can get a nice 360-degree overview of all the patrons in the place in a few seconds. And third, men tend to flock to diners because of the quantity of food they get for the money. So don't miss out.

717. POST OFFICE

Even with online bill paying, PayPal, and other convenient methods of getting things from one place to another, now and then, everyone needs to mail something. So now and then, everyone needs to go to the post office . . . handsome single men included. So instead of rolling your eyes in frustration the next time you have to wait in line for a book of stamps or to send a piece of certified mail, enjoy it. Better yet, head to the post office at the busiest times to maximize your people exposure. Look around you, smile, and be friendly. You never know who you might meet.

718. YARD SALE

To bring the men to you, hold a yard sale to get rid of some of your stuff. Ask your friends and family members if they have things they would like to unload as well, particularly items that guys would be interested in, such as golf clubs, furniture, and video game consoles. Then hang some flyers around your neighborhood a few days ahead of time and sit back and wait for the men to pour in.

O PRO *In addition to potentially meeting some nice men in your area, you will make a few bucks.*

O CON *If you're just starting out, gathering enough items for a full-blown yard sale might be tough.*

719. THE APPLE STORE

Most guys love technology and love gadgets. The Apple Store sells both. And with the popularity of iPods and MacBooks, Apple stores are more filled with men than ever. And the stores are interactive. You can take free classes on Photoshop or how to use your iPod. To find your Apple store, check out *www.apple.com*.

720. CITY BUS

When your trip across town is a little too far for a cab and you're not in the mood for the claustrophobia of the subway, jump on the city bus. The seating arrangement almost forces you to at least say hello to the person sitting next to you. And who knows . . . you may be so interested in that person that you might get off at his stop.

○ PRO *Compared to other forms of transportation, the city bus is pretty reasonable.*

○ CON *Depending on your city, some city bus systems aren't the best.*

721. HOSPITAL WAITING ROOM

Probably not on your list of favorite places in general, but a hospital waiting room offers many opportunities. First, there could be a hand-some patient there for a sports injury. There is the possibility of a single dad there with a child who needs stitches. And then, of course, there are the male nurses, physicians' assistants, and doctors them-selves. This isn't to suggest that you should hang out in a waiting room; just keep an open mind if you happen to find yourself there.

722. KOSHER DELI

If your religion takes you into a kosher deli for your sandwiches, meats, and pickles, consider shopping for your men there as well. One, you will know they share your love of good cold cuts, and two, the chances are good they are also of the Jewish faith (which will make your parents happy). Major cities are filled with kosher delis, so for maximum man exposure, visit kosher delis around town.

723. PHARMACY

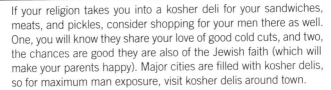

Whether it's for an antibiotic for the sinus infection you picked up on a plane, your birth control pills, or a refill on your night cream, you have to hit the pharmacy now and then. And unless he's Superman or has sworn off hygiene products, so does he. So the next time you hit the pharmacy, take a look at who else is waiting at the counter or browsing through the aisles. This is one of those places where you just might make a love connection where you least expect it.

○ PRO *If he's proactive about his health, that's a good sign—he's probably responsible in general.*

○ CON *Many pharmacies have drive-up windows—they are an option if you are in a hurry, but skip them if you are scoping for a man.*

724. SELF-CHECKOUT AT THE GROCERY STORE

If you've only got a few items and the manned aisles are full, consider the self-checkout. The line is usually a little longer, which will give you a chance to get to know the men in line who also enjoy using a scanner. Plus, you can call on them if you need a little help figuring out which kind of onion you have in your basket.

O PRO *The self-checkout may draw a more independent type of man.*

O CON *If you have a ton of produce, this method can really slow you down.*

725. SITTING ON YOUR FRONT PORCH

If your house or apartment building has a front porch, you'd be wise to sit on it now and then. You will get a great overview of the people in your neighborhood and more importantly, the men in your neighborhood. And from your front porch, you will be able to see which men walk in to their homes or stores (depending on whether you live in a residential or shopping district) alone and which men walk with wives or girlfriends. You will also learn which men have dogs, drive nice cars, exercise . . . the list goes on and on.

O PRO *This one is easy and free.*

O CON *If you sit on your front porch too often, you risk becoming one of those nosy neighbors who knows everything about everyone.*

726. SPRAY-TAN SALON

Unfortunately, as scientists have discovered how dangerous UV rays are in terms of aging and general health, the popularity of the tanned look has not faded (for men or women). In fact, it may have even deepened. Luckily, there are ways you can get that sun-kissed look without kissing your soft, smooth skin goodbye—a spray tan. And as you enter or exit your safe spray-tan booth, keep your eye out for health-conscious tan men. If you bump into someone you want to know better, you won't have to run home to take a shower before you go grab some coffee together because the spray tan leaves you sweat-free.

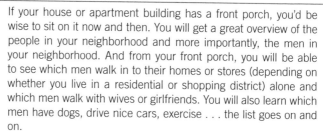

727.   UNISEX FITTING ROOM

As more and more unisex stores pop up in malls and shopping districts, there are increasingly more unisex fitting rooms. They aren't meant to put coeds in the same room together, but they do offer a nice opportunity to chat as you wait for the next available room . . . and then, of course, there is the chance to catch eyes with the man who just tried on jeans in there before you.

O PRO *As guys walk out to check out the larger mirror, they may need some friendly fashion advice . . . from you.*

O CON *The way some dressing rooms are lit these days, you may not be in the best mood on the way out.*

728.   COMMUNITY HERB GARDEN

If you have a community herb garden, you never know who might show up, especially if your community houses a number of singles. You'd be surprised at the number of men who are interested in cooking and growing their own herbs who might check out the garden for some pointers. A man who is browsing an herb garden by himself probably is single—and a pretty darn good cook—or at least, he tries. A good combination.

729.   PERSONAL ADS IN THE NEWSPAPER

Despite all the online dating sites out there these days, some people have more luck doing it the old-fashioned way—by writing an "In Search Of" (ISO) ad in the personal section of the newspaper. And it appears that good writing counts. One study showed that a well-written ISO by a woman gets an average of thirty responses. Not too shabby. So if you have tried online sites without luck or you'd rather leave technology out of your matchmaking, consider writing a personal ad.

730.   ROADSIDE FARM STAND

For delicious fresh fruit, you simply cannot beat a roadside farm stand . . . not to mention the homemade pies and other baked goods. And many times, roadside farm stands come with handsome farmers or handsome drivers who can't resist a fresh peach. Either way, it's worth your while to stop . . . if nothing more, for a nice antioxidant boost.

731.   TRAIN STATION AT RUSH HOUR

Stand in a busy city train station at rush hour and you will see a lot of men coming home from work, many of whom will likely be swinging by a Chinese restaurant or gourmet grocery store for takeout rather than going home to a wife or girlfriend. To meet one of these men and potentially become his dinner plan in the near future, break the ice by asking the time or inquiring about a train schedule.

O PRO *In a busy crowd, you can quickly slink away if you get a cold shoulder.*

O CON *A lot of these men may be in a big hurry; if he appears harried, move on.*

732.   THE BODY SHOP

A man you find at The Body Shop is probably interested in both personal hygiene and preserving the environment—a good combination. To get his attention, approach him and tell him you're having trouble deciding between two soaps. Ask him which he likes better. If he smells them willingly, the chemistry is there. If not, move on.

O PRO *He himself will probably smell pretty good.*

O CON *He could be shopping for perfume or body wash for a wife or girlfriend. If he's in the women's section, tread lightly.*

733.   IN YOUR LOBBY

If you live in an apartment building or condo complex with a lobby, you probably have gotten a good look at most of the tenants who share your street address. And you've probably gotten a sense of who's single, who's married or in a relationship, who's having an affair, and so on. If you've spotted a guy who passes all your tests (single, attractive, appears to have a steady job), approach him the next time you see him parking his car or getting his mail and ask him if he'd like to get a cup of coffee with you. Even if things don't work out romantically, you may make a nice neighbor friend.

734. ORTHODONTIST

Not everyone was lucky enough to have parents willing to shell out a few thousand bucks for braces. So as a guy accumulates more money, he may decide to spend some cash to straighten his teeth. If you are in the same boat, you may bump into this guy in the orthodontist's office. You may also bump into him if you have children or a niece or nephew with braces. And of course there are the single dads taking their kids to have their braces tightened. This is not to say that you should hang out at the orthodontist in search of a single man; but keep an open mind if you find yourself there.

735. POPCORN COUNTER AT THE MOVIES

Nothing tops off a movie experience like a bucket of popcorn with extra butter and a five-dollar soda. And on a crowded movie night, the popcorn counter line is about as long as the line for tickets. Next time you go to the movies, don't wait until the movie has already started to run back out to get your snack to avoid the line. Instead, leave a few minutes early to purposely get in the long line so you can get a preview of the movie-going men of the evening. If you spot one who catches your eye, hang around the lobby when the movie is over to see if he comes out without a date. If so, make your move.

736. TEST-DRIVING A CAR

When you are in the market for a new car, you're best off test-driving a few models before you choose the car you're going to buy. So why not have some fun with it? Cruise around to car dealerships in your area and scope for handsome salesmen. When you've found one, approach him about the model you're interested in, and make sure you invite him along for the test drive. In between questions about antilock brakes and sunroof options, you can ask him a few about himself and see where it goes.

O PRO *If things go really well, you might get a nice deal on the car.*

O CON *If you decide you like the salesman and not the car, things could get awkward if you buy at another dealership.*

 =Time =Friends $ =Expense

737. THROUGH YOUR DOORMAN

If you live in a high-rise building, you probably have formed some kind of a bond with your doorman, even if it is restricted to regular hellos and goodbyes. This doorman bond could be a nice bridge to meeting a man. Next time you see him, ask the doorman if he knows any singles in the area.

○ PRO *If you're lucky, he may name someone who lives in your very building.*

○ CON *Your doorman may mistakenly take your question as a come-on.*

738. HAIRDRESSER

If your hairdresser specializes in women, you probably won't find Mr. Right there. You may, however, find him by casually mentioning to the women in the shop that you are single and in the market for a man. People love to fix people up, so your comment will throw mothers, sisters, aunts, and friends into a mission to find you a date.

739. H&R BLOCK

Even for the math-minded person, filing income taxes can be complicated, especially if you have unusual circumstances such as a side business. So naturally, as April 15 approaches, people pour into H&R Block, including many single guys. If you meet a man at H&R Block you will know that he has income and is responsible about reporting it—two big pluses. There are H&R Blocks all over the country.

○ PRO *Beyond the men there to have their taxes done, there will be the accountants who work at H&R Block for you to meet.*

○ CON *You will have to pay a small fee to get your taxes done, and if you wait until a few days before April 15, you will probably have to wait in line (but hey—that means more opportunities to meet someone).*

740. IN A CAR ACCIDENT

This is certainly not to suggest that you should go around aiming at cars in hopes of getting in a car accident. But should you find yourself in a fender-bender, which a lot of us do, keep the exchange between you and your fellow accident victim friendly. After all, you just may hit it off with him in more ways than one. And then of course there is the trusty police officer who will show up at the scene. If you two hit it off, maybe you can grab some coffee after the accident is settled.

O PRO *Talk about being at the right place at the right time.*

O CON *After a car accident, people are often emotional and downright hostile—not the ideal backdrop for romance.*

741. MATTRESS STORE

You want to make sure the bed you sleep in is as comfy as possible. So if your mattress was passed down from an aunt or (heaven forbid) it's still a twin, a trip to the mattress store is in order. And in addition to beds ranging from fluffy to firm, you are likely to find some single men browsing the aisles for a bachelor pad bed of their choice. Or, consider the salesmen. Katie Z. of Lansing, Michigan, met her fiancé when he sold her a mattress in a local mattress store. "He gave me his employee discount, so I knew he was interested. Then he called me to make sure my mattress was delivered, and I knew he was really interested. So I asked him out for coffee and the rest is history," she says. In addition to the sale tags, keep your eyes peeled for men shopping alone because if they are picking out a mattress by themselves, chances are they are sleeping on it by themselves and may be as eager to meet someone special as you are.

742. PLANT NURSERY

In the market for some shrubbery for your home? Head to a plant nursery and start browsing. As you check out the selection of perennials, grasses, and ferns, keep your eyes open for some attractive men picking out plants by themselves. If they are at the nursery alone, the chances are good that they are single homeowners. And then beyond the customers, there will be the shrubbery experts there to answer any questions you may have about what plants do well in sun or shade.

743. WAITING IN LINE FOR THE ATM

When you're in the market for Mr. Right, waiting in line ceases to be a pain and transforms into an opportunity for love. Waiting in line for the ATM is a perfect example. As you stand in line the comfortable amount of steps behind a person making a deposit or withdrawal so as to not make him or her nervous, smile and be friendly. If a guy is waiting at an ATM it means two things: He has some cash to play with—a good sign, and he's probably local.

744. WAWA

If you live in New Jersey, Pennsylvania, Virginia, Maryland, or Delaware, surely you've made many trips to your local Wawa for a hoagie, coffee, or stuffed soft pretzel—all Wawa specialties. And because Wawa's are such popular convenience stores, they are usually jam-packed with people and lots of single men on their way to or from work. For maximum man exposure, hit the Wawa before or after work, when single guys are picking up their cup of coffee or a sandwich for dinner.

745. CELL PHONE STORE

You'd be hard pressed to find an adult American citizen who doesn't own a cell phone; and because we use them so often, cell phones only last so long. So every 18 months, on average, a cell phone owner has to turn over his or her trusty phone in exchange for a shiny new one. As a result, cell phone stores get a constant stream of customers . . . many in the form of single men who use their phones for business and/or personal use. And beyond the customers, there are the salesmen. So if your cell phone is starting to show signs of aging, get into a cell phone store early to see what's available . . . both in phones and the men who use them.

746. CHIROPRACTOR'S OFFICE

Jennifer H. from Atlanta, Georgia, fell in love with her chiropractor. "At first, I couldn't tell whether I liked him because he made my back feel so good. But when he asked me out after an appointment, I knew it was mutual." The moral of the story: Don't rule out your chiropractor or other doctor as a potential date. It's easier to find a new doctor than it is a new man! There are also the men in the chiropractor's office. Either way, your visit could turn out to be good for more than just your posture.

747. ORGANIC BREAKFAST PLACE

With all the scary information about pesticides and hormones in food these days, a lot of people are choosing to go all organic. And luckily for those people, there are all kinds of organic restaurants these days, including restaurants that serve organic breakfasts. In addition to eggs from free-range chickens, sausage from pigs that have been raised the old-fashioned way, and milk from cows that have not received daily hormone injections, you can find health-conscious men who still love a good breakfast now and then. Organic restaurants usually have a unique laid-back atmosphere, which make them more comfortable places for meeting fellow patrons.

748. PARTY SUPPLY STORE

For theme parties or children's birthday parties, a trip to a party supply store is in order. And if you catch a party supply retailer on the right day, it just may be a good venue for meeting men as well. Fun, festive men throw parties now and then, so they may be there. And then of course there are the single dads in search of the perfect Sponge Bob or Cinderella favors to make their kids smile. Either way, to meet these party-going men, you have to be right alongside of them, checking out the hats and streamer colors. So next time you're in a shopping center with a party supply store—or in the market for party supplies yourself—take a peek.

749. CARPET STORE

Men browsing around in carpet stores probably own homes. And men browsing around carpet stores alone are probably single homeowners (floor coverings are one of those things couples shop for together). So if you are a homeowner and are currently in the market for carpeting, take your eyes of the swatches now and then and take a look at the customers.

750.   CROWDED RESTAURANT AT LUNCHTIME

It's called a lunch "hour" for a reason—you technically have only 60 minutes to get to a restaurant, dine, and get back to the office. So if you go to a popular restaurant at lunch and are lucky enough to get a table before the big rush, offer to share your table with a single businessman (or businessmen) waiting in line for a table.

○ PRO *If you have a spark, wonderful—maybe you can take it to dinner.*

○ CON *If there is no spark, you are no worse off—you just helped someone get back to the office faster and shared your lunch with someone new.*

751.   ITALIAN RESTAURANT

There is something undeniably romantic and sensual about Italian food. To meet Italian men who want to celebrate their heritage and feel a hint of nostalgia as they eat, or non-Italian men who appreciate a delicious meatball Parm, head to an Italian restaurant in your area. Make sure you enjoy a delicious Chianti and mingle with the guests waiting for a table.

Five great Italian restaurants:
1. Sabatino's in Baltimore, MD: *www.sabatinos.com*
2. Carmelo's Restaurant in Austin and Houston, TX: *www.carmelosrestaurant.com*
3. Patsy's Italian Restaurant, New York, NY: *www.patsys.com*
4. Milan Italian Restaurant, Pine Brook, NJ: *www.milanrestaurant.com*
5. Christini's Italian Restaurant, Orlando, FL: *www.christinis.com*

752.   TJ MAXX

Greg S. from Seattle, Washington, met his current girlfriend at TJ Maxx. "I was confused as to whether a shirt I was looking at was the right color (I'm colorblind). She laughed, informed me that it was pink (not green, as I had thought). I was afraid she was taken because she was shopping in the men's department, but luckily for me, she was shopping for her dad. I took a chance and asked her if she wanted to grab some lunch with me, and I'm happy I did!" TJ Maxx is a great place to meet men because they sell both men's and women's clothing; plus, they have an open store where you can get a good look at your fellow shoppers. And if that weren't enough, you really do get the max for the minimum—the deals on designer clothes are worth checking out.

🕐=Time 👤=Friends $=Expense

| **753.** | **FAST-FOOD RESTAURANT** |

Fast-food restaurants probably have the highest number of solo diners of any type of eating establishment. Whether it's your businessman on the go or the golfer who stops to grab a burger and fries after he hits the course, your fast-food restaurant is bound to serve up some single guys ready to supersize and hopefully, socialize.

○ PRO *Even if you don't meet someone, fast-food restaurants have several delicious, healthful options these days.*

○ CON *Because of the "fast" nature, you will have to act quickly, especially if the guy's order is to go.*

| **754.** | **OUTSIDE YOUR FRONT DOOR** |

Your dream guy could have an address that is just a few numbers off from your own. Unless you live by yourself on a 10-acre lot, there are bound to be single men living within yards of your house or apartment—the trick is to spot them. You don't have to stare out your window with every spare moment; just keep your eyes open when you are watering your flowers, getting your mail, or walking down the street. And be friendly to all your neighbors—you never know when one of them will have an attractive single friend he or she is dying to introduce you to.

○ PRO *Convenience. If it works out with your neighbor, he will always be just a few doors away.*

○ CON *If it doesn't work out, he will be just a few doors away. There could be many awkward moments at the mailbox.*

| **755.** | **COMPUTER OUTLET** |

Most men love gadgets. And in addition to computers, computer outlets house a huge supply of gadgets at a discounted price. So you may want to attract one of these men as he browses the aisles of a computer outlet, wide-eyed with excitement at the merchandise and deals. For best results, wear red—so you'll be visible among all the black and gray.

=Time =Friends $=Expense

756. GAS STATION

Karen Jones, president of the Heart Matters and author of *Men Are Great,* tells the following story about one of her clients: Sharon had just purchased her dream car, a BMW convertible. She was at the gas station rummaging through her purse when she heard a guy's voice say, "Nice car." Without looking up, she mumbled, "Yeah thanks." Then she turned around, and saw the backside of the guy who she had blown off . . . wearing a suit and getting into his Mercedes. "The lesson," Jones says, "is to stay open and be friendly to everyone . . . even at the gas station."

757. DOG GROOMER

Many single women choose to share their lives with a furry friend. And every responsible dog owner with a curly or longer-haired dog regularly takes the pooch to the groomer. Jessica M., of Buffalo, New York, met her current flame, Nick, while picking up her pooch, Lucy, from the groomer. "It was the first time I had my dog groomed, and I barely recognized her. Half in shock by how different she looked, I turned around with Lucy in my arms and bumped into this gorgeous guy with his golden retriever. Thank goodness Lucy and his retriever, Rex, get along, because they have spent many nights playing together since then . . ." So with Jessica's story in mind, next time you drop Fido off or pick him up, look beyond the other cute, freshly cut dogs and at their dog owners.

O PRO *In a lot of cases, a guy who owns a dog eventually wants to settle down and have a family.*

O CON *Unless your dog's hair grows like a weed, you won't find yourself at the groomer too often. As an alternative, if you live close to the groomer, consider taking your dog for a walk in that neighborhood to see who walks out with a freshly coiffed dog.*

758. RUMMAGE SALE

Everyone loves a good bargain now and then. So your occasional trip to a rummage sale could be worth your while . . . for the bargains and for the men searching for bargains. Whether the guys are working at the sale or shopping for items, it's worth your while to periodically take a break from rummaging through stuff and look around you. Depending on the size of the sale, take a few strolls through sections offering items of interest to guys, such as baseball cards, wallets, and food vendors.

759. SHOPPING FOR CAR INSURANCE

With all the car insurance companies and agents out there, it's tough to know who will give you the best deal. So why not make the quest for good insurance a quest to meet a nice, single car insurance salesman as well? Walk into the agencies in your area and ask to speak to someone about a quote. There are a lot of men in the insurance business, so you are bound to meet with a single one or two.

O PRO *In a face-to-face meeting, it may be easier to charm the agent into a better quote . . . and into asking you out.*

O CON *If you have a 9-to-5, Monday through Friday job, these trips could be tough to schedule.*

760. DRUGSTORES

For some reason, drugstores always have decent-looking singles running around buying everything from hair conditioner to antacids. In fact, drugstores such as Eckerd and CVS have become such a regular necessity that many of them are open 24 hours. But don't expect to find a desirable guy lingering in the aisles at 2 A.M. Try dropping in a busy drugstore after work. That's when many of the singles are grabbing their daily drugstore necessities. You'll find men browsing for birthday cards, having pictures developed, choosing the right headache medicines, or filling prescriptions. Maybe you'll turn out to be just what the doctor ordered.

761. SALON

The days of the barbershop aren't over. However, many men of today are choosing to get the professional treatment by hairstylists. How can this benefit you? Talk to your stylist. They often arrange dates for their clients. It's not even awkward! Probably your stylist knows you better than most people, so having him or her set you up feels almost natural. It starts with you though. Just ask your stylist what he or she thinks about helping you find someone new and exciting.

762. PSYCHOLOGIST'S WAITING ROOM

$ $

You already both feel ridiculous. Why not capitalize on it? Today more than ever, people from all walks of life are seeing psychologists. For some, it's just about spilling their thoughts and feelings. For others, it's about working through problems. This one is a double-edged sword. Some women welcome a guy who has the guts to see a shrink. Others think that if he's seeing a shrink, he must be crazy. Then again, since you're there, say hello.

⊙ PRO *It could mean dating a sensitive guy—and that is probably a good thing.*

⊙ CON *There is the potential for neediness, for both of you.*

763. HOAGIE SHOP

$

It's amazing—put a few pieces of lunch meat on a long roll, add some cheese, mayonnaise, onions, and a little oil and oregano—and men go nuts. Guys love hoagies. So at a hoagie shop, you are guaranteed to find men salivating as they read the menu and place their orders. To break the ice, ask a man in line which sandwich he recommends—chances are he will offer a few favorites, and maybe keep the conversation rolling from there.

Five great hoagie shops:
1. Philadelphia Fevre Steak and Hoagie Shop, Seattle, WA
2. Andy's Bar and Hoagie Shop, Altoona, PA
3. Steak'n Hoagie Shop, Cary, NC
4. Hoagie Heaven, Gloucester City, NJ
5. Mr. Spots, Ann Arbor, MI

764. SPICE AISLE AT THE GROCERY STORE

$

Next time you find yourself in the spice aisle, don't rush—read the labels and discover the perfect flavor to add to your meals for the week. As you're looking for some ingredients to spice up your dinner, you just may bump into a guy who will spice up your dating life.

765. CHINESE TAKEOUT JOINT

$ $

This may seem like a bad place to meet men because you usually just pick up your food and leave. But instead of waiting until the end of the 15 to 20 minutes to pick up your order, head over a little early and see who else is waiting. Single men get takeout food a lot. If you strike up a good conversation, ask the guy if he would like to eat his food in the park . . . with you.

766. | LOTTERY TICKET LINE WHEN THE JACKPOT IS LARGE

When one of the lottery jackpots starts to grow, we all start dreaming of what we'd do if we won. As a result, a large jackpot tends to draw many hopeful ticket buyers. And there's no better way to kill time as you wait for your winning ticket than to make friends with the cute guy in line next to you. Even if you don't hit the big jackpot, your line buddy may buy you dinner that night!

○ PRO *You can easily get the conversation ball rolling by asking him what he would buy if he won.*

○ CON *The odds of winning the lottery are way against you.*

767. | P.F. CHANG'S CHINA BISTRO

P.F. Chang's is a stylish yet affordable Chinese restaurant that started as a West Coast chain but can now be found all over the country. The restaurant is always crowded, and the bar is a perfect place to have a drink and an appetizer, and maybe spot a cutie having some of Chang's famous lettuce wraps. So if you and a girlfriend find yourselves in the area of a P.F. Chang's, stop in and see what they have to offer—both on and off the menu.

d date flea market reunion restaurant tattoo parlor wedding auction ho
ub baby shower casino hibachi ladies night café bake sale brunch river
ambake double date culinary festival smorgasbord tavern church service
mal hospital roommates yacht club school courthouse nudist colony bee
val baseball game car show firefighting fishing tailgating poker campgr
ting contest bowling weight room military cigar shop airport london bri
eiffel tower vacation hotel cruise mardi gras times square central park
f america mount rushmore hollywood safari smithsonian online animal
e blood drive volunteering special olympics toy drive red cross soup kit
rt gallery book club cooking class library museum college campus orche
ature walk planetarium political rally shakespeare festival disney world
uarium water park caroling parents playground mini-golf county fair co
use laundromat grocery store beach gym subway deli yard sale liquor
post office personal ads company picnic conference water cooler bartend
oncert scavenger hunt karaoke comedy club biking karate softball pain
iling ymca square dancing boardwalk cookout whale watching farmer's
et party friends cafeteria open house singing group bars beach house
ting blind date flea market reunion restaurant tattoo parlor wedding au
ospital club baby shower casino hibachi ladies night café bake sale bru
iverboat clambake double date culinary festival smorgasbord tavern chu
ervice spa animal hospital roommates yacht club school courthouse nu
ony beer festival baseball game car show firefighting fishing tailgating
campground eating contest bowling weight room military cigar shop airp
ndon bridges bus eiffel tower vacation hotel cruise mardi gras times sq
ntral park mall of america mount rushmore hollywood safari smithsonian
e animal rescue blood drive volunteering special olympics toy drive red
up kitchen art gallery book club cooking class library museum college ca
rchestra nature walk planetarium political rally shakespeare festival dis
orld zoo aquarium water park caroling parents playground mini-golf co
ir coffeehouse laundromat grocery store beach gym subway deli yard
iquor store post office personal ads company picnic conference water co
rtending concert scavenger hunt karaoke comedy club biking karate so
intball sailing ymca square dancing cookout whale watching farmer's m
ty friends cafeteria open house singing group bars beach house wine ta
d date flea market reunion restaurant tattoo parlor wedding auction ho
ub baby shower casino hibachi ladies night café bake sale brunch river
ambake double date culinary festival smorgasbord tavern church service
mal hospital roommates yacht club school courthouse nudist colony bee
val baseball game car show firefighting fishing tailgating poker campgr
ting contest bowling weight room military cigar shop airport london bri
eiffel tower vacation hotel cruise mardi gras times square central park
f america mount rushmore hollywood safari smithsonian online animal
e blood drive volunteering special olympics toy drive red cross soup kit
rt gallery book club cooking class library museum college campus orche
ature walk planetarium political rally shakespeare festival disney world

work-related ways

768. SOMEBODY ELSE'S COMPANY PICNIC

If a friend invites you to his or her company picnic, go for it! Company picnics tend to be fun social events. Plus, you'll know everyone there is employed. And if that weren't enough, your friend can give you the inside scoop on all the people there (single versus married, lazy versus hard-working, body odor verses fresh-smelling, and any other pertinent information).

◑ PRO *Because you don't work at the company, you will stand out and have that "new girl" appeal. Plus, no one will fault you Monday morning for drinking too much or going home with the guy from sales.*

◑ CON *Unless you're terrifically outgoing, you're at the mercy of the friend who invited you.*

769. A WORK CONFERENCE

Regional and national business conferences are a great way to get cutting-edge information in your field, to network with coworkers . . . and to meet men from other companies. Most business conferences include cocktail hours, dinners, and optional late-night excursions around the host city with fellow conference goers—all great opportunities to meet new guys who just happen to share your profession. Just make sure not to partake in too many complimentary cocktails—these are people you want to respect you; you don't want them to see you tipsy.

770. YOUNG PROFESSIONALS MEETING

Most cities have young professionals groups these days, where people join together to mingle, network . . . and meet potential dating partners. These groups tend to attract ambitious, successful, and outgoing guys. Many members of these organizations have recently moved to the area for a job and are looking for new people—and women—to socialize with.

◑ PRO *You will know the guys you meet in these groups have decent jobs.*

◑ CON *These organizations tend to draw business-minded individuals, so if you're not interested in all-business most-of-the-time, this is probably not your best forum.*

771.   AT WORK

$

Despite all the warnings out there about dating men you work with, it's actually one of the most popular places for couples to meet. Heidi from Alameda, California, knows first hand. "I met my soul mate in the office at my last job, six years ago," she says. "We dated for about three years while at the same job, and broke up twice. It was hard working with him when things were going badly, but working together actually forced us to deal with some of the hard stuff because we had no other choice. If we hadn't worked together, we probably wouldn't have stayed in touch after our breakups, and then gotten back together for what I hope is the last time!"

PRO *Proximity: You see the people you work with more than you see your family and friends.*

CON *The breakup factor Heidi talked about: If it ended badly, it could make things terribly uncomfortable on a daily basis.*

772.   BUSINESS DISTRICT BAR

$ $

Where do single professional men go at 6:00 on a Thursday or Friday evening? The closest bars to their offices. So where should you go to meet these men? A bar, pub, or lounge in close proximity to a few large office buildings. Situate yourself close to a group of guys, smile, and be friendly.

773.   WORKING AT THE GAP

$

Jennifer from Allentown, Pennsylvania, got a part-time job at The Gap for the discounts . . . she never dreamed she'd meet so many single guys who needed fashion advice. "Usually, when guys are shopping alone, they're single," she says. "And I was right there to help them pick the sweater color that looked best." And chances are, the guy who's shopping at The Gap has at least some sense of style, even if he does need some help from a friendly associate (that would be you).

PRO *The discounts and the exposure to the very latest fashion trends.*

CON *If you have a tendency to over-shop, the proximity to all that discounted clothing could eat up your paycheck in a hurry!*

774. HEALTH SCREENING

Many health-conscious companies and organizations sponsor free health screenings for their employees. If you work for a larger one of these companies, the health screening may not only clue you in to your overall health status, it may expose you to some guys who work in your company whom you would have never met otherwise. So as you wait to have blood drawn or your skin checked for suspicious moles, smile and chat with the people around you.

775. WORK BANQUET

If you work at a large company with multiple branches, you will see lots of new faces when the locations join together at a banquet where there are hors d'oeuvres, drinks, and dinner; in other words, lots of opportunities to socialize. You will have your place of work in common with the men you meet . . . without the awkwardness of working in the same building. So don't turn down any opportunities to attend one of these events.

○ PRO *You know all guys you meet will be employed.*

○ CON *If your company is national, some of the guys could live pretty far away.*

776. WORKING AS A WAITRESS

Even if you already have a day job, if you are looking to meet new men, a part-time waitress job may be in your best interest. Sarah S. met a ton of nice men when she was working as a waitress at an upscale restaurant in Boston, including one man who she is currently dating. "Waitressing is great—you can chat and get to know your male customers and make some extra cash at the same time," she says. "And in addition to the customers, I made some wonderful friends who worked at the restaurant."

○ PRO *You will be out and about and earning money at the same time.*

○ CON *Working as a waitress can be challenging because some members of the general public can be totally rude. You will have to be prepared to take the good with the bad.*

777. CORPORATE GOLF OUTING

If you work at a mid- to large-sized company, your company probably holds a golf event. Sometimes they're for charity, but often they are just a fun way to get the company workforce out for a few laughs. If your company doesn't have a golf outing, see what you can do to put one together. You'll meet new male coworkers and get a chance to speak with them in a comfortable and fun environment. Get involved with the organization of the event and you'll be off to a great start.

778. WORKING AS A TOUR GUIDE

Working as a tour guide can be great for several reasons. One, you will get outside in the fresh air and explore a town of interest on the weekend afternoons. Two, tour guide jobs tend to pay pretty well for a part-time gig. And three, this job will expose you to hundreds of single men with an interest in the town you're showcasing.

○ PRO *You can get the conversation rolling by asking an attractive group member if he has any questions about your city or town.*

○ CON *If he's getting a tour, he's probably from out of town, so you may be embarking on a long-distance relationship if you hit it off.*

779. TEACHERS' LOUNGE

They're educated. They like kids. They have the summer off and traditionally, they have a solid pension plan. If you're a teacher, this is an easy one. If you're not, you can always find a friend who is a teacher and just tell her you want to pop in one day at lunchtime to meet her. From there, you can survey the scene and make an educated decision.

780. YOUR FRIEND'S OFFICE

Offices are crawling with single men. Your own office may not be the best place for you to find one, but your friend's office is a different story. So next time you're meeting a friend for lunch, offer to meet her inside her building, so you can get a look at her male coworkers. If you spot one you like (and you get the thumbs up that he is single), ask your friend if she can invite him to join the two of you next time.

○ PRO *If things don't work out, you won't worry about bumping into him at the printer.*

○ CON *If things don't work out, your friend might worry about bumping into him at the printer, which could make her feel uncomfortable.*

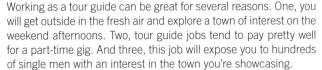

781. UNEMPLOYMENT LINE

In the topsy-turvy world of today's economy, you can find all types of people in the unemployment line. While you may think this place is one of the worst places to find a man, don't be too quick to judge. There are some fantastic guys who have had unfortunate circumstances hit them, whether they make $10 per hour or $100,000 a year. They're going to need a warm shoulder and someone who will listen to them. Maybe that's you.

782. YOUR PARENT'S OFFICE

Offices are crawling with single men. And if you are in an office other than your own, none of those men will be off limits to you. So next time you're meeting your mom or dad for lunch, offer to meet inside his or her building, so you can get a look at his or her male coworkers.

O PRO *If you are single, your parents are probably chomping at the bit to fix you up . . . so they will be happy to hook you up with an eligible coworker in their office.*

O CON *If your parent is on the more controlling side, you will be involving him or her in the process from the start—which could mean trouble.*

783. NEWS STATION

Single men with good jobs running around in ties. Just say you were always curious to see where it all goes down. Men love that. You might even see some of the men from your local news. Plus, there are many people needed to make a news broadcast come together. Probably more than half of them are younger men. This idea is definitely different, but it has a certain romance to it. Just drop by a station and say hello. You could be surprised by what you'll find.

784. NEW JOB

A new job can give you a whole new perspective on life . . . and open up a whole new group of dating possibilities. Not only do you have the men in your office, if you hang out with your new coworkers in social situations, you will meet their friends as well. If you have a fabulous job, don't change it just for the new men, but if your job has grown as stale as your dating life, it may be the perfect time for a life transformation. Check out *www.careerbuilder.com* for jobs in your area.

=Time ♦=Friends $=Expense

785. WORKING AT THE GYM

If you have some extra time in the evening or on weekends, consider getting a part-time job working at the front desk at the gym. You'll have the opportunity to greet all the members as they walk in, which may lead to a few opportunities for romance.

786. MEDIABISTRO EVENTS

If you are a writer, editor, journalist, or other type of professional who dabbles in editorial work, consider attending some events sponsored by Mediabistro.com. Not only will these seminars and parties do wonders for your career with the valuable tips and networking opportunities they provide, they will also provide the perfect forum in which to rub elbows with men who share your passion. Mediabistro parties and seminars are held across the country throughout the year. Party themes include "Media and Film" and "Bowling Leagues," and seminar topics include "Breaking Into Television News," "The TV Drama Writer's Room," and "Fact Checking Basics." For more information, log on to *www.media bistro.com* and click on events.

787. MICROSOFT OFFICE REFRESHER COURSE

Sure, you know the basics of Excel and Access, but now and then, you still feel stumped. You wish you had the manual you received when you took the Microsoft Office course eight or so years ago . . . Well, it may be time for a new course and a new manual, both to brush up on your Office skills and to meet men who, like you, spend a lot of their workday in front of a computer. Most companies will pay for you to take a Microsoft Office course, so ask your boss first in case you can get it for free. These courses tend to be fairly interactive, which will give you a chance to get to know your "neighbor" in the class.

788. STOCKHOLDER MEETING

To mix and mingle with some financially savvy stockholders, consider buying some stocks so you can make some money off of them, and then, attend stockholder meetings. Men are impressed with a woman who manages her money wisely, so you will immediately be off to a good start.

789. WORKING AS A FLORIST

Sure, florists get a lot of men coming in to buy flowers for their wives or girlfriends. But sometimes relationships don't work out. If you are extra helpful and friendly to men who come in to buy flowers, they may remember you and come back if and when they become single. And then, of course, there are the men buying flowers for their mothers, sisters, secretaries, or for a funeral, in which case you can get to know them better right away. So if you have some time for a part-time (or full-time) job and you can create a nice flower arrangement, consider a job as a florist.

790. WORKING AS A REALTOR

Successful single men buy and sell houses . . . and sometimes they rent. But either way, they may seek the assistance of a Realtor. And as that Realtor, you will get an awful lot of face-time with your clients showing them properties, going over paperwork, and if things go well, going out for a drink or a coffee to celebrate the purchase or sale. So if you are ready for a new career, consider one as a real estate agent.

○ PRO *In a good market, Realtors can make a lot of money.*

○ CON *Bad hours. As a Realtor, you have to be available to show houses when most people aren't working . . . in other words, nights and weekends.*

791. WORKING AT A DATING SERVICE

Want to get first dibs on all the hottest single guys joining dating services? Consider a job working for Match.com, eHarmony, or one of the many other dating sites out there. If you've got great Web site building or editing skills, your services will be in demand. Keep your eye out for jobs at these dating sites on job Web sites and on the dating sites themselves.

792. WORKING IN RETAIL

As an employee in a retail store, you will be exposed to a ton of single men coming in to browse or make purchases, so think about a part-time retail job if it will fit in your schedule. For best results, choose a store that draws a lot of men, such as a men's clothing store, sporting goods store, bookstore (to meet intellectual men), or outdoor supply store.

=Time =Friends $=Expense

793.   AT THE WATER COOLER

They don't call it "water cooler" chatter for nothing. People actually do frequently gather around water coolers and catch up on the latest news and office gossip. So if you're interested in someone at your place of business, you might want to make extra sure that you are hydrated by making frequent trips. Studies show that office romances have some of the highest rates of success, so don't overlook your place of work as a potential forum for meeting men.

794.   AUDITIONS

If you live close to a major city, chances are there are auditions for advertisements, movie extras, and even parts in shows and commercials held fairly regularly in your area. Even if you're not an aspiring actress, these auditions could be a fun thing to check out on a Saturday afternoon. There are sure to be at least a few attractive men with amateur talent, and who knows—you may discover you have a hidden talent and land yourself a part!

795.   WORKING AS A DOG WALKER

If you are looking to make some extra cash, think about becoming a dog walker. You may hit it off with one of the owners of the dogs you walk (and you'll already have formed a relationship with the dog, which is a good thing). And beyond that, as a dog walker, you will attract the attention of dog-loving men who want to give one or all of the pooches you are walking a friendly pet.

○ **PRO** *If you enjoy dogs, this job won't even feel like work.*

○ **CON** *It's a dirty job. When you are walking around carrying a plastic bag full of dog doo-doo, you might not feel like meeting men.*

796.   WORKING AS A POLICE OFFICER

This is not to imply that you should leave your current place of employment for the police academy. But if you do work as a police officer, you might want to open your eyes to the dating possibilities. You don't want to date the guy you pulled over at 9 A.M. for drunk driving, but the recipient of a speeding ticket or an expired inspection sticker may have some promise.

○ **PRO** *You will have an immediate upper hand.*

○ **CON** *Only after you've completed your duties as an officer can you switch gears and be friendly.*

=Time =Friends $=Expense

797. COFFEE IN ANOTHER DEPARTMENT AT WORK

If you are a coffee drinker, the coffee machine is an important part of your workday . . . in the morning and probably in the afternoon as well. To open yourself up to some new men, consider visiting the coffee machine in a different department, or, if you work at a large company, on a different floor. The energizing effects of coffee will make you chatty, and the much-needed break will make you want to hang around the coffee machine for a few minutes to avoid heading back to your desk . . . and to see who happens to hit it up for a warm-up. If you have coffee drinking in common with a guy, you will have a wonderful excuse to get out of the office together for some "real" coffee in the form of Starbucks or some other coffee shop out of cubicle range.

798. COLLEGE OR UNIVERSITY IF YOU ARE A PROFESSOR

If you loved college so much you decided to make a career out of it by becoming a professor, your career may open up more doors than research opportunities. Colleges and universities are crawling with eligible professors who have put their personal lives on hold for the sake of their research specialties. To get to know these professors, attend as many college-sponsored seminars, social events, and extracurricular classes as you can fit into your busy schedule.

799. WORKING AS A NURSE

As a nurse, you will meet—and care for—many people in your life. And because many men have a desire to be cared for, you will probably come across numerous fascinating men and gain many admirers as a nurse. So if you are confused about a career, think about enrolling in nursing school. Not only will you open yourself up to thousands of patients, you will partake in a necessary and noble profession. To find a nursing school, check out *www.allnursing schools.com*.

✪ PRO *Nursing is a well-paying and rewarding profession and you will meet many wonderful people (not just eligible men).*

✪ CON *Nursing is not for you if you have a weak stomach. Plus, going into it purely to meet men is unethical.*

=Time ₸=Friends $=Expense

800. COMPANY MEETING

If you work at a large company, you probably have a quarterly, bian-nual, or annual meeting where the entire company, which may include offices from around the country or around the globe, gets together. In addition to being a fun excuse for a trip (if the meeting takes place at an office other than yours), this company meeting could present an opportunity to meet men. First, you will know that any men who work at your company have a career interest that is somewhat similar to yours, and second, you will have plenty to talk about.

801. JOB INTERVIEW

If you get called to interview for a job you're not that interested in, you should still go for it. First, once you hear more about what the job entails, it may spark your interest. And second, your interviewer(s) may spark your interest too, and if it ends up that you don't want the job, you can always say so on the spot (the interviewer will probably appreciate your honesty) and then use his business card to contact him for a date a few days later.

802. EDITOR'S WORKSHOP

Whether you are an editor by trade and you want to polish your editing skills to help in some aspects of your job, or you'd like to do some editing on the side, an editor's workshop can provide some valuable tips to help you learn or perfect the trade. Most colleges and universities offer editor's workshops, so check out the Web sites of schools in your area to see what they have to offer.

803. YOUR COMPANY NEWSLETTER

Company newsletters are a nice way to get an overview of who works in your organization—new employees, employees celebrat-ing an anniversary, employees receiving awards, and other impor-tant events. If you work in a large corporation, these newsletters can be like a mini-dating service. The photos can help you see if there are any men you'd like to pursue. Or, on the flip side, if you can get your own photograph in the newsletter by celebrating an anniversary or winning an award, go for it. The single men are surely using the company newsletter for the very same purpose.

O PRO *If a man is in the newsletter, he's no slacker (unless he's a new employee, in which case he needs a friend to show him around).*

O CON *You will have to come up with an excuse to contact a man who catches your eye.*

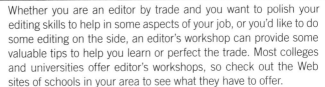

=Time ♥=Friends $=Expense

804. BARTENDING

⏰ ⏰ ⏰

$

Bartending can be a very lucrative job—and it can expose you to many interesting men. Lots of men stop by and have a cocktail or glass of wine by themselves after work or on a Saturday afternoon. And who do they chat with? The bartender. Of course bartending will also expose you to a lot of drunk losers, but you will quickly learn how to spot them.

805. WORKING AS A CAMP COUNSELOR

⏰ ⏰ ⏰

$

To meet single men in the form of fellow counselors and single dads, consider getting a job as a camp counselor. If you work as a teacher nine months of the year, the job will fit into your schedule.

◐ PRO *Men will be turned on by your love of the outdoors and children.*

◑ CON *You will have to take a CPR course before you can apply for the job.*

806. ETIQUETTE COURSE

⏰ ⏰ ⏰

$ $ $

Etiquette courses are a wonderful idea for anyone who wants to know the right fork to use at which course and appropriate topics of conversation at a business dinner. Men and women alike can use some pointers on how to present themselves in the most professional, polished manner possible. Plus, these etiquette courses tend to draw successful professionals, and they offer time for questions and interaction between class members. Think about it: If you hit it off with someone in your class, you can go out afterward to practice your table manners and social skills!

807. DALE CARNEGIE

⏰ ⏰ ⏰

$ $ $

Dale Carnegie is a club aimed at improving members' overall confidence level and public speaking skills. Dale Carnegie attracts a lot of professionals, and the supportive group atmosphere is wonderful for making new friends . . . and maybe more. For more information on Dale Carnegie or to find a chapter in your area, check out *www.dalecarnegie.com*.

◐ PRO *Even if you don't meet someone, you will most likely boost your confidence level.*

◑ CON *If you have a severe phobia of public speaking, you may not want to practice in front of guys you'd like to date, no matter how supportive they may be.*

⏰=Time ♟=Friends $=Expense

808.   MODELING AT A DEPARTMENT STORE

It's become more rare, but there are some department stores that still feature live "mannequins" in their windows or live models who walk the store and showcase the latest fashions. So if you've always dreamed of modeling, watch the paper for modeling job openings. Not only will you get to try on some fabulous clothes, you will get to meet and chat with tons of shoppers—including single male ones—all day long.

O PRO *As a model, you will get lots of attention from the men.*

O CON *You have to be reasonably tall and attractive to get a modeling job.*

809.   CORPORATE VOLLEYBALL TOURNAMENT

If you're at a mid- to large-sized company, you probably hold at least one corporate event. Sometimes they are for charity, but often they are just a fun way to get the company employees out in the fresh air for a few laughs. If your company doesn't have a volleyball outing, see what you can do to put one together. There are some great causes out there your company can represent, and no matter how you spike it, you'll meet new male coworkers and get a chance to speak with them in a comfortable and fun environment.

d date flea market reunion restaurant tattoo parlor wedding auction ho
ub baby shower casino hibachi ladies night café bake sale brunch river
mbake double date culinary festival smorgasbord tavern church service
mal hospital roommates yacht club school courthouse nudist colony bee
val baseball game car show firefighting fishing tailgating poker campgr
ting contest bowling weight room military cigar shop airport london bri
eiffel tower vacation hotel cruise mardi gras times square central par
f america mount rushmore hollywood safari smithsonian online animal
e blood drive volunteering special olympics toy drive red cross soup kit
rt gallery book club cooking class library museum college campus orche
ature walk planetarium political rally shakespeare festival disney world
uarium water park caroling parents playground mini-golf county fair co
use laundromat grocery store beach gym subway deli yard sale liquor
ost office personal ads company picnic conference water cooler bartend
oncert scavenger hunt karaoke comedy club biking karate softball pain
iling ymca square dancing boardwalk cookout whale watching farmer's
et party friends cafeteria open house singing group bars beach house
ting blind date flea market reunion restaurant tattoo parlor wedding au
ospital club baby shower casino hibachi ladies night café bake sale bru
verboat clambake double date culinary festival smorgasbord tavern chu
ervice spa animal hospital roommates yacht club school courthouse nu
ony beer festival baseball game car show firefighting fishing tailgating
ampground eating contest bowling weight room military cigar shop airp
ndon bridges bus eiffel tower vacation hotel cruise mardi gras times sq
tral park mall of america mount rushmore hollywood safari smithsonian
e animal rescue blood drive volunteering special olympics toy drive red
p kitchen art gallery book club cooking class library museum college ca
rchestra nature walk planetarium political rally shakespeare festival dis
orld zoo aquarium water park caroling parents playground mini-golf co
ir coffeehouse laundromat grocery store beach gym subway deli yard
quor store post office personal ads company picnic conference water co
rtending concert scavenger hunt karaoke comedy club biking karate so
ntball sailing ymca square dancing cookout whale watching farmer's m
ty friends cafeteria open house singing group bars beach house wine ta
d date flea market reunion restaurant tattoo parlor wedding auction ho
ub baby shower casino hibachi ladies night café bake sale brunch river
mbake double date culinary festival smorgasbord tavern church service
mal hospital roommates yacht club school courthouse nudist colony bee
val baseball game car show firefighting fishing tailgating poker campgro
ting contest bowling weight room military cigar shop airport london bri
eiffel tower vacation hotel cruise mardi gras times square central park
f america mount rushmore hollywood safari smithsonian online animal
e blood drive volunteering special olympics toy drive red cross soup kite
rt gallery book club cooking class library museum college campus orche
ature walk planetarium political rally shakespeare festival disney world

entertaining ways

810.   CONCERT

Except for Barry Manilow, Britney Spears, or any American Idol performer, most concerts are full of single men. So when a band or singer you like comes into town, snag a ticket and check it out. First, make sure you like the performers you are going to see because concert tickets usually go for at least $50 a pop these days. Second, if you meet a man there, you don't want to start off a relationship as a poser. And third, if you have a favorite band or singer in common with a guy, you are probably on a similar wavelength, so be real.

811.   LOCAL BAND PERFORMANCES

Local bands have groupies . . . both male and female ones. So if you see a striking and potentially single guy enjoying the same guitar riff you are at a local show, the chances are good you will see him at the band's next show as well.

812.   MUSIC FESTIVAL

Music festivals combine two things most guys love—beer and live music. So if you hang out at a music festival, you are guaranteed to see single men. And in addition to the plethora of men, festivals offer the perfect social environment to get to know them, says Kathryn Alice, love and relationship expert in Los Angeles, California, and author of *Love Will Find You*. To find music festivals in your area, check out your local newspaper or entertainment paper.

813.   MUSICAL

OK, this one is a little tougher. At the risk of stereotyping, most single guys don't consider an evening at a musical a fabulous night out. But there are the guys who are there with their sister, niece, cousin, or mother—guys who are nice enough to suck it up and try to enjoy a musical. So look around the theater for someone to buy a cocktail or a box of candy for at intermission. Try going to a performance around Mother's Day. There will be lots of guys treating Mom.

814. SCAVENGER HUNT

You probably have fond memories of embarking on a scavenger hunt or two as a kid, and as an adult, a scavenger hunt can be a unique way to spend an afternoon . . . and to meet men. On a scavenger hunt, you will be mentally engaged with the guys (or guy, depending on how the hunt is organized) in your group, which will instantly generate a connection. A company called Watson Adventures (*www.watsonadventures.com*) hosts scavenger hunts for singles at zoos, museums, circuses, and other interesting venues in cities such as Boston, New York, San Francisco, and Seattle.

815. CD STORE

If you are a music lover—particularly, if you are an eclectic music lover—you have probably spent many hours browsing your local CD store, the one that always has exactly what you're looking for. Music, especially eclectic music, is the perfect conversation starter. So next time you're in the market for a special CD, take a look around at the fellow shoppers and ask what they have to recommend.

816. MUSIC STORE

If you play an instrument or you just get energized by being around piles of sheet music and strings, head to your local music store. Along with a wide selection of guitars and keyboards, you will find free-spirited, and in some cases, musically gifted guys . . . not to mention the people who work there.

817. CRAFT SHOW

Craft shows are wonderful events for people who make crafts, love crafts, and for folks who just enjoy a pleasant day outdoors. In addition to creative, artistic designs in the form of jewelry, paintings, sculptures, clothing, and much more, most craft shows are held outdoors and offer food, music, drinks, and other forms of entertainment . . . as well as single guys who appreciate fine arts and crafts. Whether they are there to shop for items, sell items, or purely for the good food and atmosphere, there will be single men walking around a craft show. You just have to find them.

 =Time =Friends $=Expense

818. KARAOKE NIGHT

If you've always dreamed of a singing career and only get to fantasize about making it come true in the shower, you probably already love karaoke night at your local bar or club. But you might not have thought that at karaoke night, you could meet guys who share a similar fantasy . . . and who aren't afraid to indulge it with an occasional karaoke number themselves.

O PRO *A guaranteed fun night out.*

O CON *There are people who hang out at karaoke night who take it a little too seriously. Keep it lighthearted and fun, and you will keep yourself from falling into this category.*

819. TV SHOW PREMIERE PARTY

Some television shows are attracting such a cult following that bars are sponsoring premiere parties where people can gather with fellow fans, and eat, drink, and enjoy the show. *Lost,* for example, has sparked some of these parties across the country. And in a room full of people who love a show as much as you do, there will be no shortage of conversation. To find out where these parties are being hosted, check your local newspaper, or listen to or call your local radio stations.

820. LATE-NIGHT TALK SHOW AUDIENCE

Be it Jay Leno, Jon Stewart, or David Letterman, almost everyone has a favorite late-night talk show host. And your favorite late-night guy actually says a lot about your personality. So by attending a taping of your favorite show, you may put yourself smack in the middle of a group of guys with whom you are very compatible. Look into how you can get a pair of tickets to one of these tapings, grab a girlfriend who shares your love of the show, and go for it.

O PRO *The most you have to lose is a lot of laughs.*

O CON *Tickets to late-night talk show tapings can be hard to get—you might have to be patient.*

821.   PIANO BAR WITH DUELING PLAYERS

For an entertaining evening full of great music and competition, you can't beat a piano bar. Because of the "dueling" nature, piano bar patrons tend to mingle and get to know each other as they watch the battle between the musicians unfold. For maximum single guy exposure, be open and friendly—don't huddle in a corner with your girlfriends; instead, walk up to someone you find attractive and ask him which player he thinks is better.

822.   COLLEGE PLAY

Colleges with good theater departments generally put on some really impressive plays . . . so impressive, in fact, that you will forget you're at a college play. And compared to Broadway, tickets for college plays are quite reasonable. So you have no excuse not to check out a college rendition of *The Taming of the Shrew* on a Friday night. Plus, at intermission, you might meet some open-minded single guys looking for an alternative to the bar scene or cheering on his younger sibling.

823.   COMEDY CLUB

Sharing a similar sense of humor is one of the things that can keep couples happy, laughing, and together. So if you meet a guy at a comedy club when one of your favorite standup comedians is performing, you are off to a great start. Look around and see who seems to appreciate the same lines and jokes . . . you could have more in common with him than a similar funny bone. If he's sitting with friends (and no apparent girlfriends), send the table a round of drinks or wait until he gets up from his table to approach the bar.

824.   PING-PONG TOURNAMENT

If you can hold your own behind a Ping-Pong table, consider putting your skills to the test in a Ping-Pong tournament. Aside from the excitement of the competition, you will have an opportunity to meet tens to hundreds (depending on the size of the tournament) of players, of whom the majority will probably be male.

○ PRO *If the tournament is for a charity, you stand to help raise money for a good cause; if it's not for a charity, you stand to win some money for yourself.*

○ CON *Some of these tournaments are pretty competitive, so if you've only picked up a Ping-Pong paddle a few times in your life, just go as a spectator.*

⏱=Time 👥=Friends $=Expense

825. SUNDAY AFTERNOON DOUBLE FEATURE

Don't waste a Sunday afternoon in the dead of winter on your couch—use it as an opportunity to see a double feature. It's perfectly acceptable to go to the movies by yourself . . . twice. Plus, movies tend to draw fellow singles looking for a pleasant way to spend their free Sunday. So check the paper for a lineup that sparks your interest and head out. Make sure you check out the other patrons in the lobby and at the concession stand. If you spot someone interesting, try to find a seat close to him for the shows.

826. THANKSGIVING DAY PARADE

Before or after you've stuffed yourself with turkey, filling, and football (or the televised dog show), why not head out and enjoy the nearest Thanksgiving Day parade? Between the floats and the festive crowd, you are guaranteed to leave full of holiday spirit. And if you keep your eyes open, you may leave with a new friend, too . . . or more than a friend. At the parade, you'll likely be shoulder to shoulder with numerous people, so why not make the most of the situation and get to know them? You just might meet someone with whom you can spend the rest of the holiday season . . .

O PRO *If you live near New York City, you may get your first up-close and personal shot of the Cat in the Hat balloon.*

O CON *The crowds can be downright stifling. If you're claustrophobic, stay away.*

827. AT THE JUKEBOX

When you're hanging out at a bar, a great way to meet people is by playing songs on the jukebox. Take your time picking out your selections, and if a cute stranger approaches you with a suggestion for a song, by all means, play it. Music is one of the fastest ways to connect with strangers. On the flip side, if you spot someone interesting picking out songs, approach him with a suggestion yourself. If he plays it, you've got the green light to talk to him.

 =Time =Friends $=Expense

828. GETTING YOUR CARICATURE DRAWN AT A FAIR

If you opt to sit down and allow a caricature artist to sketch an exaggerated version of your face, your courage may pay off. For one, you will draw attention to yourself. Onlookers may stop to check out the likeness of you and turn into instant admirers. And there's always the potential for hitting it off with the artist himself. So next time you're at a festival or fair that features caricatures, see what the artist comes up with.

○ PRO *These drawings are usually reasonably priced and take less than 30 minutes to draw (so you won't be in the spotlight too long).*

○ CON *If you are self-critical, stay away from caricatures. They sometimes exaggerate a person's most unflattering features.*

829. HARLEM GLOBETROTTERS SHOW

Believe it or not, the Harlem Globetrotters are still playing their unique form of basketball all over the world, and it's a great show. For some good, wholesome entertainment and the potential to meet lots of Globetrotters fans—of which there are a lot more guys than girls—pay attention to when the team is playing in your area. For more information, check out *www.harlemglobetrotters.com*.

830. ROCK CONCERT

A rock concert is a great place to meet people. For one, you know you share a taste in music, so you have an instant topic of conversation. Before the show starts, get to know the people sitting around you. Ask them if they have seen the band before, what their favorite albums are, and so on. If things go well, you may share a drink or a cup of coffee and talk about your favorite parts of the concert when it's over.

○ PRO *More guys attend concerts than girls, so the ratio will be in your favor.*

○ CON *Some concerts can be really loud. If you are easily bothered, bring some earplugs.*

831.   WAX MUSEUM

Staring at wax likenesses of celebrities like Brad Pitt and Angelina Jolie could be a fun bonding experience. Stroll through a wax museum by yourself or with a girlfriend and check out the live figures around you as well as the inanimate ones. If you spot someone you'd like to get to know, make your way over to him in the crowd. Then when you get a chance, ask him if he thinks a particular figure looks like the real person. If he's no friendlier to you than the wax figures, quickly move on.

832.   BACKSTAGE AFTER A CONCERT

Nothing feels better than scoring a few tickets to a concert by one of your favorite bands or artists . . . except, of course, scoring backstage passes to the show. If you get a chance to get backstage passes, grab them. Not only will you get the opportunity to see the stars of the concert up close and personal, you will mingle with fellow fans, whom you may very well be just as excited to meet as the musicians themselves.

833.   FILM FESTIVAL

Love independent films? There are many like-minded single guys like you, singles who flock to film festivals to check out the latest in cinematic creativity. To meet these potential soul mates, you have to be at the film festival yourself, laughing at the same parts and appreciating the same camera angles. So if there's a film festival in your area, try your hardest to score some tickets.

◊ PRO *If you meet someone, the two of you can enjoy independent films together for the rest of your lives and live happily ever after. The end.*

◊ CON *If you live in a more rural, remote area, finding a film festival to attend may be a struggle. Check local colleges and universities.*

834.   COOKING SHOW TAPING

Many television cooking shows are taped in major cities, so the next time you are visiting a big city, drop by one of the cooking studios. They're always looking for audience members. Take a chance and see if they seat you next to some unsuspecting guy who also wants to try some new dishes. For example, check out *http://nycvisit.com* for more information on getting tickets to New York cooking shows.

=Time ♦=Friends $=Expense

835. MEDIEVAL RESTAURANT

If you ever have the opportunity to go to one of these fun, theme restaurants, you should definitely seize the opportunity to go back in time—at least for a few hours. In addition to seeing a medieval show (typically involving knights swordfighting), your waiter or waitress will be wearing medieval garb, and will keep in character—you'll feel like you're part of the show! Often, these restaurants serve you at a banquet-style table, so you may find yourself seated with a cute, single guy. These places tend to attract groups, so grab a few girlfriends and head out for a night of medieval fun!

O PRO *You'll have a blast, and enjoy great food and beer served in large steins.*

O CON *Keeping with medieval times, you'll eat your food the old-fashioned way—sans utensils. If you like a more refined dining experience, skip this one.*

836. REALITY TV CASTING CALLS

Reality TV casting calls are relatively easy to find. Check out *www.realitytvworld.com* and think about the type of man you'd like to meet. Would he try out for *American Idol*? How about *The Apprentice*? Maybe he's attempting to be the country's next heartthrob as *The Bachelor*. No matter which show he's choosing, or which casting call you check out, you'll find an array of men looking their best and hoping for approval. Make an appearance and make yourself noticeable. It will be worth it.

O PRO *You may just land yourself a spot on a TV show.*

O CON *The statistics on reality-show love successes aren't great.*

837. TALK SHOW AUDIENCE

Make your trip to New York or Los Angeles a memorable one. Do your man-hunting while enjoying yourself! Check out sites like *http://nycvisit.com* and become a part of the best shows on television—from *Late Show with David Letterman* and *Saturday Night Live* to *The Daily Show* and *Last Call with Carson Daly* and more. Think about the kind of man you want to meet. Would he be a fan of Jon Stewart? Would he like Regis? Choose which show you'd like to see and go for it. There isn't a more entertaining way to meet a guy.

838. IMAX THEATER

Want to see a film you can completely immerse yourself in? Grab a friend and head to an IMAX theater, where you will view an action-packed film in crystal clear images up to eight stories high. To maximize your man exposure at an IMAX film, go see a feature that is manly in nature, such as the film that follows climbers on Everest, the one that simulates the weightlessness of space, or the one that allows viewers to slam-dunk with Michael Jordon. For more information, check out *www.imax.com*.

839. ROCKY HORROR PICTURE SHOW

Since 1975, the *Rocky Horror Picture Show* has been entertaining wacky cult audiences with its quirky, catchy music and plot. And it's still being shown in cities across the country. People in the audience have usually seen the show numerous times, and they shout out responses to the characters in the movie. Whether you've seen the *Rocky Horror Picture Show* repeatedly yourself or you're hungry for a new experience, you are in for a fun, bonding experience with some eccentric men. To find out more about the show, check out *www.rockyhorror.com*.

○ PRO *If anyone ever asks you if you've seen it, you can say "Yes!"*

○ CON *Some of the people who regularly go to the Rocky Horror Picture Show are a little . . . out there. Be prepared.*

840. SATURDAY NIGHT LIVE TAPING

Good old Lorne Michaels and his teams of comedians have been making live audiences laugh for decades. And a lot of men—especially men with a good sense of humor—enjoy a Saturday night full of laughter and live entertainment. To meet these men, try to score tickets to a taping of *Saturday Night Live* in New York City. Check out *www.nbc.com/Saturday_Night_Live*.

○ PRO *If you meet a guy at the taping, you have a huge city full of restaurants and clubs in which to get to know him better. Plus, you may get to see a hot celebrity host (recent ones have included Justin Timberlake and Ben Affleck) in person.*

○ CON *Some critics say* Saturday Night Live *isn't as funny as it used to be, but even if you only get a few laughs, it will be worth it for the experience.*

 =Time 📍=Friends $=Expense

841. SATURDAY AFTERNOON MATINEE

Nothing to do on a dreary Saturday afternoon? Don't watch reruns on the couch—instead, head out to a Saturday afternoon matinee. It's perfectly acceptable to go to the movies by yourself, especially when it's light outside. Plus, daytime movies tend to draw fellow singles looking for a pleasant way to spend a free weekend day. So check the paper for a matinee that sparks your interest. When you arrive at the theater, scan the other patrons in the lobby and at the concession stand. If you spot someone interesting, try to find a seat close to him for the show.

842. DOG SHOW

If you are an extreme dog lover, you probably stop on the channel with the dog show as you're skimming through on a Saturday afternoon. So why not go see the show in person? In addition to the fluffed-up show dogs, you will be under one roof with other diehard dog owners and lovers, and you could find your match in the single man group.

O PRO *As a dog lover, you will be thoroughly entertained.*

O CON *The movie Best in Show was pretty accurate—some dog show people are a little over the top. And some of them are also gay.*

843. LORD OF THE DANCE

Believe it or not, Michael Flatley's performances (*Riverdance, Lord of the Dance*) are dancing shows that men actually enjoy. Maybe it's the bagpipes, or maybe it's the multiple girls in skirts hopping in unison, but a higher proportion of men seem to pop up at these performances. So the next time you have an opportunity to go to a Flatley show, don't turn it down. And make sure you hang around the bar or snack stand at intermission to get a load of your fellow audience members. For show information, visit *www.lordofthedance.com*.

844. OPENING NIGHT OF A POPULAR ACTION MOVIE

Some men revert back to little boys when it comes to movies—they repeatedly watch the trailer of *Star Wars, Oceans 12,* or another movie, anxiously awaiting opening night. Then when opening night arrives, these men are lined up in droves in front of the theaters. So where should you be in order to meet these men? Lined up in front of the theaters alongside them. Even if you have no interest in seeing the movie, you may want to jump in line for a little while to see if any of the moviegoers sparks your interest.

O PRO *If you do make it into the theater, you may enjoy the movie.*

O CON *Some of the more cultish films like Star Wars tend to draw a few men who still live in their parents' basements.*

845. COMMUNITY THEATER

Many small cities and towns offer community theaters where local actors put on plays and musicals. If your area hosts one of these theaters, you're wise to get tickets to a Friday or Saturday night performance, both for the inexpensive entertainment and for the opportunity to meet fellow audience members in line or at the snack stand or bar at intermission. You'd be surprised at how many men appreciate a good live play now and then, and even the single men who aren't thrilled to be there should get credit for taking their mother or sister for a night out. So for a good overview of what your community has to offer—both in terms of acting talent and men—check out your local theater.

O PRO *Compared to New York prices, you will get a lot of action for your buck.*

O CON *A large portion of the audience may be married or gay.*

846. GALLERY OPENING FOR A HOT NEW ARTIST

Art galleries are wonderful places for meeting singles, so pick up brochures now and then to see who's coming in with a new exhibit. In addition to the artist himself, the opening night will attract his friends, family members, and other community members interested in art.

O PRO *With music, food, and drink, art galleries present the perfect setting for meeting new people.*

O CON *If you're not particularly fond of the artist's paintings or sculptures, you will have to fake it or bite your tongue to be polite.*

847.   FASHION SHOW

With the whole metrosexual thing becoming more in vogue, you can find a surprising number of (straight) men at fashion shows these days. After all, men like watching models. And beyond the audience members, a fashion show may present handsome male models (to drool over if nothing else). If you receive an invitation, dress to the nines and keep your eyes peeled. A great fashion show extravaganza is Fashion Week in New York City, where people gather from all over the world to see famous designers' latest creations. To find out more, visit *http://nymag.com/fashion/fashionshows*.

848.   OSCAR PARTY

If you love the glitz and glamour of the Oscars, and you also love the movies they celebrate, throw an Oscar party. It's a great excuse to invite some friends to your house. To make it extra festive, ask people to dress in tuxes and gowns for the occasion. And here's the important part: In the invitation, ask your friends to bring a surprise single guest of honor. It's important to create situations to meet men. "Instead of waiting for invitations to parties, create an event that you can invite people to yourself," says Karen Jones, president of the Heart Matters and author of *Men Are Great*. "And it doesn't have to be a party," she says. "Be it brunch, a softball game, or a group outing to clean up trash in the park, all you need to do is get a small posse together and ask people to bring a few male friends."

○ PRO *With everyone gathered around the TV, you will all get to know each other.*

○ CON *You only have this excuse to throw a party once a year.*

849.   ANTIQUES ROAD SHOW

Got antique jewelry or other items you think might be worth something? It could be worth it to try to get them on *Antiques Road Show*, both for the potential profit and for the potential of meeting men at the show. First there are the appraisers. Then there are the men there for the same reason that you are—they own an antique item and would like to know how much it would bring at an auction. The scene is bustling and social—people are eager to meet each other and see what they're interested in having appraised. Keep your eye out for when the show is coming to your area. For more information, log on to *www.pbs.org/wgbh/pages/roadshow*.

850. MURDER MYSTERY DINNER THEATER

For those of you who like something a little different on a Friday night, there's murder mystery theater. You'll enjoy a three-course meal while you watch actors play out a murder scenario, and then you'll get to guess who did it. If you are looking to meet new people, the best way to approach the murder mystery dinner is to come with a friend or two, but not enough to fill a table. That way, you'll be seated with strangers (hopefully, a single one).

○ PRO *Even if you just end up hanging with your friends, the murder mystery theater promises to be a fun time.*

○ CON *You will probably have to shell out $50 to $100 per ticket.*

851. BYOB MUSIC VENUE

There are some venues out there where you can see excellent live music . . . and bring your own booze. These places tend to draw bands with a cult following and free-thinking, laid-back patrons—usually guys—who prefer to spend money on good music than on five-dollar beers. Wait until a band is playing whose style of music you enjoy—that way, you will be likely to meet a guy who has a similar taste in music.

852. THEATER/LOUNGE

Some theaters combine a cozy lounge atmosphere with an entertaining show—a fabulous combination for meeting men. These theaters offer a full bar and leather couches perfect for conversing in between acts. And the men who are attracted to these venues tend to be successful and intellectual—another fabulous combination.

○ PRO *These lounges frequently host parties and receptions perfect for mingling and meeting.*

○ CON *This is a fairly expensive evening, so you may want to reserve this outing for a few times a year.*

853. MAGIC SHOW

Everyone enjoys a good magic show now and then. So if there is a child in your life who you can take to a magic show, or if you just want to attend one for fun with a friend or two, go for it. You just might magically meet someone who is also there with a niece or nephew, or a few friends. And beyond the audience, if David Copperfield is your type, there's always the magician himself.

=Time =Friends $=Expense

854.   ON-SITE RADIO PROMOTION

They're always up to something outrageous and they're often right around the corner. Your local rock, hip-hop, or sports talk station is throwing a promotion near you. You just need to find it. Find some of your favorite stations' Web sites and look to see where they're having special promotional events. Men and women come out in droves to see their favorite DJ, enjoy food and drink specials, improve the community, lend a hand with a food or toy drive, and more. Why not check it out?

O PRO *These events sometimes give out some really cool prizes.*

O CON *If you live in the middle of nowhere, your local radio station's events may not be so happening.*

855.   TRIVIA NIGHT AT A BAR

Trivia nights are becoming more popular in pubs and bars, and they provide a great opportunity to meet guys. First, you get a preview of the trivia contestants' basic knowledge. Second, you can team up with interesting new strangers and feel an instant bond. Third, trivia nights draw a lot of repeat customers, so you know there's a good chance he'll be there next Thursday, too.

O PRO *Trivia nights provide a lighthearted, fun atmosphere for meeting new people.*

O CON *They are almost always held in bars, so if you have a thing about not meeting guys in watering holes, this isn't your place.*

date flea market reunion restaurant tattoo parlor wedding auction ho
ub baby shower casino hibachi ladies night café bake sale brunch river
mbake double date culinary festival smorgasbord tavern church service
nal hospital roommates yacht club school courthouse nudist colony bee
al baseball game car show firefighting fishing tailgating poker campgro
ting contest bowling weight room military cigar shop airport london bri
eiffel tower vacation hotel cruise mardi gras times square central park
america mount rushmore hollywood safari smithsonian online animal r
e blood drive volunteering special olympics toy drive red cross soup kitc
t gallery book club cooking class library museum college campus orche
ature walk planetarium political rally shakespeare festival disney world
arium water park caroling parents playground mini-golf county fair co
se laundromat grocery store beach gym subway deli yard sale liquor s
ost office personal ads company picnic conference water cooler bartend
ncert scavenger hunt karaoke comedy club biking karate softball paint
ling ymca square dancing boardwalk cookout whale watching farmer's
t party friends cafeteria open house singing group bars beach house w
ing blind date flea market reunion restaurant tattoo parlor wedding au
spital club baby shower casino hibachi ladies night café bake sale bru
verboat clambake double date culinary festival smorgasbord tavern chu
rvice spa animal hospital roommates yacht club school courthouse nuc
ny beer festival baseball game car show firefighting fishing tailgating p
mpground eating contest bowling weight room military cigar shop airp
don bridges bus eiffel tower vacation hotel cruise mardi gras times squ
tral park mall of america mount rushmore hollywood safari smithsonian
animal rescue blood drive volunteering special olympics toy drive red c
o kitchen art gallery book club cooking class library museum college car
rchestra nature walk planetarium political rally shakespeare festival disn
rld zoo aquarium water park caroling parents playground mini-golf cou
r coffeehouse laundromat grocery store beach gym subway deli yard s
uor store post office personal ads company picnic conference water coo
tending concert scavenger hunt karaoke comedy club biking karate sof
tball sailing ymca square dancing cookout whale watching farmer's ma
y friends cafeteria open house singing group bars beach house wine ta
date flea market reunion restaurant tattoo parlor wedding auction hos
b baby shower casino hibachi ladies night café bake sale brunch riverb
nbake double date culinary festival smorgasbord tavern church service
al hospital roommates yacht club school courthouse nudist colony beer
al baseball game car show firefighting fishing tailgating poker campgro
ing contest bowling weight room military cigar shop airport london brid
eiffel tower vacation hotel cruise mardi gras times square central park
america mount rushmore hollywood safari smithsonian online animal re
blood drive volunteering special olympics toy drive red cross soup kitc
gallery book club cooking class library museum college campus orches
ture walk planetarium political rally shakespeare festival disney world

activeways

856. BIKING

One of the best ways to meet a man you are compatible with is to do the things you love . . . in groups. If you love to road bike, mountain bike, or both, look around for people to meet as you take in the scenery on a ride. If you normally bike on deserted roads (which isn't a great idea anyway), switch to more public areas, such as neighborhoods, popular bike trails, and parks.

857. DRIVING RANGE

If you are looking for single guys, especially if you are looking for single guys older than thirty, you can't beat the driving range. "For the life of me, I can't figure out why more single women don't go to their local driving range," says Abby, a thirty-something single. "There are nothing but men there, and most of them are more than willing to give you advice on how to straighten out your slice."

○ PRO *The male to female ratio is guaranteed to be in your favor.*

○ CON *Some men use golf as an excuse to get away from the women in their lives, so you may get some cold shoulders.*

858. SPORT YOU LOVE

Marit F., an avid swimmer and senior account executive in Salt Lake City who never was a big fan of the bar scene, met her boyfriend Tom at the indoor pool where Tom is a master swim coach. "I walked in, took one look at the coach, and thought, 'oh my god, he is beautiful.' I passed him on the deck and he sort of croakingly said, 'warm up.' I knew that he liked me from that moment—it's funny how you just know. We've been together for a year and a half and he just moved in with me." Marit's advice to all women: "Be who you are and do what you love. It's the best way to meet someone who will share your interests and passions."

859. KARATE CLASS

As a single woman, the more methods of self-defense you learn, the better. And the coordination, power, and workout associated are all bonuses. Not to mention the potential for clicking with a karate classmate or instructor. "Martial arts classes are usually full of men and offer a social environment conducive to connecting," says Kathryn Alice, a relationship and love expert in Los Angeles, California, and author of *Love Will Find You*. To find a karate class in your area, check your newspaper, local YMCA, or community college.

---

860. SOFTBALL

Softball leagues are some of the most popular adult sports leagues in the country. Whether you join a league at your company or in your neighborhood, you are bound to find some single guys in the mix of the twenty- to sixty-year-old slow-pitch players.

⭕ PRO *The after-game happy hours and good wholesome fun of the game.*

◐ CON *You have to be able to hit the ball now and then.*

---

861. ADULT SKIING LESSONS

If you have never skied, it is in your best interest to take a lesson before you hit the slopes. Skiing is not an intuitive motion, so you will need some instruction. As a bonus, skiing lessons are often full of adventurous, fun-loving adults. Not to mention the handsome instructors.

---

862. GOLF

The best way to meet men is to go where the men are, and you can't find a spot more full of XY chromosomes than your local golf course. It's surprising that more women don't take up the sport because it is perfect for our gender—it's gentle, requires patience, and allows for socializing while you are walking or driving from hole to hole.

⭕ PRO *Golf is also a great sport to know if you are in the business field.*

◐ CON *To avoid having 18 holes take up an eight-hour day, you will want to take some lessons before you hit the course. Plus, it can be an expensive sport.*

---

863. ADULT ICE-SKATING LESSONS

If you skated as a kid and want a refresher course, or if you always wanted to glide across the ice but never learned how, there are adult lessons out there just for you. And better yet, these lessons sometimes attract open-minded, adventurous single men. Skating lessons are usually held weekly for a period of time (usually six to eight weeks), so you will have plenty of time to get to know your classmates and instructors.

⭕ PRO *You will learn a fun recreational sport you can practice for the rest of your life.*

◐ CON *The single men in your class may not be straight.*

864. BIKE TOUR

If you are a biker, a bike tour—for example, one of the rides held to benefit multiple sclerosis—could be the perfect place to meet someone new. Guys who do these types of tours are generally in good shape, friendly, and nice. If you are an avid cyclist, consider a ride that involves a weekend stay somewhere. Or if you are a beginner, think about doing a shorter ride that includes a post-event meal.

O PRO *These tours usually raise money for a good cause, so your time will be well spent.*

O CON *Even if you are just beginning, you have to be in relatively decent shape to do one of these tours.*

865. BRAZILIAN DANCE CLASS

Part samba, part reggae, Brazilian dancing combines energy, sensuousness, and rhythm—a perfect combination to get you and your fellow classmates in the mood for love. And pairs need not apply—it's perfectly acceptable to attend some of these classes solo—just make sure you call and ask before you sign up. If you're single, chances are, you'll be paired with multiple partners, and you will instantly be able to tell if the two of you have chemistry. Brazilian dancing is becoming increasingly more popular for both sexes, especially in big cities. So check out your local YMCA, other community organization, or dance studio to find out when Brazilian dance classes are available.

866. BIKING GROUP

Biking groups are a great way to meet people who share a love for the activity. To find a good biking group, stop in at your local bike shop. Explain your experience level and preferred type of riding (road versus mountain versus racing). Even if you don't meet your life partner, you are guaranteed to meet some fabulous riding partners.

=Time =Friends $=Expense

867.   PARACHUTING

$ $ $

If you have an adventurous spirit and are searching for a guy who is a thrill seeker as well, consider parachuting. You will have an experience of a lifetime and may end up hitting it off with your instructor or fellow 'chuters.

○ PRO *For the rest of your life, you will be able to say, "I have jumped out of a plane."*

○ CON *At the risk of stating the obvious, this is a dicey and expensive sport.*

868.   RUNNING GROUP

$

Running groups are a great way to meet people who share a love for the activity. To find a good running group, stop in at your local sporting goods or running shop. Explain your experience level and preferred type of running (racing, trail, or just for fun). Even if you don't meet your life partner, you are guaranteed to meet some fabulous running partners. And for the edgier runner, there is an activity that is growing in popularity called "hashing," which combines drinking a few beers with a nice trail run. Sounds dangerous, but there are those wacky runners who love it.

869.   SPEED BOWLING

$ $

Speed bowling is one of the latest methods of meeting fun-loving singles. It usually works like this: After a few icebreaker events, the women and men are split into teams of three, respectively. One male and one female team are stationed at each bowling lane. The teams then continue to rotate through the lanes so that everyone gets to know each other. To find speed bowling, check with your local alleys or dating organizations.

870.   SPINNING CLASS

$ $ $

Spinning is an ideal form of exercise if you are outgoing and looking to meet new people (including men)—it's a fabulous workout put to great music, and it still leaves you with enough wind left to socialize with the people around you. Spinning classes tend to draw a lot of regulars . . . sometimes to the point where class members have their own bikes. Some spinning classes become so close knit that they get together after class and on weekends to do other nonspinning activities as a group.

871. VOLLEYBALL

Guys who join volleyball leagues tend to be athletic, fun, and social—a great combination! And groups like this tend to go out for a snack or a drink after games and sometimes socialize even beyond that, which will give you plenty of opportunities to get to know your teammates better. And you will naturally feel a bond with your team members because, well . . . you are on the same team!

O PRO *Volleyball is a great way to keep your body and your social life in great shape.*

O CON *You have to have some spiking and setting skills to join one of these teams; if all you can do is run from the ball, you will be wasting everyone's time. There is also the potential for awkwardness if you try and fail to date one of your team members.*

872. YOGA CLASS

Any guy who takes a yoga class is not only open-minded and comfortable with his masculinity, he is probably pretty strong and flexible. Yoga also builds self-esteem, so you will have no problem marching over to the handsome guy on the mat after class and asking him out. Plus, you will get a good preview of his body since yoga clothes are generally pretty formfitting.

O PRO *Muscular men in tight clothing.*

O CON *A lot of guys think yoga is wimpy, so there will probably be more females than males in your class.*

873. DANCE CLUB

If you actually enjoy dancing, dance clubs can be a blast. Guys you meet at dance clubs may be there for a few different reasons. They may genuinely love to dance (the good kind of dance club guys), or they may be trying to get laid (the bad kind of dance club guys). One drawback of dance clubs is that at first glance, these two polar opposite guys can be hard to decipher. Tip: Make sure to bring a friend or two with you to a dance club—with roofies flying around, these are not the safest places to hang out alone.

874. | SURFING COMPETITION

If you love the beach and you love to watch surfing and attractive men, you can't beat a surfing competition. These things are crawling with handsome, laid-back surfers who are really good on a board. And there is usually some down/mingling time that provides the perfect opportunity for you to approach a surfer you have your eye on and compliment him on his last hang 10.

○ PRO *Surfers . . . everywhere.*

○ CON *Competition in the form of girls strutting around in bikinis. This is a place where you probably will not be outnumbered in the male to female ratio.*

875. | TENNIS COURTS

If you enjoy tennis and can hold your own in a game, head to the courts one afternoon by yourself. Practice on the wall and wait to see if any single players (preferably, male ones) show up to do the same. Or see if you can hop in on a doubles game if a group needs a fourth.

○ PRO *Tennis is a great social sport because you can converse as you play.*

○ CON *You may have to wait a little while before an uneven number of players shows up.*

876. | WHITE WATER RAFTING

Got an adventurous spirit? You will love white water rafting. And if you go by yourself or with just a few friends, you are bound to share a raft with a few strangers—hopefully, single ones. Most white water rafting trips take several hours, so you will have plenty of time to cooperate with your team members through the rough spots . . . and get to know them at the same time.

○ PRO *Most white water rafting courses have several routes based on experience level, so you can go even if you are a beginner.*

○ CON *If you are less than adventurous, don't go for this one— unless it's a really smooth river, white water rafting is not for the faint of heart.*

 =Time   =Friends $=Expense

877. GOLF TOURNAMENT

A lot of charities are going with the golf tournament fundraiser these days—you join a team, play some golf, have some food and drinks, and socialize—all for a good cause. Most of these golf tournaments are coed, with a strong sway toward the male side, so you are almost guaranteed to be way outnumbered by guys at a golf tournament. And the full day you spend golfing and talking with them is a great preview.

O PRO *A nice day spent outside for a good cause.*

O CON *You'll need some basic golf skills for this one; if you absolutely cannot play, you will just hold people up. Consider driving the carts instead.*

878. PLAYING VOLLEYBALL ON THE BEACH

If you are hanging out on the beach and see an opportunity to dive into a beach volleyball game, by all means, do so. Kathryn J., a publicist, met her current husband Labor Day weekend while she was playing volleyball on the beach in Martha's Vineyard. "We eloped on our fourth date on Valentine's Day, and we celebrated our 15th anniversary in 2007," she says.

879. SALSA CLUB

A salsa club is a fabulous place to meet men who like to dance. The atmosphere is energetic and sexually charged, and it's perfectly acceptable to boldly dance right up to a guy and see what he is made of on the salsa floor. Grab a few friends, put on your dancing shoes, and have a blast.

O PRO *Unless you hate salsa music, it is almost impossible to have a bad time at a salsa club.*

O CON *Just like any bar or club, salsa clubs can attract some shady characters—don't go alone, and watch out for your friends.*

880. TENNIS LESSONS

Tennis is a great sport to know for social reasons . . . and it is a great sport to learn for social reasons, too. Group tennis lessons tend to attract a nice mix of men and women, and as you improve, you may want to take your matches beyond the class and test out your skills one-on-one with a nice single tennis novice. Even if you know the basics, there is a tennis lesson out there for you—lessons are usually available for all skill levels.

⊕=Time ♦=Friends $=Expense

881. APARTMENT POOL

If you live at an apartment complex that has a pool, you may want to use it for more than a summertime cool-off. Apartment pools are a wonderful place to meet people in your complex and their friends—potentially friendly, single men. Most apartment pools are surrounded by lounge chairs, so get a feel for the lay of the land, so to speak, before you choose your spot. The closer you are to the man or men, the better your odds of talking to them.

○ PRO *Even if you don't meet a man you are interested in, you could make some great friends.*

○ CON *If you date someone in your building and it doesn't work out, there could be some uncomfortable moments in the elevator.*

882. SINGLES GOLF

Meeting people through golf is a great way to begin any relationship, personal or business; so consider the American Singles Golf Association, an organization composed of real people you can meet face-to-face while you play golf. There are American Singles Golf chapters throughout the United States and Canada. Chapters hold monthly membership meetings and multiple group golf outings and social-only events throughout the year. Golf outings consist of 32 people gathering on a Saturday afternoon to play golf and have fun . . . followed by dinner at a local restaurant. For more information, check out *www.singlesgolf.com.*

883. BODY SURFING

Nothing will bring you back to your childhood faster than body surfing on a few powerful waves at the beach. The smell of the ocean, the sharp shells under your feet, the feeling of being swept away by the current—you just can't beat the beach. And at peak season on a beautiful day, the ocean is so full of body surfers and boogie boarders that you might have to fight for a spot, which is a good thing if those body surfers are attractive single guys. So don't be afraid to accidentally wipe out in one of these guys' paths . . . it may lead to a summer romance like the one you had when you were sixteen.

884. HIGH SCHOOL TRACK

For people who like to mix a few sprints into their runs or who want to know exactly how much ground they've covered, there's the high school track. If you head to your local high school track on a Saturday or Sunday morning, you are sure to find some serious and/or detail-oriented runners. The lane situation on the track will provide the perfect opportunity for you to reel someone in just long enough to strike up a conversation. If all goes well, the two of you can run to a coffee shop for some breakfast together afterward. Tips: Be sure to hit the high school track on an off time; if you go near it during a track meet or other high school sporting event, you'll only cause annoyance and a scene. And if you spot a guy running serious sprints, wait until he is doing his cool-down jog to approach him—serious runners are pretty, well . . . serious about running.

885. MOTORCYCLE LESSONS

"I took motorcycle lessons last fall," says Lori Gorshow, president of Dating Made Simple. "The class was a mix of men and women, but there were more men by far. The men in the class really respected the women because most women choose to ride on the back rather than drive the bike." In other words, if you meet a guy while taking a motorcycle lesson, your relationship will already be off to a good start.

886. SINGLES ROLLER DERBY

Talk about a memorable night full of a fun, nostalgic activity! Throw on a pair of skates, glide across the floor, and enjoy the roller disco party. The skates and tunes will make for great conversation starters with your fellow skating singles. A roller derby will also attract open-minded guys only, so if a macho guy is your type, look for the singles demolition derby instead. For more information on singles roller derby and other singles events, check out *www.meetmarket adventures.com*.

887. BIKE RACE

Some bicycle races draw quite a crowd. A good example is the Philadelphia Bike Race, where people gather early in the morning to line the streets and cheer on the bikers. The atmosphere is festive, fun, and competitive—a perfect combination for bonding with your fellow race watchers. Bicycle races also attract a lot of men, so you will likely be standing near a few eligible guys as you watch the wheels zoom by.

888. SALSA LESSONS

Salsa lessons are a great place to meet men for a few reasons. One, the class will be a fun bonding experience. And two, you will learn a skill you can practice with your partner for years to come . . . maybe a partner you met in the class! Salsa bars frequently offer salsa lessons, so if there's a salsa bar in your area, you're bound to get expert instruction there. Salsa lessons are also available from dance instructors and at most colleges and universities.

889. CROSS-COUNTRY SKIING

Cross-country skiing is one of the very best full-body workouts you can get. And if you head to a popular area to glide across the snow on a winter day, you are likely to bump into others who prefer to exercise on skis. If you spot a skier who piques your interest, ski on over to him and ask him if he knows any new trails. Maybe he'll show you, and then the two of you can warm up over a cup of hot chocolate and get to know each other better.

○ **PRO** *Nothing is better than cross-country skiing for toning your legs. Say goodbye to the winter flab!*

○ **CON** *Cross-country skiing equipment is expensive—be sure you're serious about it before you make the investment.*

890. FRISBEE TOURNAMENT

For a day full of fun, exercise, and competition, consider entering a Frisbee tournament. These events are often held as charitable fundraisers, and their setups range from just a few teams to hundreds of teams. Some tournaments organize coed teams, and others split up teams by gender. Either way, with all the interaction, you are bound to meet a ton of new people—probably more guys than girls—at a Frisbee tournament.

=Time =Friends $=Expense

891. HIGH DIVING LESSONS

If you are adventurous, check out a high diving class, where you will learn the best techniques for hurling into water from a high place. These lessons usually draw similarly adventurous types, so if you're into risk-taking guys, you'll probably be in luck with this one.

○ **PRO** *If you are ever running from the authorities and come to a cliff, like in The Fugitive, you'll be able to dive with confidence to escape.*

○ **CON** *If you are afraid of heights, this may not be the best activity for you (unless you want to tackle your fear, of course).*

892. SCUBA LESSONS

  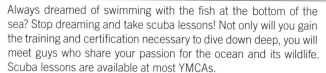

Always dreamed of swimming with the fish at the bottom of the sea? Stop dreaming and take scuba lessons! Not only will you gain the training and certification necessary to dive down deep, you will meet guys who share your passion for the ocean and its wildlife. Scuba lessons are available at most YMCAs.

○ **PRO** *You will meet people who you can actually go scuba diving with once you're certified.*

○ **CON** *The bends.*

893. INDOOR TRACK IN THE WINTER

If you love to run or jog but you hate doing it in cold weather, head to an indoor track. Not only will you be able to run in shorts and a T-shirt and measure exactly how far you've gone, you will run alongside guys who don't use the winter doldrums as an excuse to get out of shape. And because indoor tracks are usually fairly small, you will run in close proximity to these guys.

○ **PRO** *An indoor track will take away your "it's too cold outside to run" excuse and you will stay in better shape.*

○ **CON** *Men in short running shorts—sometimes, they are as bad as a Speedo.*

894. PAINTBALL

For the more adventurous, this activity forces you to dress in combat and run through the woods, shooting and dodging paint bullets. Paintball provides nonstop excitement, as well as an opportunity for you to meet others who enjoy a heart-pounding, competitive activity like paintball. And as a female, you will be way outnumbered by guys at this event; there aren't too many girls into this pastime. You can show up alone, with a friend, or in a group; for best results, show up alone or with a small group, so you will be paired with opponents you don't know.

○ **PRO** *Guys you meet during paintball will see you as tough—a good foot to get off on if you start a relationship with one of them.*

○ **CON** *It hurts to be hit with a paintball, and the balls often leave welts.*

895. PLAYING DARTS

Instead of hanging at a table or at the bar with your girlfriends, which may scare off guys (men are hesitant to approach a group of women engulfed in conversation), get yourself out there by playing a few rounds of darts. If there are guys playing, ask them if you can form some teams. Or get the darts started yourselves and see who joins in. Men love games, so they will be all over the chance to get to know you over a game of baseball (the darts kind).

896. ROLLERBLADING

The benefit of rollerblading when it comes to scoping for men is that you can cover a lot of ground in a little time (as compared to walking or jogging). This only works, of course, if you rollerblade in an area where there are lots of single men to scope. So lace up your blades and head out to a busy park on a Saturday afternoon; if you spot a group that interests you, stop to take a break. If nothing materializes, skate on.

○ **PRO** *Rollerblading is great exercise.*

○ **CON** *A lot of parks and public areas have banned rollerblading. Makes sure the areas you choose are blade friendly.*

897. | SNORKELING LESSONS

Want to check out what's lurking in the more shallow parts of the sea? Learn how to snorkel, and you can spend hours looking at fish, shells, and the coral reef. And when you take snorkeling lessons, you may come face to face with a few of the interesting creatures lurking above the sea as well . . . creatures in the form of attractive guys who also want to learn to snorkel.

❍ PRO *If you meet someone special, you will have the perfect excuse to vacation in the Caribbean.*

❍ CON *If you live in a landlocked part of the country, these lessons could be hard to find.*

898. | A FITNESS WALK IN THE PARK

Walking through the park, you will pass guys doing all sorts of parkish things—such as walking their dogs, jogging, rollerblading, or grilling out. So for the perfect combination of exercise and guy-scoping, put on your cutest matching workout outfit and hit the pavement. And leave the iPod at home—you will appear much more approachable without it.

899. | FLYING A KITE

To attract the right kind of attention to yourself, take a kite down to the beach as people are starting to leave at the end of the day, when the transition from bathing-suited beach bums to clothed dog-walkers just begins. That way, your chances of meeting a nice guy who admires your kite will still be good, but you won't blend in with all the other beach-goers.

❍ PRO *If you don't meet anyone, you will still have entertainment in the form of your kite.*

❍ CON *This activity is limited to days with wind; take a kite out on a still day and you will just look clueless.*

900. | GROUP DANCING LESSONS

Many group dancing lessons give you the option to sign up solo or with a partner. Sign up sans partner so you can get fixed up with all the other single dancers in the class. If you have chemistry on the dance floor, you might just want to grab a drink or some dinner after class.

 =Time ♦=Friends $=Expense

901.   MARATHON

If you're running a marathon and spot an attractive guy in your pacing group, move into the spot next to him. Not only will his presence take your mind off which mile you are on, you may get the urge to strike up a conversation to pass the time (if you're not suffering, that is). And even if you don't get the nerve to talk to him during the race, you will have a chance to approach him over the post-race water and bagels to ask him what he thought.

O PRO *Big marathons draw tens of thousands of people—think of all the guys you might hit it off with . . .*

O CON *Some people don't like to talk when they run; if you sense a cold shoulder, move on or wait until the end of the race.*

902.   RACQUETBALL COURT

Love a heated game on a small, indoor court? Play racquetball. Racquetball is a popular sport among successful businessmen—they use the sport as a forum for meetings. You can play racquetball with three players, so head to a club and try to get involved in a businessman game (if you're good enough, that is). If you hit it off with one of the players, you can take it to one-on-one.

O PRO *Racquetball offers great exercise and exciting competition.*

O CON *Some racquetball clubs are really exclusive. If you have a friend who belongs to a club, ask him or her if you can tag along.*

903.   SAUNA

As you are sweating through your sauna session, why not make the time pass faster by chatting with the guy on the bench across from you? Saunas provide the perfect small, intimate setting for getting to know someone. Marie from Myrtle Beach, South Carolina, knows firsthand—she approached her man for the first time in a sauna. "I had been watching Chad at the gym for weeks. I thought I saw him noticing me as well, so I followed him into the sauna one day. I was miserable in there (I am claustrophobic and hate heat), but it was worth it. He asked me out and we've been together ever since!" So the next time that guy you've been chasing heads into the sauna, by all means, follow him.

O PRO *You'll brew up a good sweat.*

O CON *You'll brew up a good sweat—not the most flattering first impression.*

904.   WATER POLO

For a great aquatic workout coupled with some good competition, consider playing water polo. There are a lot more men than women who engage in this sport, so you will be pleasantly outnumbered. To find water polo leagues and clinics in your area, check out *www. usawaterpolo.com.*

905.   BATTING CAGES

If you want to go where the boys are, you simply can't beat the batting cages. So grab a hard hat, get in there, and start swinging. Chances are, there will be a man hitting balls to your left and your right. So in between rounds, smile and be friendly. Be bold and ask him for a few pointers. If you're feeling extra daring, ask him if he wants to grab a hot dog with you when you're both finished hitting. Even if you don't meet someone, you'll give your hand-eye coordination a workout.

906.   CROQUET CLUB

Interestingly enough, croquet seems to be making quite a come-back. It's not just for your grandparents' outdoor parties anymore. So consider joining a croquet club where you will improve your hand-eye coordination and get to know your fellow players at the same time. To find a croquet club in your area, check out *http:// dmoz.org/Sports/Croquet/Clubs/United_States.*

◐ PRO *Because it's a fairly low-key sport, croquet allows for plenty of time for socializing.*

◑ CON *There aren't a whole lot of croquet clubs out there, so you may have some trouble finding one in your area.*

907.   HIKING CLUB

Hiking clubs attract athletic, adventurous people who love the outdoors. If this describes you, you just might meet your perfect match by joining a hiking club. These groups typically go on long, organized hikes together, which will give you plenty of time to get to know your fellow hikers. Plus, you will get to explore paths you may not have known about otherwise. To find a hiking club in your area, check out *http://hikingandbackpacking.com.*

908.   LIFEGUARDING

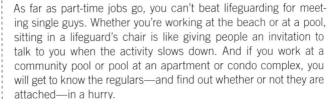

As far as part-time jobs go, you can't beat lifeguarding for meeting single guys. Whether you're working at the beach or at a pool, sitting in a lifeguard's chair is like giving people an invitation to talk to you when the activity slows down. And if you work at a community pool or pool at an apartment or condo complex, you will get to know the regulars—and find out whether or not they are attached—in a hurry.

○ PRO *The CPR and lifeguarding certification courses could also be a great place to meet guys.*

○ CON *Boredom . . . and sunburn.*

909.   PLAYING FRISBEE WITH YOUR DOG IN THE PARK

On a sunny weekend, grab your pooch and head to the park to play Frisbee. First, your dog will absolutely love you for it. And second, you will open yourself up to be approached by friendly, dog-loving guys. For maximum guy exposure, take frequent breaks to stroll around the park to see who is there. If a guy comes up to you and your dog, he is probably also a dog lover—a big plus!

910.   SINGLES CANOE TRIP

Some singles groups sponsor all-singles canoe trips, where you jump into a canoe for a day full of paddling and flirtation as you float down the river. For a trip that includes exercise and meeting men, consider taking part in a singles canoe excursion. To find a singles canoe trip in your area, type "singles canoe trip" into any search engine, or register (for free) at *www.fitness-singles.com*.

911.   SNOWMOBILING

Snowmobiling is one of those activities that instantly makes you feel like a kid again. And if you snowmobile in a popular snowmobiling area, you may bump into other "big kids" having as much fun as you are. So take a break in between rides, break open a thermos of hot chocolate, and get to know your fellow 'bilers.

○ PRO *Fun, fun, fun. And if you meet someone who shares your passion for fun sports like snowmobiling, you will have fun doing lots of other things together too.*

○ CON *Snowmobiling in a crowded area can be on the dangerous side. Be careful.*

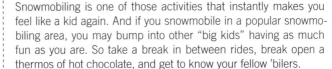

🕐=Time 👤=Friends $=Expense

912. WALKING TO WORK

$

Some of us are blessed to live within walking distance of our places of employment. And despite this blessing, a lot of people still climb in their cars and drive the five or so blocks back and forth to work every day. This is acceptable when it's freezing or raining, but on a nice day, this is not only lazy and a waste of resources, it's a waste of an opportunity to meet men. During rush hour, there are numerous athletically minded guys who would rather hoof a few blocks with their attaché cases than waste the gas . . . guys you will only meet if you are out there walking beside them. Make sure you walk to work on National Walk to Work Day, on the first Friday in April, when the highest number of American workers will be getting there on foot.

○ PRO *The added exercise will be good for you.*

○ CON *Depending on the length of your walk and the formality of your job, you may have to wear sneakers and bring the heels with you.*

913. WALKING TOUR

$

If you live in or near a big city with lots of history, such as New York or Boston, check out the historical walking tours. Not only are you likely to meet single male history buffs from your city, you may also meet available guys who have some free time during a business trip. If you hit it off during the tour

Five great walking tour cities:
1. Boston, MA
2. New York, NY
3. Chicago, IL
4. Portland, OR
5. Washington, DC

of historical sites and buildings, you may keep on strolling to a cozy restaurant to get to know each other better.

914. WORKING OUT WITH A PERSONAL TRAINER

$ $ $

If you want to whip yourself into shape, consider hiring a personal trainer who can show you just how to target your "problem areas," so to speak. And if you want to potentially take your relationship beyond the gym, consider hiring a single male personal trainer. To find one, do some research by scoping out the personal trainers at your gym and asking the other members of the staff some subtle questions about them. Even if you don't have a romantic connection with your trainer, he might have a single friend to introduce you to.

915.   ANY BIG HILL IN WINTERTIME

It's true. When the first significant snowfall hits, people of all ages return to their youth. Many twenty- and thirty-somethings have pre-snowfall cocktail parties and celebrate the accumulation with a sledding party. It's a great way to get fresh air, exercise, and laugh more than you have in years. Get on your gear, grab a toboggan, and just go for it. Don't let the man of your dreams just slip away. He could be just one sled over from you!

916.   DANCE STUDIOS

Taking dance lessons doesn't have the stigma it once had. Although Tony Manero might have scared off a few women in *Saturday Night Fever*, dancing was considered cool then—and with shows like *Dancing with the Stars*, we're seeing a whole new crop of men who like to get out there and boogie. Here's the move. Call a dance studio that's in a busy part of town. Talk to the manager. See what kind of people come in and if any singles ever attend the classes. Some dance studios offer a Singles Night. Also, grab a friend—you don't have to go alone! Take something fun like swing dancing or hip-hop. You have nothing to lose but a few calories.

917.   INTRAMURAL LACROSSE

Enjoy heated competition with a splash of romantic intrigue? Consider intramural lacrosse, where you will bond with your team members on and off the field. Lacrosse usually draws athletes that are serious enough about the game to make for good competition . . . but not serious enough to sacrifice fun. And these intramural groups tend to socialize outside of practice and games, as well—a great opportunity to get to know your male teammates better.

918.   STEAM ROOM

Many gyms offer coed steam rooms where gym rats can sit and "take a steam" and wonder just what the point is of getting a "good sweat." Before you go into a panic, know that it's not a deviant experience. It's simply a great way to loosen and relax the muscles after an invigorating workout. Unwind, be yourself, and say hello to someone new.

919. KITE SURFING

No, you don't have to do the kite surfing, but if you want to meet a guy at the beach, keep your eye out for kite surfers. For those unaware, kite surfing has become the latest beach craze in terms of "gnarly" physical activities. Sometimes called "kite boarding," kite surfing applies elements of surfing, wake boarding, and kite flying to produce a thrilling and seemingly never-ending ocean ride. For the purposes of meeting a guy, however, you don't need to learn to ride one, you just need to look up in the sky while you're at the beach. These guys know that all eyes are often on them, so your attention is definitely welcomed. Go for a walk and as they pull their board to the shore, simply walk up and ask them about kite surfing. They will be more than happy to explain it to you and probably even give you a lesson.

920. ROLLER-SKATING RINK

Every fad is cyclical, right? Well, guess what's back? Roller-skating. It's true. As an adult, roller-skating rinks present an odd combination of competition, skating, and sex appeal which draws men of all kinds. Who knows? Maybe you have some of that competitive spirit and want to take a spin around the rink in a mini-skirt while a girl with a lip ring tries to take you down. And if not, you can always sit on the sidelines and flirt with some of the spectators.

◑ PRO *It's a good place to go have some fun with your girlfriends, no matter who you meet.*

◑ CON *Weird long-haired men who like to skate backwards and perform other tricks by themselves on the rink.*

921. SKYDIVING

Skydiving trips offer an incredible rush. Add a number of single men to the mix, and you've got something special. Skydiving trips require a few hours of learning before you take the big leap. This means that several people are in the class together, many of whom are single men.

◑ PRO *You will immediately connect with everyone in your class, as jumping out of a plane tends to bring people closer!*

◑ CON *This activity is obviously not without its risks and it tends to attract thrill-seekers, so if they are not your type, consider meeting a man at a coffee shop instead.*

922. DISC GOLF

Here is a fun way to socialize. Basically, picture a beautiful country setting with several "goals" located sporadically throughout. The goals are metal posts containing chain-linked baskets. The idea is to throw a Frisbee into the goal after a number of attempts and then record your score. It's golf, but with a Frisbee. It's a relaxing sport that's sweeping the country for both men and women. Plus, you can chat with your teammates or competitors during the match. In other words, it's a country walk that allows you the opportunity to get to know the men with whom you're playing. You can't beat that for a fun first date. Visit *www.pdga.org* to find a match near you. They have rules, message boards, and everything you need to understand and pursue the sport.

923. SNOW TUBING

Want the thrill of flying down a snowy mountain with a reduced risk of falling and breaking a bone? Try snow tubing. You'll have access to the same mix of single ski-loving guys in the lodge, but when it comes time to hit the slopes again, you'll do so on a soft, padded snow tube. Grab a few girlfriends and have a blast.

Five great snow tubing sites:
1. Mount Snow, West Dover, VT: *www.mountsnow.com*
2. Moonshine Mountain in NC: *www.moonshinemountain.com*
3. PolarWave Snow Tubing, Batavia, NY: *www.polarwave snowtubing.com*
4. Papoose Discovery Center, Portland, OR: *www.squaw.com*
5. Soldier Hollow, Midway, UT: *www.soldierhollow.com*

924. WALKING THE MALL

This doesn't mean walking the mall during normal hours to shop, but walking it for exercise early in the morning. Most of the walkers will probably be women, but you may bump into the occasional man, and you are likely to see businessmen swinging into the mall coffee or bagel shop that's open a few hours before The Gap and Foot Locker. Plus, you may meet some female walking buddies with eligible sons or friends.

PRO *The mall offers a climate-controlled, safe place to walk, and you can scope out the sales at the same time.*

CON *If you have a shopping problem, walking the mall could tempt you to return later in the day.*

=Time ♦=Friends $=Expense

925.   WALKING YOUR NEIGHBORHOOD

Not only will you get valuable exercise and fresh air as you stroll through your neighborhood, you'll get more information about your male neighbors . . . including how well they keep up their homes and whether or not they have a girlfriend (or girlfriends) coming in and out. If multiple walks reveal that a guy is available and responsible with his home, consider leaving a nice fruit basket and a note on his doorstep.

⊙ PRO *If things work out, you may gain a mate and a neighborhood walking partner!*

⊙ CON *If things don't work out, you may have to change your walking route.*

926.   SERIOUS SWIMMING CLUB

If you love swimming but get bored doing laps back and forth across the pool at the Y, consider joining a swimming club that will take you into rivers, channels, or the ocean for some exercise. Plus, it will introduce you to men who enjoy a more adventurous swim. For more information on swimming clubs in your area, check out *www.active.com*.

927.   SQUASH

Squash is a wonderful game for heated competition. To meet men who love the fast-paced, sweaty workout that is squash as much as you do, head to your local YMCA and sign up for an open court. Squash is a fairly male-dominated sport, so your chances of being paired with a member of the opposite sex are good. If you two hit it off on the squash court, you can take the relationship out for coffee afterwards.

928.   CHIP AND PUTT

If you enjoy golf, but don't enjoy four-plus hours on the course, then chip and putt may be perfect for you. Even the best golfers hit the chip and putt course to practice their chipping and putting now and then. To meet these men, and maybe to break the ice by asking them for some pointers, you have to be a hole ahead or behind them. A good time to catch these guys may be in the evening, when they decide to chip and putt because they can't fit in a full 18.

 =Time   =Friends $ =Expense

929. FENCING LESSONS

$ $ $

Fencing is an exciting way to get a workout, and it's great for hand-eye coordination and to pick up some self-defense pointers. And because it involves fighting with swords, fencing attracts men; so in a fencing class, you are likely to be paired with a member of the opposite sex as your opponent. Most colleges and universities hold fencing classes, and you may want to also check at your gym or the YMCA. If you find yourself falling for someone in your fencing class, just don't spear him. . . . For more information on fencing, check out *www.fencing.net.*

930. GHOST HUNTING

$ $ $

Yes, this is for real. There are people who enjoy hunting down ghosts in their free time, and you might just find some fascinating men in the mix if you decide to join them. In addition to searching for spirits, ghost hunters attend paranormal conventions, and stay in haunted bed and breakfasts. So if you've always been fascinated by the paranormal, give it a try.

931. TAE BO

$ $ $

A combination of martial arts, boxing, and dance, Tae Bo classes tend to draw a nice mix of men and women. They are a great workout, and they show you some self-defense techniques in the process. For maximum guy exposure, attend a Tae Bo class at your gym right after work or on Saturday mornings. If you're extra daring, ask the instructor which class includes the most men—if he is a guy, maybe he'll ask you out!

932. HIKING TRAILS

$

To get some good exercise and enjoy the fresh air and scenery—men included—of a mountain, get up early and hit the hiking trails. Most hiking areas offer trails of all skill levels, so you don't have to be an expert climber to hit the trails. Hiking is a very popular sport among men, so grab your boots and a backpack (filled with extra snacks you can share with handsome hikers along the way), and get going.

933. ICE-SKATING RINK

To get a little exercise and bump into some single guys (perhaps even literally), head to an ice-skating rink with a few girlfriends on a Saturday afternoon—you'll find single dads, practicing ice hockey teams, and so on. Take frequent breaks to grab a snack or drink in the common food area to check out who the place has to offer.

934. SINGLE PARENTS SPORTS LEAGUE

If you are a single parent, you know how valuable time with other single parents can be. Sharing stories and offering support to one another is great for stress relief. And if you take that relationship onto a field or court in a single parents sports league, you will feel even better. Some single parents groups offer sports competitions; if you are an athletic person, consider finding a single parents sports league for good competition, and potentially, good romantic companionship with a nice single dad on your team.

935. FOLK-DANCING LESSONS

For some great exercise, some fun moves, and a fast-paced class that allows you to dance with many different partners, try folk dancing. Contrary to popular belief, folk dancing attracts people of all ages. And if there are partnerless men in your class, you can bet they are single. If you have good chemistry in the class, take your relationship out for a cup of coffee afterward and see where it goes. To find a class in your area, check out *www.folkdancing.org.*

936. SWIMMING LESSONS

If you grew up in a city, you may not have had too many swimming experiences and therefore, you may not feel all that confident in the water. Or maybe you just want to learn how to perfect your breast stroke. Either way, there are adult swimming lessons out there for all skill levels, and they attract men and women alike. So to brush up on your swimming and potentially meet a man you can hang out with at the pool this summer, take some swimming lessons. To find lessons in your area, check your local YMCA or high school.

937. SNOWSHOEING

They say, if you can walk, you can go snowshoeing. Snowshoeing is great exercise, and it attracts people from all different walks of life. Similar to cross-country skiing, snowshoeing is usually done through woods or fields. On a perfect winter day, you will find fellow friendly snowshoers out on the trails with whom you can meet over a mug of hot chocolate. So grab an adventurous friend and your gear, and go.

938. ROCK-CLIMBING WALL

Since it became big in the 1990s, climbing has really taken off as a sport, and climbing walls have become increasingly more popular places for people to meet potential dates. At a climbing wall, you know people are there for the right reasons—to challenge themselves and focus on the task at hand. But in between calculated foot and hand placements, you can also look to your left or right and smile at the climber next to you. After all, he might be able to give you some pointers to help you get to the top . . . and then ask you out once you get to the bottom.

○ PRO *Climbing is a great workout and is wonderful for your self-esteem.*

○ CON *This sport requires some basic strength and coordination, so if you haven't worked out in ten years, a climbing wall may not be the best place for you.*

939. TRAINING FOR A MARATHON

If you are training for a marathon, you're wise to join a marathon-running group, especially if you are training from scratch. These groups offer carefully scheduled training, so you will be at the right stage at the right time. Plus, they are great for moral support—a lot of people who train with groups end up running the entire race with their group members. And if there are attractive, available guys in your training group, you will have plenty of miles to get to know them better. To find a running group in your area, check out *www.coolrunning.com*.

○ PRO *Completing a marathon is a wonderful feat.*

○ CON *If you hate running, it could be a long few months of training—all the more reason to join a group with whom you can suffer through it.*

=Time *=Friends* *$=Expense*

940. SURFING LESSONS

West Coast, East Coast, even river surfing has become popular across the globe. And wherever there are surfers, there are surfing lessons. This is a great way to get some physical exercise, try a new hobby, and possibly meet a new love interest. The next time you're visiting the beach, call around and find someone to give you a surfing lesson. If you're not interested in your teacher, ask when he and his friends go surfing, since you'd like to watch some of the experts take on a few waves. After that, you'll have your choice of single men. Plus, your new teacher and his friends will be happy to have you come observe. Just be prepared to get up early. Many surfers begin hanging 10 just after dawn.

941. TAI CHI

Tai chi, a traditional Chinese mind-body relaxation exercise consisting of intricate exercise sequences performed slowly, is becoming increasingly popular, among both men and women. Men love it because it is a form of a martial art, which appeals to their macho sides, and women love it because its movements are soft and relaxed. You can buy a tai chi DVD, but for best man-meeting results, enroll in a class. For best results, find a laid-back instructor, says Ron Knaus, DO, psychiatrist in Largo, Florida, and author of *A B Chi*. "You want someone who is just happy that you are moving—not someone who will be compulsive about the positioning of your elbow," he says. Plus, a relaxed instructor won't mind that you're trying to get to know your male classmates a little better.

942. TRAPEZE SCHOOL

As a child, did you watch the trapeze artists in the circus wide-eyed with admiration, hoping some day you too could glide through the air? Well, there's a way you can make your dreams come true, possibly in more ways than one. Trapeze schools offer courses such as flying trapeze, static trapeze, and

Five great trapeze schools:
1. Trapeze School New York:
   http://newyork.trapezeschool.com
2. Trapeze School Baltimore:
   http://baltimore.trapezeschool.com
3. Trapeze School Bean Town:
   http://boston.trapezeschool.com
4. Trapeze High, Escondido, California:
   www.trapezehigh.com
5. Trapeze Experience, Miami, Florida:
   www.trapeze-experience.com

ropes. In addition to learning the ropes, so to speak, you will meet men who share your love of acrobatics and adventure.

=Time =Friends $=Expense

943. JUJITSU

Martial arts classes tend to attract a lot of men. Just think of the story you could tell your grandchildren: After I kicked his butt in jujitsu class, we went out for coffee and fell in love. And even if you don't fall in love, you will learn a method of self-protection, which any single woman can benefit from.

944. RACQUETBALL CLUB

Racquetball clubs are perfect for people who love to play racquetball, or for those who want to join a higher-end gym with racquetball courts, state-of-the-art equipment, pools, Jacuzzis, and other amenities. If you can afford to spend a little more per month on a gym membership and you want to meet guys who play racquetball or appreciate a nice fitness club as much as you do, consider joining a racquetball club. Beyond the exercise facilities, a lot of these clubs offer social events for club members to meet and mingle.

945. HORSEBACK RIDING

Whether you've never been on a horse before or you've been riding since you were a kid, horseback riding can be a wonderful way to meet a handsome cowboy—either the wrangler who leads you through the trails or the fellow riders in your group.

○ PRO *Horseback riding is something you can do solo, which will increase your chances of meeting new people.*

○ CON *Horseback riding isn't ideal for people with a fear of horses.*

946. SAILING CLUB

See if there are local marinas or clubs that offer sailing lessons during the summer months. The costs are often affordable, you don't need your own boat, and the larger sailboats can always use an extra crew member. You might just meet your "first mate." Jennifer K. of Boston, Massachusetts, takes sailing lessons and says it's a wonderful place to meet guys. "Every time I've gone out on a boat for instruction, I've been with a new person—usually a guy," she says. "The last time I went, the skipper and I had such a fun time that we made a date to sail again together the next weekend!"

Five great sailing clubs:
1. Club Nautique (nationwide)
2. Sailtime (nationwide)
3. Community Boating Inc. (Boston, Massachusetts)
4. Odyssey Sailing (St. Louis, Missouri)
5. Club Nautique (San Francisco, California)

⊕=Time ⍥=Friends $=Expense

947. YMCA

🕐 🕐 🕐

👤

$ $ $

The Y can be a great alternative to a gym membership—the rates are usually fairly cheap, and most YMCAs offer a range of exercise options, from swimming to weight lifting to treadmills. . . . Not to mention the opportunity to meet men in your neighborhood who want to stay in shape without having to hang out at a muscle-head gym.

948. SKATEBOARD SHOP

🕐

👤

$ $

You don't have to be a skateboard chick to shop in a skateboard shop; these shops have plenty of cute, trendy clothes, flip-flops, sneakers, and beach necessities. Not to mention the cute guys who are actually in the market for skateboard equipment. If you actually do skateboard, great! You will have plenty in common with the guys you meet in a skateboard shop. If not, no problem—they will appreciate your taste in clothing. Don't be shy.

949. SKI LODGE

🕐

👤

$ $

After a hard day on the slopes, most guys will want to unwind in the ski lodge with a coffee or a beer and some appetizers. And with the toasty fireplace and cozy atmosphere, they will be extra-relaxed and ready to socialize, especially with an adventurous ski bunny like you. So make it a point to warm up in the lodge in between runs or before you're ready to call it a day.

○ PRO *If your friends don't feel like staying, a ski lodge is a perfectly acceptable and non-threatening place for a girl to grab a drink or coffee solo.*

○ CON *If you don't ski, this probably isn't the most convenient establishment for you to patronize.*

950. SURF SHOP

🕐

👤

$ $

You don't have to be a hard-core surfer girl to shop in a surf shop; in addition to bathing suits, board shorts, surf boards, and other surf gear, many of these shops have accessories such as mugs and beach towels, as well as surfing-themed home décor. Not to mention the attractive dudes who are actually in the market for surf boards and fresh wax.

951.   WIND SURFING LESSON

The next time you take a Caribbean vacation, consider taking a wind surfing lesson. Not only will you get one step closer to mastering a sport that is primarily male-dominated, you will meet fellow adventurers in the lesson. Most guys are attracted to women who will try something, if only once, so you will get kudos for getting up on the board in the first place.

952.   KITE SHOP

Whether it's a fancy stunt kite or your traditional triangular shape, men love the challenge of flying a kite. Therefore, you will find many men shopping for their weapon of choice at a kite shop. And you may find a fun kite for yourself to try, which may lead to an encounter with an interested kite flyer or passerby at the beach or park. Or, you may just pick out a nice windsock with the help of a handsome kite shop employee. Either way, a trip to a kite shop is in order.

953.   SKI SHOP

If you ski, wonderful—you will have plenty in common with men you meet in a ski shop. And if you don't ski, no problem. You don't have to be a ski bunny to shop in a ski shop; these shops have plenty of cute, trendy clothes, ski jackets, snow boots, and other winter necessities. Not to mention the handsome men who will actually be shopping for ski equipment.

⏱=Time 👤=Friends $=Expense

d date flea market reunion restaurant tattoo parlor wedding auction ho
b baby shower casino hibachi ladies night café bake sale brunch river
mbake double date culinary festival smorgasbord tavern church service
nal hospital roommates yacht club school courthouse nudist colony bee
al baseball game car show firefighting fishing tailgating poker campgro
ing contest bowling weight room military cigar shop airport london bri
eiffel tower vacation hotel cruise mardi gras times square central park
america mount rushmore hollywood safari smithsonian online animal r
blood drive volunteering special olympics toy drive red cross soup kitc
t gallery book club cooking class library museum college campus orches
ature walk planetarium political rally shakespeare festival disney world
arium water park caroling parents playground mini-golf county fair co
use laundromat grocery store beach gym subway deli yard sale liquor s
ost office personal ads company picnic conference water cooler bartend
ncert scavenger hunt karaoke comedy club biking karate softball paint
ling ymca square dancing boardwalk cookout whale watching farmer's
t party friends cafeteria open house singing group bars beach house w
ring blind date flea market reunion restaurant tattoo parlor wedding au
spital club baby shower casino hibachi ladies night café bake sale bru
verboat clambake double date culinary festival smorgasbord tavern chu
ervice spa animal hospital roommates yacht club school courthouse nuc
ny beer festival baseball game car show firefighting fishing tailgating
mpground eating contest bowling weight room military cigar shop airp
don bridges bus eiffel tower vacation hotel cruise mardi gras times squ
tral park mall of america mount rushmore hollywood safari smithsonian
animal rescue blood drive volunteering special olympics toy drive red
o kitchen art gallery book club cooking class library museum college ca
rchestra nature walk planetarium political rally shakespeare festival disr
rld zoo aquarium water park caroling parents playground mini-golf co
ir coffeehouse laundromat grocery store beach gym subway deli yard s
quor store post office personal ads company picnic conference water coc
tending concert scavenger hunt karaoke comedy club biking karate sof
ntball sailing ymca square dancing cookout whale watching farmer's ma
y friends cafeteria open house singing group bars beach house wine ta
d date flea market reunion restaurant tattoo parlor wedding auction ho
b baby shower casino hibachi ladies night café bake sale brunch river
mbake double date culinary festival smorgasbord tavern church service
nal hospital roommates yacht club school courthouse nudist colony bee
al baseball game car show firefighting fishing tailgating poker campgro
ing contest bowling weight room military cigar shop airport london bri
eiffel tower vacation hotel cruise mardi gras times square central park
america mount rushmore hollywood safari smithsonian online animal r
blood drive volunteering special olympics toy drive red cross soup kitc
t gallery book club cooking class library museum college campus orche
ature walk planetarium political rally shakespeare festival disney world

outdoorways

954. PUBLIC POOL

It was the perfect place to meet new friends and socialize when you were still wearing plastic Swimmies to stay afloat, and that doesn't have to change now that you are an independent woman who is actually happy to hear the "adult swim" whistle blow. So bring a chair, a towel, and a book and keep your eyes peeled for single men. You'll be surprised at how many go swimming solo.

PRO *The bathing suit nature of the public pool leaves nothing to the imagination, so you will know exactly what you are getting into.*

CON *The bathing suit nature of the public pool leaves nothing to the imagination, so you will be forced to put it all out there before you've even had a first date.*

955. BOARDWALK

For an entertaining hour of people watching, you can't beat a trip to the boardwalk. Once a place for people to get dressed up and promenade by the sea, the boardwalk now draws people of all walks of life, in all shapes and sizes. In the group, you may just spot someone who catches your eye in a good way. Maybe he's there for an ice cream break from the beach . . . or a trip to the casino or arcade. For whatever reason, the two of you just might be at the right place at the right time.

PRO *Depending on where it is located, the boardwalk may offer some fun little shops to peruse as well.*

CON *If there aren't many people strolling the boardwalk, the pickings may be slim.*

956. GREENHOUSE

Regardless of whether or not you are a fan of feng shui, plants add positive energy and color to your living space. And where better to find the best selection of the perfect plants to complement your rugs and wall hangings than at a greenhouse? As you peruse the temperature-controlled aisles for the perfect plants, keep your eye out for like-minded green-thumbed men who are doing the same. You can always break the ice with a question about which plants do best in your lighting conditions.

957. BANK OF A LAKE

With water skiers, boaters, swimmers, fishermen, and other guys enjoying the lake, you will have plenty to look at as you sit on the bank. So pack a nice picnic and head down to the lake with a friend on a sunny weekend afternoon . . . there's no telling who you will meet. Who knows—you may even end up on a Jet Ski or boat yourself by the end of the day.

958. SANDBAR

Now and then, there are those picture-perfect days at the beach where the air and the water are both warm, there's a nice breeze, and there's a sandbar a few yards out that you can hang out on. When these sandbars form, they usually attract a lot of beach-goers. So swim out there and check out the sandbar yourself— there will probably be a few single beach cuties to choose from. And the island-like setup of the sandbar will force you to get to know them.

959. FOURTH OF JULY PICNIC

What better place to meet the man of your dreams than at a celebration of our great nation? With summertime cocktails and fireworks, a Fourth of July celebration can be a really romantic setting. And since the Fourth of July is such a family holiday, if a guy shows up to a picnic solo, chances are good he's available. So don't be shy.

Five great celebrations:
1. Philadelphia Welcome America Celebration
2. Fourth of July in Amelia Island, Florida
3. Phoenix Fourth of July Celebration
4. San Francisco Fourth of July
5. Boston's Fourth of July Celebration

960. JEWISH SINGLES OUTDOORS

If you are looking for a single Jewish guy and you love the outdoors, this organization is for you! This club joins Jewish adults together for hiking, biking, camping, rock climbing, scuba diving, horseback riding, and more. They also sponsor purely social events for members. For more information, check out *www.mosaics.org*.

○ PRO *Lots of opportunities for fun in the sun with a potential match, both in terms of your interests and your religion.*

○ CON *These clubs also welcome families and married couples, so you won't be spending time outdoors with purely singles.*

=Time =Friends $=Expense

961. EXPLORING A CAVE

$

You don't have to be a world-class spelunker to enjoy a few hours in a cave. Depending on where you live in the country, there are a number of tourist-friendly (a.k.a. non-spelunker) caves for you to explore. You usually have the option of walking through these caves yourself or joining a guided tour. For maximum single guy exposure, you probably want to opt for the guided group tour, which will give you plenty of chances to catch eyes with the other singles in your tour as you duck under stalactites.

962. CITY PARK

$

If you live in the heart of a busy city, you may crave an outdoor space with grass and trees. And unless you want to drive a few hours, your central city park is the fastest way you can get some natural scenery . . . not to mention the other "scenery" you will get in the form of guys jogging, walking their dogs, biking, and so on. Lots of single men spend time in city parks, and they may be just as anxious to meet someone to share a picnic or stroll with as you are. So forego the headset if you are exercising in the park, and opt to eat your lunch at a picnic bench instead of at your desk. There is no telling who you will meet.

○ PRO *Outdoor fun in the sun.*

○ CON *At the wrong hour, city parks can be quite dangerous. Never go by yourself at night.*

963. TIKI BAR

$ $

For a fun, festive night outside among friends, head to the closest tiki bar. A lot of tiki bars serve "cook your own" grill food, where you pick out your cut of chicken, steak, or fish and throw it on a big center grill yourself. This situation is ideal for meeting men for a few reasons. One, most men love to grill, so they will flock to the tiki bar to make sure their steak is cooked just right (by themselves, of course). And two, as you stand and watch your meat sizzle, you will have some time to chat with the fellow grillers around you, many of whom will just happen to be guys.

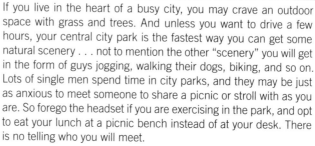

=Time =Friends $=Expense

964. TOP OF A MOUNTAIN

The top of a mountain is one of the most romantic places on earth to meet someone. And thanks to gondolas and other means of mountain transportation, you don't have to be an expert hiker to get to the top of most mountains. An example: Mount Pilates in Switzerland. You will take an exciting pulley-cart ride to the top with a group of ten or so strangers (a great opportunity to make friends). And once you're at the top, you won't believe the view. You'll fall in love instantly. Plus, there are restaurants and shops that provide bonus chances for socializing.

965. BACK-YARD COOKOUT

They're fun, laid back, and great for some hearty laughs. You could say this about back-yard cookouts . . . or the men who frequent them. Life is busy, and it's easy to decline invitations to informal affairs like back-yard barbecues. But to meet men, back-yard cookouts are ideal, so you should accept as many invitations as you can. At a back-yard cookout, you can chat informally over a soda and hot dog, you can rest assured that you have some friends in common (so he's not a freak), and if things go well, you can always go home to throw on your dancing shoes and hit the town.

966. HOT AIR BALLOON

If you have always gazed up at hot air balloons in wonder, dreaming of the day you'll get the chance to take a ride . . . stop dreaming and plan your ride now. Not only will you get an amazing adventurous experience, you may get to share it with some fascinating people. The typical hot air balloon basket holds a few folks, so if you sign up alone, you will share your ride with strangers. If you are feeling daring, ask the person who is organizing your trip if you can ride with a group that contains a single guy.

967. ON THE BEACH, AT SUNSET

There is something irresistibly romantic about a stroll on the beach at dusk . . . even when you are by yourself. So put on some comfortable clothes, grab your dog (if you have one), and head on down. You may very well bump into some guys with the same appreciation for the beauty of nature. And if they are alone, they are probably single. For safety's sake, make sure you only walk on the beach when there are plenty of others out there strolling with you. A desolate beach at any hour is not a safe place.

🕐=Time ♦=Friends $=Expense

968. OUTDOOR MARKET

Whether you live in the big city or a small town, if you have an outdoor market to peruse on a Saturday afternoon, go. These markets usually offer a nice spread of fresh foods, flowers, and other items . . . and often, single guys perusing fresh foods, flowers, and other items. And beyond the shoppers, there are the vendors. Maggie B. from Emmaus, Pennsylvania, hit it off with the free-spirited guy selling organic vegetables at her outdoor market. "We exchanged a few glances for a couple of weeks in a row as I paid for my items . . . then I finally got the nerve to ask him what he was doing when the market closed," she says. "I could tell he was shy, so I bolstered myself up to make the first move. It paid off—we've been seeing each other ever since!"

969. PARK BENCH

A park bench in a busy area of the city or park is a great place to sit and people watch. Grab a book or magazine and enjoy the sun . . . and take a break every once in a while to enjoy the scenery. You may see men running, walking their dogs, throwing a football with a nephew, or simply taking a stroll. Smile at these guys and they may decide to take a break and sit on the park bench next to you.

○ **PRO** *At a busy time, you will observe tons of people. And if you're at a loss for words, you can always ask for the time.*

○ **CON** *If you spot someone interesting, you may have to abandon your bench, walk up to him, and make the first move.*

970. STREET VENDOR

Whether you live in a big city or just visit big cities from time to time, you know all about the bargain street vendors. If you're in the market for a sweatshirt, baseball hat, or knockoff Louis Vuitton, you can find it for a decent price at a street vendor. And on the weekends, these vendors are busy with people looking for a bargain . . . including men. For maximum guy exposure, make a quick purchase at the purse or jewelry stands and spend some time browsing the vendors that sell things that guys are interested in—food, paintings, caps, and so on.

---

971. WHALE WATCHING

If you get a thrill from spotting a school of dolphins in the ocean, just think of how you'll feel when you spot a whale! And who better to share your excitement with than a single male animal lover standing next to you on the whale watching boat? Whale watching boats sail off the East and West Coasts, with some of the best whale sightings off of Cape Cod. An afternoon on a whale watching boat is reasonable—around $50, and it will give you the opportunity to check out your fellow whale watchers as well as the giant sea creatures. For more information on Cape whale watching, check out *www.whalewatch.com*.

---

972. MEMORIAL DAY PICNIC

What a better place to meet the man of your dreams than at a picnic kicking off the start of the summer season? With summertime cocktails and fireworks, a Memorial Day celebration can be a really fun and potentially romantic setting. So throw back a hot dog and a fruity drink in celebration of the red, white, and blue.

---

973. ZOO CONCESSION STAND

If you like animals, take an afternoon stroll through your local zoo. And make sure you take a break at the concession stand. If you spot a guy waiting for a hot dog by himself or with children only, chances are good that he is single. And watching animals could be a great first bonding experience for the two of you. So when you are finished with your snack, head to the same animal as the hot dog guy . . . even if you saw it already.

---

974. SITTIN' ON THE DOCK OF THE BAY

This one is perfect for anyone who loves the beach. All kinds of people are coming and going from the docks around a bustling beach locale. Sometimes you'll see party boats heading out for a night of fun on the water. Other times you'll see groups of men going out for a day of deep-sea fishing. Plus, sometimes there are fabulous little eateries with fresh delicacies from the sea. The point is, the entire area is crawling with men! Normally, men of all kinds too. Some are locals who fish for a living. Some will head out and come back as green as can be. Hey, at least they're trying something new—and so should you. Say hi and strike up a conversation. You never know what you'll catch.

975. SPRINGTIME LAWN PARTY

Life is busy, and it's easy to decline invitations to informal affairs like springtime lawn parties. But to meet men, these parties are ideal, so you should accept as many invitations as possible. At a springtime lawn party, you can chat informally over a keg of beer and a hamburger or hot dog with no strings attached, and you can take things beyond the lawn if all goes well.

976. POOL PARTY

Surely you loved pool parties as a kid—the fun in the sun, splashing, refreshing summer snacks, and so on. And you can still have a blast at a pool party as an adult. So grab your suit and a towel, and keep your eyes peeled for single men at the party. They will no doubt be in the mood to chat over a cold drink and a cool pool.

○ PRO *There's something about a pool that makes the atmosphere more relaxed and fun.*

○ CON *You'll have to let a man meet you for the first time with wet hair and no makeup, which may be hard for some women.*

977. LABOR DAY PICNIC

What better time to meet the man of your dreams than the day that almost everyone has off? With the last summertime cocktails and fireworks of the season, a Labor Day celebration can be a romantic setting to meet someone. And since Labor Day tends to be a family holiday (and again, one that almost everyone has off), if a guy shows up to a picnic solo, chances are good he's unattached.

○ PRO *Meeting a guy at a friend's picnic guarantees you that he has some normal friends.*

○ CON *Since Labor Day picnics are frequently on a Monday, if you hit it off with someone new, you'll most likely have to call it an early night due to having to work the next day.*

978. NATURE PRESERVE

People visit nature preserves for all kinds of reasons. And because the reasons are so vast, so are the kinds of people who visit them. Some go to simply get away from it all and be one with nature. Others like to meditate or perhaps get into a little yoga. Some like to take pictures, some simply go for a walk, and some can be found walking their furry friend. No matter the reason, you will find a friend here. And chances are, he could be single.

⏱=Time ♛=Friends $=Expense

979. SUNBATHING ON ANY BEACH OR AT ANY PARK

$

Why do men sunbathe? Because women are around, most likely also sunbathing. If it's above 80 degrees and you're barely dressed, and there's no sign of gawkers and/or stalkers, you'll find a man. So find the right spot and let it all hang out. You'll be able to find what you're looking for, while he is also looking for you. It's a two-way street when you're half-naked in the heat.

O PRO *You'll be able to get a nice preview of men's bodies.*

O CON *You will have to give them a nice preview of yours. If you're the modest type, you may not feel completely comfortable.*

980. LOCAL OUTDOOR SHOP

"As a married woman, I am kicking myself that I didn't know the value of an outdoor shop when I was single," says Dr. Trina E. Read, sex expert in Alberta, Canada. "My husband is an outdoors kind of guy and usually for his birthday or Christmas, I go to our local outdoors shop (here in Canada, it's called Mountain Equipment Co-op) to buy him a piece of gear. Inevitably, every time I go in some good-looking guy strikes up a conversation about whatever piece of equipment I'm buying, whether it's at the counter, on the show floor, or waiting in line to pay," she says. So as a single woman, you might want to look for an excuse to buy—or at least browse through—some outdoor equipment.

981. STANDING UNDER SOMETHING IN THE RAIN

It's probably happened to you many times in your life. You are walking down the street enjoying a day of shopping or browsing when all of a sudden . . . boom: thunderstorm out of nowhere. So what do you do? Run for the nearest cover, which may be as simple as a small roof or awning on the sidewalk. Instead of cursing at the situation, look at it as an opportunity to get to know the others who have also taken cover at the same spot. If you're lucky enough to be near a coffee shop, ask a handsome stranger if he'd like to wait out the storm over a java with you.

O PRO *In a busy city, you'll probably never see the person again, so you have nothing to lose.*

O CON *Thanks to the rain, your hair probably won't be looking its best for a first meeting, but oh well.*

=Time ♟=Friends $=Expense

982. STROLLING THROUGH A HISTORIC DISTRICT

Most old towns and cities have a charming historic district for you to explore. Next time you have a Saturday afternoon to spare, take a walk through a historic district near you. If you spot an attractive stranger who appears to be comfortable in the neighborhood, approach him and ask him some questions about the buildings. If things go well, he could be telling you his life story over coffee shortly after.

983. DOG PARK

The combination of a park and people with their dogs is perfect for meeting animal-loving men. If you have a dog, grab him or her and head to the dog park for some fresh air and a stroll. And your dog's friendly nature will be the perfect icebreaker for meeting dogs paired with good-looking male owners. To find a dog park in your area, log on to *www.dogpark.com*.

◑ PRO *As soon as you see your buddy's smile and wagging tail when you get to the dog park, you will know how much he or she appreciates the quality time with you.*

◑ CON *Doggie doo-doo. Watch where you walk—dog parks sometimes draw inconsiderate dog owners who don't bring a bag and a scooper.*

984. FARMER'S MARKET

For fresh fruits, vegetables, and meats, you simply cannot beat a farmer's market. As more farms become fields full of houses, these types of markets are becoming scarce these days, so if you are lucky enough to live near one, by all means, take advantage of it. Not only will you get good deals on delicious farm-fresh food, the interactive nature of a farmer's market will provide the opportunity to meet fellow patrons and the farmers themselves. At the apple stand, ask a nice-looking stranger which variety he recommends. Then ask him if he would be interested in sharing a freshly ground coffee with you at the coffee stand. Even if you don't meet the man of your dreams, you will be supporting the local farmers in your area.

🕐=Time 👤=Friends $=Expense

985.   POLAR BEAR CLUB

A jump into cold waters with the Polar Bear Club will give you a real rush—because of the frigid water and because of the adventurous guys shivering around you. It takes a special type to join the Polar Bear Club and appreciate the thrill of an icy swim, so if it sounds like fun to you, you just may make a love connection with one of your fellow bears. For more information, check out *www. polarbearclub.org.*

○ PRO *Contrary to its older man image, the Polar Bear Club includes members of all ages and genders.*

○ CON *Shrinkage.*

986.   FREE CONCERT IN THE PARK

You have absolutely nothing to lose at a free concert in the park. First, it's free, so you won't be disappointed if the performance is subpar. Second, men love live music, so a free concert is likely to attract many of them looking to check out the performance. And if men are in the park near where you live for a concert, they are likely your neighbors, so these guys are worth getting to know.

987.   WATCHING THE SUN SET

No matter where you live in the country, there is occasionally a breathtaking sunset that makes you want to climb to the highest peak in the area to get the clearest view. So why not do that? As soon as you see the sky start to show shades of pink and orange, hop in your car and speed to the nearest lookout point. Chances are, if you find a man there who has done the same, he is as romantic and appreciative of nature as you are—it could be a perfect match.

988.   WATCHING THE SUN RISE

If you are an early riser, you have surely caught a few sunrises that have stopped you in your tracks and made you think, "Wow, that's beautiful." To potentially meet a man who also rises early and appreciates a beautiful sunrise as much as you, head to a spot where the horizon is nice and clear. For example, head to an open field, or, if you are lucky enough to live near a beach, head to the water's edge for a sunrise. Even if there's no one there to appreciate it with you, your day will be off to a glorious start.

=Time   =Friends $=Expense

989. NUDE BEACH

$

There's a reason little kids are eager to lose their diapers and run around—it feels really good to be naked, which may be why some people prefer to hit the sand in the buff. If this is you, you may just meet your

Five popular nude beaches:
1. Formentera, Spain
2. Wreck Beach in British Columbia
3. Firefly Beach in Negril, Jamaica
4. Black's Beach, La Jolla, California
5. Rooftop Resort, Hollywood, Florida

soul mate on a nude beach. Nude beaches leave nothing to the imagination, so you will have no question as to what you are getting into.

990. PICNICKING IN THE PARK

$

Whether you're on your lunch break or looking for some fresh air on a weekend afternoon, pack yourself a picnic, and head for the park. Enjoy the scenery of men jogging, walking, throwing a football, or engaging in other park activity. If you sit down in a crowded area, the men just may come up to you. Be sure to pack some extra snacks and drinks just in case.

991. CARRYING A LARGE UMBRELLA ON A RAINY DAY

$

On a rainy day, people on a crowded street will be running for cover during a downpour. So turn a negative into a positive by carrying a large umbrella, opening it up, and offering some space to a handsome stranger. The proximity will force the two of you to exchange some chitchat until the downpour passes.

992. IN A GONDOLA

$ $

Lilly S. from Indianapolis, Minnesota, met her love in a gondola climbing to the top of Mt. Pilates (part of the Swiss Alps) in Switzerland. "We were both traveling in small groups, and we had to mix together in our gondola rides up the mountain. I don't like heights, and Mike was nice to me as I peeked over the side. We connected during the 20 to 30 minute ride to the top, and we spent the rest of the day exploring together. He's from Chicago, so it's been a bit of a long-distance relationship, but nothing considering we met in a foreign country!" she says. There is something about the face-to-face setup of a gondola that makes it easy to meet your fellow passengers, whether you are riding it to the top of a ski slope or to enjoy the view off of the top of a mountain. Next time you find yourself in one, get to know your gondola-mates.

=Time =Friends $=Expense

993. LOOKING FOR SHELLS ON THE BEACH

Love often strikes when you least expect it . . . like when you head back down to the beach in the evening to do some quality shell searching. As you engulf yourself in combing through piles of broken shells, make sure you glance up now and then to see who's on the beach walking his dog, jogging, or engaging in some other evening beach activity. The beach is often best for meeting men when the daytime sunbathers have gone and you have some room to check out the lay of the land. Just make sure there are enough fellow beach combers out there—a beach that is too quiet could be unsafe.

994. HAWK WATCHING

If you're an animal lover, you are probably excited when you spot a hawk flying above . . . or better yet, perched on a branch in front of you. To increase your chances of seeing a hawk soaring or sitting—and to better your chances of meeting a bird-appreciating man—consider going on a hawk watch.

Five great hawk watching areas:
1. The Grand Canyon, AZ
2. Cadillac Mountain, Acadia National Park, Bar Harbor, ME
3. Hawk Ridge, Duluth, MN
4. Mount Pisgah, Asheville, NC
5. Hawk Mountain Sanctuary, Kempton/Berks and Schuylkill counties, PA

995. RUNNING A 5K

Even if you're not a runner, next time you hear about a 5K in your area, consider taking part. Since they're short (just over 3 miles), 5Ks often attract all sorts of people—not just the marathon-type who work out more than you'd like. They're often held in the spring or summer, so it's a great chance to be outdoors with lots of active people—including some single guys. Keep an eye on the local papers or ask at a gym to hear about the next 5K held in your area.

○ PRO *You'll get in better shape, which will make you more attractive overall.*

○ CON *You'll have to spend some time training in order to finish the race running.*

996.   IN A TUG-O-WAR

$

Although you probably haven't participated in one since elementary school (or not at all), next time you have the opportunity to participate in a tug-o-war, go for it! Whether at a company cookout, an alumnae get-together, or an event at a beach, tug-o-wars are by nature silly and fun. Plus, since they're most often coed, you may find yourself teaming up with some cuties. Take this opportunity to laugh, get a little exercise—and flirt! Just be careful—if you fall down and end up with a mouthful of sand, you may be a bit too red-faced to spark any love connections.

997.   HARPOON BREWERY EVENTS

$ $

Love beer? Even if you don't, consider attending one of the Harpoon Brewery events, because if there's one thing guys love, it's a cold brew. Whether it's their Saint Patrick's Day party, Oktoberfest, summer Brewstock, or any of the dozens of tastings they hold, Harpoon knows how to put on a fun, outdoor party with music, food, beer, and lots of guys. Their events take place all over New England so if you're going to be in the Northeast, check out *www. harpoonbrewery.com* to find out what's scheduled.

998.   POSING FOR A SPENCER TUNICK PHOTO

$

Spencer Tunick takes pictures of large groups of people. So what? Well, it just so happens that these people pose naked. He has been arrested, broken records, and produces stunningly beautiful photographs—and he's always looking for volunteers. So if you hear that Spencer Tunick is coming to your area, consider baring all to take part in a momentous artistic occasion. Who knows? You may find yourself next to a daring, artistic, naked cutie. Tunick's photo shoots draw crowds of more than 15,000 people all over the world. You can say you've done at least one extremely bold thing in your life, and if you end up meeting your mate there, you'll have one heck of a story to tell!

999.   RUNNING THROUGH A SPRINKLER

$

Unless you live on the water, it can be tough to find a way to cool down in the summer months. Why not revisit your youth and take a run through the sprinkler? It's a great way to cool down, and you'll instantly feel like a kid again. If a cute guy happens to walk by, offer up the sprinkler. Even if he turns down your offer, he won't be able to repress a smile.

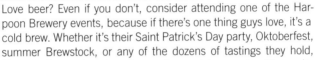
=Time =Friends $=Expense

1,000. AS AN EXTRA IN A MOVIE

If you live in or near a major city, at one point or another, you'll most likely hear about a movie being filmed in the area. More often than not, these movies require extras. While getting a walk-on part usually requires some kind of screening, if directors are looking to fill a public area with people, anybody will do. So, next time you hear of a movie being shot, why not head down to wherever they're filming and make your own movie history? There will be lots of people—including single guys—thinking the same thing. If you end up on film, you'll always have a way to remember the day. And if you end up on film *and* you get a date, you'll be able to share your first date with the entire world!

1,001. JUST BEING YOU

They say love most often strikes when you least expect it. And in many cases, this is true. When you're at the gym for your daily workout, walking on a busy street on your lunch hour, or shopping for dinner at the grocery store—if you open up your eyes and your heart, there are men all around you. And many of them are as eager to meet someone as you are.

=Time 〒=Friends $=Expense